# THE PROFILE METHOD
# FOR THE CLASSIFICATION
# AND EVALUATION OF
# MANUSCRIPT EVIDENCE

# STUDIES AND DOCUMENTS

Founded by Kirsopp and Silva Lake

## VOLUME 44

EDITED BY

IRVING ALAN SPARKS

in Collaboration With

| | |
|---|---|
| J. NEVILLE BIRDSALL | ELDON J. EPP |
| SEBASTIAN P. BROCK | GORDON D. FEE |
| †ERNEST CADMAN COLWELL | |

# THE PROFILE METHOD FOR THE CLASSIFICATION AND EVALUATION OF MANUSCRIPT EVIDENCE
as applied to the continuous Greek text of

# THE GOSPEL OF LUKE

BY

FREDERIK WISSE

GRAND RAPIDS, MICHIGAN
WM. B. EERDMANS
1982

*In memoriam Ernest Cadman Colwell*

**Library of Congress Cataloging in Publication Data**

Wisse, Frederik.
   The profile method for the classification
and evaluation of manuscript evidence, as
applied to the continuous Greek text of the
Gospel of Luke.

   (Studies and documents; 44)
   1. Bible.   N.T. — Manuscripts, Greek.
2. Bible.   N.T.   Luke — Manuscripts, Greek.
3. Bible.   N.T.   Criticism, Textual.
4. Bible.   N.T.   Luke — Criticism, Textual.
I. Title. II. Series.
BS1939.W57        225.4'8        82-7448
ISBN 0-8028-1918-4        AACR2

# PREFACE

The development of the Profile Method has been integrally connected with the International Greek New Testament Project (IGNTP). When I began my graduate studies at Claremont Graduate School in 1965, the American office of this British-American project had just been moved to the School of Theology at Claremont by Ernest C. Colwell, Chairman of the American Executive Committee of the IGNTP and President of the School of Theology. During my volunteer work for the project in the summer of 1966 I had the idea of profile as a method for the classification and evaluation of MS evidence. Soon after this occurred to me I was joined by Paul R. McReynolds, a fellow graduate student and an assistant of the IGNTP, who has shared the often tedious work of selecting test readings, profiling hundreds of MSS, and classifying and studying the profiles. In a separate study he has applied the Profile Method to the various groups in the Lucan MS tradition.

Due to its connection with, and relevance to, the work of the IGNTP, I was in the fortunate position of receiving expert advice on, and criticism of, the Profile Method from its very beginning. Above all I am indebted to the late President Colwell, who proposed that I make the Profile Method the topic of a doctoral dissertation and who was my thesis advisor. Two other scholars associated with the IGNTP, Eldon J. Epp and I. Alan Sparks, closely followed the development of the Profile Method with their encouragement and advice. No less helpful were James M. Robinson and Ernest W. Tune, who with President Colwell formed the dissertation committee.

By the time my dissertation was submitted in the spring of 1968,[1] McReynolds and I had profiled and classified about 550 MSS which were available to us in collation or on microfilm in the files of the IGNTP in Claremont or which we consulted in American rare book collections.[2] Thanks to a generous grant by the Calvin Foundation of Grand Rapids, Michigan, I was able to spend the fall and winter of 1968-69 at the Institut für neutestamentliche Textforschung of the Wilhelm University in Münster, Germany. This institute has assembled a microfilm collection of all known Greek MSS of the NT insofar as these are available for photography. I am most grateful to Professor Dr. Kurt Aland, the director of the INTF in Münster, who extended to me the hospitality of his institute and gave me full access to its enormous microfilm collection. This made it possible to profile and classify an additional 816 Lucan MSS. The only microfilms left undone involve MSS of which

[1] "The Claremont Profile Method for the Classification of Byzantine New Testament Manuscripts: A Study in Method" (Ph.D. dissertation, Claremont Graduate School and University Center, 1968).

[2] A number of less accessible MSS were profiled for us from the original by Jacob Geerlings during study trips to Greece.

v

the biblical text cannot easily be distinguished from the commentary and late MSS from the sixteenth century onward. The latter is a relatively small group of MSS which postdate the printed Greek text of Erasmus; the chance of anything of value among them is rather small. This leaves about two hundred fifty MSS of which the microfilm in Münster was illegible, or of which the present location is unknown, or for which the INTF in Münster has not been able to acquire microfilms. This makes the Gospel according to Luke the part of the NT of which the available Greek MS evidence has been most extensively classified. The results, involving 1385 MSS, are presented in Chapter V.

Eldon J. Epp was the first to report on the Profile Method in a paper presented before the Society of Biblical Literature, Pacific Coast Section, in May 1967.[3] In December of the same year Paul McReynolds and I had the opportunity to present the Profile Method to the Textual Criticism Seminar of the Annual Meeting of the Society of Biblical Literature in New York.[4] In 1970 we published another brief explanation and defense of the Profile Method.[5]

It was our intention to publish our dissertations in one volume soon after their completion.[6] The addition of more than 800 MSS that I profiled in Münster, however, necessitated a major revision of the group studies that formed the basic part of McReynolds's dissertation. Since he soon became preoccupied with administrative duties, and I with the study and publication of the Nag Hammadi texts, little progress was made during the following ten years. In the meantime references to, and use of, the Profile Method by some scholars indicated an imperfect understanding of its principle and intent — no doubt partly because of our failure to publish. This led to the decision to work toward separate publications without major revisions.

The first two chapters of the book are taken from my dissertation with only minor revisions. Chapters III and IV have been updated and revised where this seemed appropriate. Chapter V presents the classification of all profiled Lucan MSS in the order of the Gregory-Aland numeration. Approximately 550 of these were profiled and classified jointly by McReynolds and myself and were already included in McReynolds's dissertation. I have rechecked and adjusted these classifications after the 816 MSS that I profiled and classified in Münster had been integrated. Chapter VI presents the groups and clusters in the Lucan text tradition with a list of their members. For detailed group studies the reader is referred to the dissertation of Paul R. McReynolds. Chapter VII includes suggestions for the use of the Profile Method with other texts. In this connection I discuss an objection to my use of the Profile Method voiced by W. L. Richards.

Appendices I and II give the basic data necessary to classify and evaluate

[3]It was published as "The Claremont Profile Method for Grouping New Testament Minuscule Manuscripts," *Studies in the History and Text of the New Testament in Honor of Kenneth Willis Clark, Ph.D.* (ed. Boyd L. Daniels and M. Jack Suggs; SD 29; Salt Lake City: University of Utah, 1967) 27-38.

[4]This report was published as part of "The International Greek New Testament Project: A Status Report" by Ernest C. Colwell, I. Alan Sparks, Frederik Wisse, and Paul R. McReynolds, in *JBL* 87 (1968) 191-97.

[5]"Family E and the Profile Method," *Bib* 51 (1970) 67-75. This was a response to the incorrect use made of the Profile Method by Jacob Geerlings in *Family E and Its Allies in Mark* (SD 35; Salt Lake City: University of Utah, 1968); see below, pp. 27-28.

[6]McReynolds finished his dissertation at the end of 1968; it is called "The Claremont Profile Method and the Grouping of Byzantine Manuscripts."

Lucan MSS that have not yet been profiled. After some experience it should be possible to classify a Lucan MSS within half an hour. It proved impracticable to provide the complete profiles of all the classified Lucan MSS. They are included only in the case of the significantly mixed MSS. Readers who would like to consult the actual profiles of certain Lucan MSS or groups, in order to check classifications or engage in special group studies, should write to me. Appendix III evaluates the witnesses to the continuous Greek text of the Gospel of Luke in the UBS edition. It also discusses the general issue of MS citation.

Though the Profile Method was originally designed to classify and evaluate Byzantine NT MSS, its use is by no means limited to these. It can be applied with profit to any ancient text that has a large MS attestation. It is my hope that it will help textual critics make full use of the MS evidence of a wide variety of texts.

Thanks are due to the Social Sciences and Humanities Research Council in Canada, the funding agency of the McMaster Project on "Normative Self-Definition in Judaism and Christianity" with which I was associated during the revisions of this study.

Frederik Wisse
McGill University, Montreal
August, 1980

# CONTENTS

# ABBREVIATIONS

| | |
|---|---|
| ANTF | Arbeiten zur neutestamentlichen Textforschung |
| *Bib* | *Biblica* |
| Cl(s) | Cluster(s) |
| corr | corrected reading or text |
| Def | Defective |
| *Exp* | *Expositor* |
| fragm | fragmentary |
| Gr(s) | Group(s) |
| *HTR* | *Harvard Theological Review* |
| IGNTP | International Greek New Testament Project |
| Illeg | Illegible |
| *Int* | *Interpretation* |
| INTF | Institut für neutestamentliche Textforschung in Münster, Germany |
| *JBL* | *Journal of Biblical Literature* |
| *JTS* | *Journal of Theological Studies* |
| Kmix | Mixed text close to group $K^x$ |
| Mix | Mixed text at some distance from group $K^x$ |
| MS(S) | manuscript(s) |
| *NTS* | *New Testament Studies* |
| NTTS | New Testament Tools and Studies |
| *RTP* | *Review of Theology and Philosophy/Revue de théologie et de philosophie* |
| SBLDS | Society of Biblical Literature Dissertation Series |
| SD | Studies and Documents |
| *SE* | *Studia evangelica* I (TU 73) |
| TextsS | Texts and Studies |
| TR | Textus Receptus |
| TU | Texte und Untersuchungen |
| UBS | United Bible Societies |
| *ZNW* | *Zeitschrift für die neutestamentliche Wissenschaft* |

CHAPTER I

# THE ROLE OF MINUSCULES IN NEW TESTAMENT TEXTUAL CRITICISM

Of all the spectacular developments in NT textual criticism since Tischendorf the least advertised has been the phenomenal increase in the number of known minuscules. There must be a reason for this curious situation. It cannot simply be due to the fact that the finds of a considerable number of early papyri have tended to overshadow all other NT textual developments. Certainly the bringing to light of more than 1700 minuscules in less than a century could have shared top rating with the few hundred newly discovered papyri and uncials, most of which are mere fragments, if only lower critics had chosen to do so. The underlying reason is that the ever-swelling mass of minuscules has been a real embarrassment to the textual critic. Every additional minuscule, however high its market price might be, has made the critic's task more confusing and difficult.

The mass of minuscules creates a dilemma for the textual critic. Either he will try to take all MS evidence into account without hope of ever finishing his task, or he will ignore the great majority of existing MSS and be accused of basing his results on partial and probably biased evidence. No wonder, therefore, that the role of minuscules in NT textual criticism has become the most frustrating problem facing the scholars in that field.[1]

The problem posed by the minuscules can be divided into two parts. First, the question must be answered whether minuscules deserve to play a role in the search for the best text of the NT, and consequently, whether they should be represented in a full *apparatus criticus* to the Greek NT. In case this first question is answered in the affirmative, it still must be shown that the great quantity of MSS does not make any kind of meaningful and representative use of minuscules impossible or impractical.

In a situation where MS evidence runs into more than 5000 separate items and a time span of more than fourteen centuries, it should be questioned whether all this evidence is relevant for the establishment of the original text. It may well be that the oldest copies in existence are adequate representatives of the MS tradition so that the rest can be ignored. After all, why start more than thirteen centuries after the autographa were written, and wade back through literally thousands of MSS in an

---

[1]This problem may well be the main cause of the decline in textual studies in the last thirty years. The immensity of the work to be done — much of it unexciting plodding through late MSS — and the prospects of having to interpret all the evidence once it is available, seem to have driven scholars to greener pastures, or to monographs on marginal but manageable issues.

immensely complicated process, if at best one can only arrive at a fifth-century text which is already well represented by copies of that time. To find the foundation of a building one does not first climb the roof; one starts somewhere below the ground floor.

This argument, obvious and tantalizing on the surface, forms the background for all those who consider it justified to ignore all, or almost all, minuscules.[2] Yet they must first prove that the MS tradition after, let us say, the ninth century, does not add any pertinent information for the recovery of the original text of the NT. Whether one holds that this proof necessitates a complete study of the more than 2700 known minuscules depends on one's viewpoint. Naturally the opponents of the use of minuscules do not consider this time-consuming process to be necessary at all.

There is basically only one argument which can circumvent the task of studying all the late minuscules to make sure that they are indeed of no value for textual criticism. This argument is that among the early uncials there are MSS which stand in a relatively uncorrupted tradition, and which show all other text-types of that period to be secondary and corrupted. Only if this argument can be proved, and if it is clear from some sampling that late minuscules fall predominantly in the tradition of one of the corrupted texts, can we safely omit a full study of these MSS.

The first and best representative of this position is Fenton John Anthony Hort.[3] His view stands out from that of many who share his attitude toward minuscules in that he knew what was at stake and was willing to face the consequences. With some danger of caricaturing Hort, we shall attempt to summarize his evaluation of the mass of minuscules in four points. It should be borne in mind that Hort knew of the existence of fewer than one thousand cursives, and that only 150 of these were available to him in complete collation, though he sampled some more in a few selected passages.[4]

a) An analysis of the text of the major uncials, the NT quotations of the Fathers, and the early versions shows that there were three text-types in existence during the fifth century A.D.: the Neutral or Alexandrian text,[5] the Western text, and the Syrian text. Patristic attestation shows the Syrian text to be the latest of the three, though it eventually won out and became the text found in the great majority of the minuscules.

b) A study of conflate readings — Hort used four from Mark and four from Luke — conclusively proves that the Syrian text is a recension which made use of the Western and Neutral texts.[6] Hort knows of no case where a Neutral reading is a conflation of a Western and Syrian reading, or where a Western reading is a conflation of Neutral and Syrian readings. Thus Hort has internal evidence proving not

---

[2]There is no question among scholars about including the very few ninth-century minuscules and the relatively small number of "Neutral" and "Caesarean" cursives. It should be noted that the latter group is usually included in a textual apparatus, not because they represent a text not found among earlier uncials, but because they have a text like those uncials which pushed aside the TR.

[3]Brooke Foss Westcott and Fenton John Anthony Hort, *The New Testament in the Original Greek: Introduction and Appendix* (New York: Harper & Brothers, 1882). Without wishing to deny or ignore the contribution made by Westcott we will simply refer to "Hort."

[4]Ibid., 77-78.

[5]Differences between Neutral and Alexandrian readings can be ignored for our purposes.

[6]Westcott and Hort, 93ff.

only that the Syrian text is posterior to the Western and Neutral texts, but also that it is secondary in nature.

The conflate readings imply a further point about the work of the editors of the Syrian text, for "it is morally impossible that their use of documents of either or both classes should have been confined to those places in which conflation enables us to detect it in actual operation."[7] Hort at this point is still forced to leave open the possibility that the Syrian text had a source, or sources, beyond the Neutral and Western texts that was both ancient and good.

c) As elsewhere, Hort closes this remaining loophole by means of both transcriptional and intrinsic evidence. Transcriptional evidence indicates that no Syrian readings existed before A.D. 250. This means that even if the Syrian recension had sources beyond the Western and Neutral texts, these sources did not go back farther than the middle of the third century, and thus were later than the two non-Syrian text-types.[8]

It was left up to the intrinsic evidence to give the final death blow. Readings peculiar to the Syrian MSS proved to be smooth; they never offend, are free from surprises and seemingly transparent. Therefore, taking the negative side of the *lectio difficilior* principle, Hort can conclude that the internal evidence of Syrian readings is "entirely unfavorable to the hypothesis that they may have been copied from other equally ancient and perhaps purer texts [than the Western and Neutral] now otherwise lost."[9]

d) Thus the die was cast against the minuscules. We again quote Hort: "Since the Syrian text is only a modified eclectic combination of earlier texts independently attested, existing documents descended from it can attest nothing but itself."[10] And one page later: "All distinctively Syrian readings must be at once rejected." Still, Hort laments the fact that so few minuscules have been studied, but his sorrow does not go deep. True, some "valuable texts may lie hidden among them," but "nothing can well be less probable than the discovery of cursive evidence sufficiently important to affect present conclusions in more than a handful of passages, much less to alter present interpretations of the relations between the existing documents."[11]

Only after these carefully reasoned and convincing steps did Hort limit himself to the early uncials and especially to the "Neutrals" among them. It speaks for Hort's power of persuasion and influence that, though scholars today would question almost every point of his argument, yet the result still stands. After a few halfhearted attempts for supremacy by the Western text, Codex Vaticanus and its allies have become the new "Textus Receptus."

A prominent contemporary textual critic, Professor Kurt Aland, has also taken a generally negative view of the minuscules.[12] His position is sufficiently different from Hort's to deserve separate treatment. Unfortunately, we have no

---

[7]Ibid., 106.
[8]Ibid., 113.
[9]Ibid., 115.
[10]Ibid., 118.
[11]Ibid., 77.
[12]We ignore the many lower critics since Hort who have largely or completely left minuscules out of consideration, but who have not justified or explained this omission. One may assume that, besides Hort's legacy concerning the Syrian text, the reasons were primarily practical ones.

comprehensive introduction, like that of Westcott and Hort, from Aland's hand. Conclusions will have to be drawn from scattered remarks in a number of articles.[13]

An a priori rejection of the mass of minuscules would have been impossible for Aland. He and the INTF in Münster took on the difficult and important task of publishing an up-to-date list of all extant papyri, uncials, minuscules, and lectionaries of the Greek NT.[14] Hence, one could hardly expect him to pass by the majority of MSS without at least a preliminary study.

Yet Aland's interest in the minuscules is not for their own sake. He is no longer satisfied with Hort's judgment that the discovery of important cursive evidence is most improbable. He wants to find the few hypothetical nuggets which Hort did not think were worth the effort. Aland wants to be able to say that he has searched the minuscules exhaustively for anything of value.[15] This search, of course, presupposed that the minuscules as such are of little value. Only the exceptional MSS warrant the concerted effort.

Thus with Aland no less than with Hort a value judgment is at work. Minuscules have to pass a test before they are considered worthy of inclusion in a textual apparatus. All MSS which are generally Byzantine[16] will fail. Aland sees the Byzantine text as a unit which, in spite of all its internal differences and developments, should be treated as one. This text-type is for him already well enough represented by some of the late uncials. He believes that the character and readings of the Byzantine text are so well established that its members can be represented under a siglum M (Majority text).[17] In order to separate the sheep from the goats Aland proposes a list of readings which will readily identify a minuscule as being Byzantine or non-Byzantine.[18]

In many ways Aland's attitude toward the minuscules is a step forward from Hort. Greater certainty is necessary than Hort's "probabilities" to eliminate the possibility that new evidence will invalidate conclusions drawn from a selection or sampling of MSS. Aland is trying to provide this certainty. The question remains, however, whether Aland is not still too restrictive. Aland believes that von Soden tried to do too much in dealing with the whole history of the text.[19] Yet this criticism does not focus on von Soden's inaccuracies and questionable results. Rather, Aland implies that a large part of von Soden's effort was unnecessary. The Byzantine text, and particularly the Byzantine minuscules, can be left out of consideration. They are

[13]A number of relevant articles have been collected by Aland in book form (*Studien zur Überlieferung des neuen Testaments und seines Textes* [ANTF 2; Berlin: Walter de Gruyter & Co., 1967]). The article in this volume most relevant to the use of minuscules ("Die Konsequenzen der neueren Handschriftenfunde für die neutestamentliche Textkritik," 180-201) is a somewhat modified form of Aland's paper, "The Significance of the Papyri for New Testament Research" read at the 100th meeting of the Society of Biblical Literature in New York and published in *The Bible in Modern Scholarship* (ed. J. Philip Hyatt; Nashville/New York: Abingdon, 1965) 325-46.

[14]Kurt Aland, *Kurzgefasste Liste der griechischen Handschriften des neuen Testaments* (ANTF 1; Berlin: Walter de Gruyter & Co., 1962).

[15]Kurt Aland, "The Significance of the Papyri," 339.

[16]From here on I will use Kirsopp Lake's designation, "Byzantine text," for what critics have called Syrian, Antiochan, Delta, Kappa, Koine, or Ecclesiastical text ("The Byzantine Text of the Gospels," *Mémorial Lagrange* [Paris: J. Gabalda et Cie., 1940]) 253.

[17]Kurt Aland, "The Significance of the Papyri," 342.

[18]This list is the long-promised "1000 cursives examined in 1000 passages with a view to evaluate their text." Since this is in fact a method for classifying MSS, it will be scrutinized, insofar as that is possible, along with other methods in Chapter III.

[19]Kurt Aland, "The Significance of the Papyri," 341.

of no use in establishing the original text of the NT.[20] But this is a conclusion to be drawn from evidence, not to form the basis for the selection of evidence.

The point of contention is not whether the Byzantine text, whatever that exactly may be, is of greater or equal value than the great Egyptian uncials. The real question is whether the time has come to speak about the value of Byzantine MSS at all. Except in von Soden's inaccurate and unused pages, the minuscules have never been allowed to speak. Once heard, they may well be found wanting, but at least their case will have been presented, and then for good and necessary reasons they will be content to grace libraries and rare book collections. Textual critics deserve to have all the evidence before them, evidence which has not first been prejudged.

It is an ironic fact that today basic MS evidence of the NT is less available to the textual critic than it was fifty years ago. Editions of great uncials have long been out of print. Tischendorf's *editio octava maior* has never had serious competition, let alone a complement. Though the casual user of a critical text of the Greek NT has been well provided for, the expert and serious student is at the mercy of highly selective and incomplete *apparatus critici*. This situation could only be defended if the task of establishing the best possible NT text had been accomplished, and if the history of the transmission of that text was clear. But it is not.

The much-needed new and unbiased look at all the evidence available demands the use of a good representation of the minuscules. To condemn the great majority of them by means of a single siglum will not suffice. The situation up to the ninth century is too uncertain. The fact that among the early uncials and papyri there is only one clearly defined group of MSS has made any objective judgment impossible.[21] The well-trained choir of the "Neutral" group, recently strengthened by P[75], has drowned out all the solos. The long overdue dethronement of the Textus Receptus (TR) by Hort and others suffered from overkill of the only group of MSS that could have put up a fight. Since that time lower criticism seems to have become the study of what to do when Codex Vaticanus and P[75] disagree.

A study of the minuscules could change this situation. They promise hope of discovering the several lines of textual tradition which fed into the tenth and eleventh centuries. The few extant late uncials give no sufficient clues to this tradition.

The late minuscules also give us a case study of the forces involved in the transmission of the text. The word "mixture" still covers a large blank space lined with question marks. In the medieval tradition enough MSS remain to observe and study these unexplained phenomena. Certainly we may expect to receive some answers about the growth of groups and recensions, about scribal habits and early attempts at textual criticism. When used with care, these answers can help us to understand what went on at earlier, less well-attested stages of the transmission of the text.

All these considerations are secondary to the overriding need for complete and unbiased evidence. There has never been such evidence. The bulk of the minuscules may well be of little value for textual criticism, but how can one be sure

---

[20]Ibid., 342. It must be kept in mind that Aland's purpose is to construct a large apparatus to a critical text of the Greek NT.

[21]Although, in theory, a single MS may be as valuable as a group, in practice a single divergent MS is suspect.

before studying them? No one has ever presented a conclusive argument against the use of the Byzantine text. Certainly Hort's case against the late minuscules no longer convinces,[22] and Aland is begging the question. Therefore, until there is proof to the contrary, minuscules ought to play a meaningful role in the lower criticism of the Greek NT.

Up to this point we have discussed only the desirability of using the evidence of the minuscules in textual criticism. Little was said about its feasibility. Ultimately, every textual critic might well agree that it would be useful to have the evidence of the cursives available if only he could be convinced that this could be accomplished within his lifetime.[23] If the number of minuscules had been no greater than that of the uncials the issue would never have arisen. Only because the number of late minuscules seemed unmanageable did scholars like Hort and Aland try to avoid using them.

Several factors play a role here. The realities of mid-twentieth-century existence no longer favor projects which demand half a century or more. There is a constant clamoring for results, not only by the intended public, but also by the scholar who is eager to see the publication grace his bibliography. Of no less importance is the fact that financial contributors, hard enough to come by in the field of text study, do not favor endless research projects, and for understandable reasons.

A second factor is the proposed evidence of the minuscules itself. One could imagine making collations of some 1700 MSS extant in one of the Gospels, but how will anyone ever make sense out of them? The purpose of a critical apparatus must be kept in mind: this purpose is not primarily to publish a large number of collations, though this is part of the picture. If these collations cannot be weighed, compared, and interpreted, they are useless. Too large a number of MSS renders any apparatus meaningless.

Ideally, a critical apparatus gives all pertinent MS evidence necessary for the establishment of the best possible text, and nothing more. Since the number of MSS used in an apparatus must be kept within reasonable limits, it is clear that only a fraction of the total number of Greek MSS of the NT can be included. This could easily lead to arbitrariness — and it often has — unless somehow true representation could be assured. Selection is defensible only if the user of the apparatus can be convinced that the number of MSS presented spans and represents the whole tradition in text, date, and, insofar as this is known, provenance.

Thus the conditions under which cursives can be used profitably have become very limited. If there is no assurance that a relatively small number of minuscules can be selected that will accurately represent the whole Byzantine tradition, then we may as well ignore the whole group altogether. It would justify a return to the time when the compiler of an apparatus picked and chose minuscules according to his fancy and opportunity. Aland would then be in his right to ignore the differences among Byzantine MSS.

[22]Some of the weaknesses in Hort's line of reasoning were pointed out by E. C. Colwell in "Genealogical Method: its Achievements and its Limitations," *JBL* 66 (1947) 109-33.

[23]For the NT only in the case of the book of Revelation has all evidence available at the time been assembled; the basic compilation was done by H. C. Hoskier, *Concerning the Text of the Apocalypse* (London: Bernard Quaritch, 1929). Josef Schmid built his *Studien zur Geschichte des Griechischen Apokalypse-Textes* (München: Karl Zink, 1955) on Hoskier's work. Both authors frankly admitted in the introductions to their works that they chose the Apocalypse because the subject matter was limited enough — about 250 MSS at the time of Hoskier — that it could be handled in their lifetime.

This narrows the whole problem of minuscules down to the question of balanced representation. Is it possible to represent the late medieval text with a number of MSS that is large enough to do justice to the whole range of available MSS and yet not so large that it clutters up and confuses a critical apparatus? And further, if the answer to this question is positive, can these representatives be found through a simple but accurate process within a reasonable amount of time? Certainly, if it presupposes a complete study and comparison of all medieval MSS, no purpose will have been served, for it will postpone the actual selection of representative MSS beyond the horizon.

Fortunately we are no longer in the dark about either the theoretical or practical possibilities of this venture. More than half a century ago a great textual critic made a serious attempt to represent the whole Byzantine tradition in the apparatus to his text. This scholar was Hermann von Soden, and he almost succeeded. At this point[24] we may ignore the weaknesses of von Soden's grandiose venture, and simply point out what he proved relevant to selecting representatives of the Byzantine text.

a) The late medieval text, i.e., from the tenth through the fifteenth centuries, includes a considerable number of groups or families of MSS, varying in size from a few MSS to several hundred. Relatively few minuscules have such a peculiar text that they fall outside of these groups.

b) In order to determine to what group a MS belongs, it is not necessary to survey the complete text of a MS. The distinctive characteristics of a group are often visible in short selections of text. Thus a MS can be classified with relatively little effort once the text of each group in the test passages has been established.

c) The character of most groups is such that the range of its text can be represented by only a few of its members. Thus the minuscules can be adequately represented in a critical apparatus by choosing some strategic members of each known group, and by including those MSS which did not conform to any of these groups.

Although the actual results of von Soden's labors can be and have been challenged, these three conclusions have never been seriously contested. On the contrary, scholarship since von Soden has proved him right repeatedly at these crucial points.[25]

Even though von Soden did not leave the scholarly world an accurate and practical tool with which to classify the text of the minuscules,[26] he left a tempting promise. At least he proved that the venture was possible and profitable. In all fairness it must be admitted that without the example and promise of von Soden's work there would not have been a Profile Method for the classification and evalua-

---

[24]Chapter II consists of a detailed analysis of von Soden's treatment of the minuscules.

[25]H. C. Hoskier came to a similar conclusion after completing his thorough study of the MS evidence of the Apocalypse. He states: "Toward the close of our labors, it becomes apparent that the task we suggest to others of the collation of the existing rich material of the other books of the N.T. is not at all super human, and ought to have been undertaken long ago. Take the 2000 manuscripts of the Gospels. It will doubtless be found, as here, that after 100 have been carefully collated, the rest fall into well-defined groups, with perhaps here and there an exception. Let the latter then be carefully and thoroughly collated in full, but a quicker examination of the others (if properly carried out) will soon classify them with other groups" (*Concerning the Text of the Apocalypse* 1. xii).

[26]See below, Chapter II.

tion of MS evidence. Even where he failed, von Soden was instructive, and where he was correct, he proved to be of great help.

It has been the contention of this chapter that minuscules can and should figure prominently in the task of lower criticism. They deserve to be represented in a textual apparatus to the Greek NT that attempts to present the complete range of evidence without prejudgment. In view of this demand and background the Profile Method was developed. The method claims to be an accurate and rapid procedure for the classification of the MS evidence of any ancient text with large MS attestation, and to present an adequate basis for the selection of balanced representatives of the whole tradition. In addition, a new basis for group study as well as intergroup study has been presented. If this claim is substantiated by the following chapters, it will have delivered lower criticism from its present dilemma and impasse, and it will have restored the minuscules to their rightful place.

CHAPTER II

# VON SODEN'S LEGACY

Few scholarly enterprises have suffered a more curious fate than that of Hermann Freiherr von Soden. On the one hand, criticism could hardly have been more unanimous, more vociferous, and more devastating. Nonetheless, almost all of von Soden's critics have made extensive use of his work, and that in a surprisingly uncritical fashion. The reasons for this ironical fact readily suggest themselves.

An immediate and apprehensive reaction to von Soden's *Die Schriften des Neuen Testaments* (1902-13) was inevitable.[1] The work claimed to be an exhaustive and definitive study of the MS tradition of the Greek NT, with as its culmination a reconstruction of a text which was as close as possible to the original. Thus it seemed that all previous textual work had become obsolete, and that the main task of lower criticism of the NT had finally been accomplished. No textual critic could leave such a claim untested and unchallenged.

The manner of publishing *Die Schriften des Neuen Testaments* contributed to the general apprehension. The first volume, which appeared eleven years before the critical text, gave little clue as to von Soden's presuppositions, methods, and results, but made it abundantly clear that the project was all-encompassing, both in scope and depth. Nor was this first volume immune to a charge of scholarly arrogance. So sure was von Soden of the finality of his work that he adopted a totally new notation system for Greek NT MSS. Though the old Tischendorf-Gregory system had little to say for itself except the blessing of time, von Soden's system would necessitate working for a long time with the cumbersome conversion tables and to dubious advantage.[2] It is no doubt helpful to know from the MS notation the

---

[1]H. H. B. Ayles, "A Recent Attempt to Determine the Original New Testament Text," *The Interpreter* 11 (1915) 408-14; H. C. Hoskier, "Von Soden's Text of the New Testament," *JTS* 15 (1914) 307-26; Kirsopp Lake, "Professor H. Von Soden's Treatment of the Text of the Gospels," *RTP* 4 (1908-1909) 201-17 and 277-95; Hans Lietzmann, "H. Von Sodens Ausgabe des Neuen Testamentes; Die Perikope von der Ehebrecherin," *ZNW* 8 (1907) 34-47; idem, "Hermann Von Sodens Ausgabe des Neuen Testamentes: Die drei Rezensionen," *ZNW* 15 (1915) 323-31; idem, "Bemerkungen zu Hermann Von Sodens Antikritik," *ZNW* 8 (1907) 234-37; A. Souter, "Von Soden's Text of the Greek New Testament Examined in Select Passages," *Exp* 8/10 (1915) 429-44.

[2]The most obvious disadvantage of this notation system as compared to earlier ones is that the difference between papyri, uncials, and minuscules is no longer visible from the MS number. For a detailed critique, see C. R. Gregory, *Die griechischen Handschriften des Neuen Testaments* (Leipzig: Hinrichs, 1908) 3-5.

general content and date of a MS, but even if von Soden's judgment of date can be trusted, is it helpful enough to warrant a complete change in notation and enumeration? The answer of the scholarly world was negative. Von Soden's new notations have been the least used of all his contributions.

Another early reaction to von Soden's first volume involved his use of the *pericope adulterae,* John 7:53–8:11, which von Soden called μ (μοιχαλίς). Again critical comment was to be expected, for this chapter was the only one in the first volume which seemed to indicate von Soden's methodology. Although the role of μ within the whole enterprise was far from clear, even when further volumes were published, yet it gave the critics the impression that this chapter was a comprehensive sample of the quality and underlying method of von Soden's work. As such it was fair game for criticism.

The complaint about the elusiveness and obscurity of von Soden's procedure was voiced early enough. Already in 1907 Hans Lietzmann charged:

> The author prefers to present first the results after which he discusses for each group the readings which vary from it. As a consequence one never gets an over-all view of the situation, except through one's own inferences. In o her words, the critical user of the book must reconstruct for himself the apparatus of variants on which von Soden based his judgment.[3]

Lietzmann had identified von Soden's main weakness. His further critique of von Soden's reconstruction of the original text is, in comparison, of little importance. Unfortunately von Soden defended himself on the fine details of the *pericope adulterae's* recension and forms, and not on methodology and procedure.[4] The Lietzmann-von Soden debate, which could have been a meaningful and necessary exchange on methodology, ended with both sides being hardened in the belief of their own correctness and the other's incompetence.

Time has proved that von Soden's main failure was that of communication. He failed to communicate to his fellow textual critics his methodology at a time when changes could still have been made. He failed to elucidate in his publication the procedures by which he had reached his conclusions. He left the user of his volumes with no way of testing and probing his results. Finally, he even failed to communicate the MS evidence of his critical apparatus in an accurate and lucid fashion. This grandiose failure in communication goes a long way in explaining the vehemence of von Soden's critics.

Realizing the general disapproval of von Soden's work, one is the more surprised that some of his conclusions have been widely, and rather uncritically, used.[5] Part of the reason for this situation was that it is almost impossible to use von Soden critically! Yet much more it shows that a study of the Greek NT text with the scope of von Soden's work, whatever its quality, was highly necessary. Perhaps to his own dismay, von Soden's greatest contribution proved to be in grouping and classifying MSS. Although for von Soden classification of MSS was only a means toward an end, this means proved to be valuable enough to establish his name in the

---

[3]Lietzmann, "Die Perikope," *ZNW* 8 (1907) 40.

[4]Hermann von Soden, "Hermann von Sodens Ausgabe des Neuen Testaments: Die Perikope von der Ehebrecherin," *ZNW* 8 (1907) 110-24.

[5]Chapter III will give examples of this kind of use of von Soden.

field of text studies. This aspect of von Soden's work deserves some further scrutiny and evaluation.

Von Soden's conception of the task before him was clear and praiseworthy.[6] He realized that the central task was to analyze the history of the transmission of the NT text. In contrast to his predecessors and contemporaries, he was willing to go all the way. He intended to use, as far as this was possible, all available MSS, both uncials and minuscules. Yet he was enough of a realist to recognize that no historical view will evolve from a record of individual MSS. Only if MSS can be related will the venture be possible and profitable.

All those who have themselves tried to find relationships in text among the mass of NT MSS can appreciate the difficulties and pitfalls involved. Von Soden was well aware of the complexities. He realized that all the parts of the NT do not have the same textual history. The four Gospels, Acts, the Epistles, the Catholics, and the Apocalypse must all be treated separately. Then, if groups are found and tested, their text must be reconstructed and defined. Judgments must be made as to whether a group is a recension or whether it arose through "evolution," where and when it arose, and where it exerted its influence.[7] It is a great tribute to von Soden's energy, scholarship, and determination that he was willing to perform this immense task.

Though he is sparing in his recognition of the work of textual critics before him, von Soden admits that collations made by Scrivener, Tregelles, Ferrar, Abbott, Hoskier, Rendel Harris, Tischendorf, and others helped him to form a rough picture of the situation and gave him a starting point. Unfortunately, from here on matters are much less clear. He reports that he started with the Pauline letters since their textual history is less complicated than that of the Gospels.[8] The three traditional text-types formed the basis for analysis. The uncials ℵ and B headed Group I. Group II, the "Western" Text, was formed from a combination of Codex Bezae, the Itala, and the Syriac Sinaiticus. Finally, the Byzantine text was represented as Group III. The next step seems to have been the collation of many MSS in selected passages according to their agreements or disagreements with these three basic groups.[9] Through this process the outline of some further groups became visible. More important, this procedure gave a standard to determine whether a MS was a candidate for complete collation or collation only in a few selected passages. Understandably, almost all members of Group III fell into the latter category.[10]

This rough tool could have done little more than distinguish generally Byzantine MSS from other text-types. A more refined tool was necessary to distinguish groups within the Byzantine text. Again the reader is left guessing exactly how von Soden found his Iota and Kappa groups. It is clear that the analysis of the *pericope adulterae* was meant to play an important role, but how and to what extent

[6]Von Soden, *Die Schriften des Neuen Testaments in ihrer ältesten erreichbaren Textgestalt hergestellt auf Grund ihrer Textgeschichte I. Teil: Untersuchungen. I. Abteilung: Die Textzeugen* (Göttingen: Vandenhoeck und Ruprecht, 1911) 14-16.

[7]Ibid., I/1, 14.

[8]Ibid., I/1, 17.

[9]This is by no means clear from von Soden's description. He used Matthew 21–22, Mark 10–11, Luke 7–8, and John 6–7 as test passages to spot K$^x$ MSS (ibid., I/2, 775). Whether these are the *Stichkapiteln* is anybody's guess.

[10]Von Soden, I/1, 18.

remains a question. No doubt the choice of John 7:53–8:11 was ingenious. This passage is not found in the oldest Greek witnesses, and thus its history is largely limited to the Byzantine MSS. This promised a unique case of genealogical development without complicating influences from other text-types. Because of this peculiarity and its extraordinary number of variant readings, this pericope seemed to lend itself particularly well to the analysis of the Byzantine text-type.

Von Soden compared the text of almost one thousand MSS in μ. Through an analysis not disclosed to the reader, seven basic forms became visible, representing different stages of the evolution of the text. On the basis of these Von Soden claimed to have been able to reconstruct the *Urform*. The by now thoroughly frustrating habit of giving only a defense of the result without divulging the process of getting there received the deserved wrath of Hans Lietzmann.[11]

Curiously enough the seven forms of μ do only in a few cases correspond to Iota and Kappa groups.[12] This gives rise to the suspicion that the analysis of μ was not so helpful after all. In the discussion of individual groups in *Die Schriften* I/2 members of the same group often part in the *pericope adulterae*. Apparently μ did not live up to its promise. The influence of non-Byzantine text-types was felt anyway, for a significant number of Kappa and Iota MSS omit μ. Furthermore, the unique history of the passage must have been known to many scribes, and thus special efforts were made to correct and standardize this passage. Indeed, in hindsight von Soden could hardly have picked a worse passage for group analysis than this one which has been for centuries the playground of scribes and correctors.[13]

This suspicion about μ's value for group analysis is strengthened by the fact that, though transitions are never very clear in von Soden's treatment, the transition from the analysis of μ to the Iota and Kappa groups is completely absent. Perhaps von Soden used some other way which defied scientific description to find most of his groups.[14] But in whatever way it was done, he found the groups and for that we must be thankful.

Apart from the *pericope adulterae,* we know that von Soden used the "equipment" or nontextual material for the grouping of MSS. Yet there is no evidence that von Soden used an analysis of "equipment" to find groups. Only Iᵏ and Kʳ have distinctive equipment. Especially the late Kappa recension Kʳ has a distinctive lectionary equipment and numbering of sections, so that most members of that group can be readily spotted even without looking at the actual text.[15]

[11]Lietzmann, "Die Perikope," *ZNW* 8 (1907) 34-37. Lietzmann took the μοιχαλίς passage to be a sample of von Soden's method of reconstructing the original text. This interested him more than von Soden's stated purpose of finding groups and families. Hence Lietzmann's questions whether von Soden's *Urform* of μ can really be defended by the data. Allen P. Wikgren attempted to establish the text of μ in the lectionaries. He concluded that more than one form was involved ("The Lectionary Text of the Pericope, John 8:1-11," *JBL* 53 [1934] 188-98).

[12]The only clear case of a form of μ being limited to one group is Kʳ. However, von Soden admits that he did not discover Kʳ through his analysis of the forms of μ, but from the remarkable agreement between Scrivener's collation of "l," "m," and "n." As a contrast, at least four of the seven μ forms are found among Kˣ MSS (*Die Schriften* I/2, 735). The problem is usually not that members of close-knit groups have different μ forms but that they share their form with many unrelated groups.

[13]Von Soden admits the unusual complexity and confusion of the *pericope adulterae* (ibid., I/2, 717). One wonders if he would have given this passage as prominent a place in his introduction if he had published it after his group studies were finished.

[14]Three important groups had been established before von Soden's time, the Ferrar group, Kirsopp Lake's Family 1, and the group which later became known as Family Π. Von Soden almost totally ignored the discoverers of these groups though probably not the discoveries.

[15]Von Soden, *Die Schriften* I/1, 405.

It is unfortunate that von Soden's splendid achievement of finding and establishing a significant number of MS groups was overshadowed by the justified criticism of the I-H-K text-type hypothesis. Von Soden believed that the third century saw the rise of three recensions. "I" presumably was made by Origen and published by Eusebius and Pamphilus in Palestine. "H" was made by Hesychius in Egypt and "K" by Lucian in Antioch. The critic's task, therefore, according to von Soden, is to reconstruct the original text of the three recensions, and from these the common ground text which then, in most cases, is the same as, or the closest possible approximation to, the autographa. Since von Soden put the heaviest weight on Iota, the least certain of the recensions, and a great deal more weight on Kappa than had been the custom since Westcott-Hort, the critics remained singularly unconvinced about his whole hypothesis. Textual critics were most unhappy about the Iota type. The Eta type, corresponding roughly to a combination of Hort's Neutral and Alexandrian texts, was not questioned apart from its connection with the name Hesychius and the elimination of Hort's subdivisions.[16] Also Kappa was already well established before von Soden's time. Thus the criticism at this point focused on the question of its origin in the third century and its independence from other text-types. Especially Lietzmann questioned whether K was as old as H. But in the case of Iota the existence of the text-type itself was vigorously denied.[17]

As if the I-H-K recensions were not enough speculation, von Soden proposed that Tatian's Diatessaron was the main corrupting influence on the pre-I-H-K text. The influence of Tatian was meant to explain the differences between the pre-third-century Fathers and versions and the text underlying the I-H-K recensions.[18] All this theorizing would have been relatively harmless had von Soden not made the presentation of his introduction and critical apparatus dependent upon it. Even his groups of MSS are pushed into this questionable mold.

Added to the confusion is the fact that von Soden's groups are not all of the same type and quality. Some are recensions; others are families of which the archetype can be reconstructed with a great deal of certainty. This matters little as long as the group members have sufficient distinctive characteristics to form a coherent whole, and thus are clearly set apart from all other groups. However, some of von Soden's groups, particularly $I^\alpha$, $I^\sigma$, and $I^o$, do not live up to these standards. Von Soden, of course, knew that the members of these "groups" differed greatly among themselves, but he defended their coherence in terms of different degrees of corruption by another text-type, usually K. This in turn depended on his reconstruction of the history and development of the three major recensions.

Of these "pseudo-groups," $I^\alpha$ was questioned very early by Kirsopp Lake and others, since it combined Codex Bezae with MSS which later were called "Caesarean."[19] Yet Lake himself later followed a similar procedure.[20] Like von Soden, Lake also had to give a prominent place to the different degrees of corruption of the Caesarean members by Kappa in order to establish the integrity of the group. No wonder then that the Caesarean group has become as controversial as von Soden's $I^\alpha$ used to be.

[16]Kirsopp Lake, 282-84.
[17]Lietzmann, *ZNW* 15 (1914) 328-31; also K. Lake, 282.
[18]Von Soden, *Die Schriften* I/2, 1536-44 and 1632-48.
[19]K. Lake, 282.
[20]Kirsopp Lake, Robert P. Blake, and Silva New, "The Caesarean Text of the Gospel of Mark," *HTR* 21 (1928) 207-404.

The criticism of $I^\alpha$ had the result that serious doubt was thrown on von Soden's other groups, which were not as obviously wrong, but which could not be readily tested due to the author's impenetrable description. This goes far in explaining why von Soden's groups have never been used wholeheartedly by textual critics. Usually they are introduced in textual studies because nothing better is available, and then only with careful qualifications about the certainty of the classification.[21]

Nevertheless, several of von Soden's groups have been independently verified by textual critics. Family $\Pi$ ($I^\kappa$) Family 13 ($I^\iota$) and Family 1 ($I^\eta$) were established well before von Soden's time. After the final publication of *Die Schriften des Neuen Testaments* $K^r$ was conclusively verified by David O. Voss,[22] and E. C. Colwell found $I^\beta$ to be an authentic group.[23] Detailed studies have been published on Family $\Pi$ and Family 13 by Kirsopp and Silva Lake and Jacob Geerlings.[24] In general, therefore, von Soden's groups stand up remarkably well if von Soden's own qualifications of the integrity of $I^\alpha$, $I^\sigma$, and $I^o$ are kept in mind.

Thus the question presents itself whether *Die Schriften des Neuen Testaments* can be used as the basis for further study and MS classification. The answer depends on two factors, completeness and accuracy. It must be granted from the outset that von Soden did not expressly design his volumes to be used for further group study or for the classification of previously unstudied MSS. He presents, therefore, no handy tool for this purpose. This does not exclude the possibility that, after testing and trying, a way can be found to use von Soden's volumes for this task. After all, von Soden himself classified more than 1200 MSS and his treatment of the Iota and Kappa groups shows great detail.

In spite of these promises, group study on the basis of von Soden has proved to be futile. The author seemingly assumes that no one would want to do any work on MS groups beyond his contributions. He presents his reader with lists of readings which distinguish one group from another or contrast a group against the hypothetical archetype. Since neither the text of the contrasted group nor the text of the archetype is given completely and independently, reconstruction is impossible. Lietzmann reports that he worked two days to reconstruct $\mu^2$ without feeling that he was correct. And with $\mu^2$ only twelve verses were involved and many more data were given than in the case of the groups!

Compounding the problem is the fact that the lists of differences between groups are usually only partial. Von Soden analyzed most groups only in selected chapters (*Stichkapiteln*). The text of groups is not given outside the critical apparatus to the text. This does not mean that the detailed description of groups in *Die Schriften* I/2 is of no value at all. David O. Voss found von Soden's lists of differences between $K^x$ and $K^r$ helpful in proving the existence of $K^r$ as an inde-

[21] Chapter III gives several examples of the use of von Soden's MS classifications.

[22] David O. Voss, "Is Von Soden's $K^r$ a distinct type of Text?" *JBL* 57 (1938) 311-18. The distinctive traits of $K^r$ escaped Kirsopp Lake in an analysis of 119 Byzantine MSS in Mark 11 (Lake, Blake, New, 341).

[23] E. C. Colwell, *The Four Gospels of Karahissar, I: History and Text* (Chicago: The University of Chicago, 1936) 170-77.

[24] Kirsopp and Silva Lake, *Family 13 (The Ferrar Group): The Text According to Mark* (SD 11; Philadelphia: University of Pennsylvania, 1941); Jacob Geerlings, *Family 13 in Matthew, Luke, and John* (SD 19, 20, 21; Salt Lake City: University of Utah, 1961-62); Silva Lake, *Family $\Pi$ and the Codex Alexandrinus: The Text According to Mark* (SD 5; London: Christophers, 1936); Jacob Geerlings, *Family $\Pi$ in Luke* (SD 22; Salt Lake City: University of Utah, 1962).

pendent group. However, the main evidence for the verification of von Soden's groups used by Voss, Colwell, and others was of necessity from sources outside von Soden.

This leaves only the critical apparatus to von Soden's text as a source for group study and classification of unstudied MSS. Perhaps this was the most obvious place anyway, for it seems most suitable for these purposes. The elaborate group studies in the introductory volumes gave von Soden the distinct advantage of citing, in his apparatus, groups of MSS with the necessary exceptions instead of long lists of meaningless numbers. In the introductory pages to the text volume all groups used were mentioned with the MSS which were chosen to represent these groups. The advantages are obvious. Not only does it shorten the apparatus significantly, but it also presents the evidence in a form which can be readily interpreted by the reader.[25] The difficulty of getting used to the system is easily compensated for by the advantages.

Theoretically, for group studies on the basis of von Soden's critical apparatus one would only need to follow the entries in the apparatus and to look for the siglum of the group. The groups are always quoted in the same order, and exceptions are spelled out when one or more members of a group depart from the majority.[26] In this way not only the majority text of a group can be established in a relatively short time, but also the variations within the group can be registered. Hopefully, after this has been accomplished, the detailed discussion of groups in Vol. II will then surrender many of its well-kept secrets.

The classification of previously unclassified MSS on the basis of von Soden's apparatus would present no more difficulties than group studies. The MS will have to be collated against von Soden's text in a few chapters. The variants must then be compared with the support of these same variants in the apparatus. By recording each time the group or groups which share the variant with the MS in question, one will draw up a meaningful list. If the MS belongs to one of von Soden's groups, that group will appear most often in the list. If other chapters support the conclusion, the classification will be assured.

Thus, theoretically, the prospects look promising. Von Soden's apparatus would have to be reasonably accurate, however. An occasional mistake is inevitable and would not influence the outcome, but extensive inaccuracy could not be tolerated. Unfortunately, the severest criticism of von Soden has been the lack of accuracy in his apparatus. Hoskier, one of the few critics who was in a position to check von Soden extensively, was horrified. Giving abundant evidence to back up his charge, he states, "It can only be said that the apparatus is positively honeycombed with errors, and many documents which should have been recollated have not been touched, others only partially, and others again have been incorrectly

---

[25] As a contrast the UBS edition of *The Greek New Testament* (edited by K. Aland, M. Black, B. M. Metzger, and A. Wikgren; London, 1966) uses a large number of minuscules either completely or cursorily, but supplies the reader only with the general content and date of the MSS used. Thus the reader is left completely in the dark as to what value he should attach to the minuscule evidence. Listing witnesses with variants in this way is confusing rather than enlightening. See Appendix III for comments on the selection of Greek MS evidence for the UBS edition of the Greek NT.

[26] The MSS representing $K^x$ and $K^r$ were treated as a group without ever mentioning the exceptions. More disconcerting is the statement that single exceptions to other groups were ignored if it involved a less valuable witness which read with the Kappa text (von Soden, *Die Schriften* II, xxv).

handled."[27] Summing up his feelings and impressions he closes in his characteristically devastating way: "es ist zum Weinen."[28]

In order to make an independent judgment of the matter, a test was run to measure the extent of von Soden's inaccuracy. Luke 1 was chosen, since it is one of the sample chapters of the Profile Method, and, more importantly, hundreds of twice-checked collations were available with microfilms through the office of the IGNTP in Claremont.

A careful count revealed that von Soden claims to use 120 MSS in the apparatus to Luke 1. It should be borne in mind that von Soden does not always use a MS throughout. A significant number of MSS were only partially collated. Why these MSS were not used *in toto* is not clear, but time and opportunity must have been the determining factors. In the introduction to the text volume von Soden lists all the MSS used in the apparatus with reference to the groups to which they belong, and specifies the books and chapters in which they were collated.

Through the good offices of the IGNTP, 99 of the 120 MSS could be checked by means of collations and microfilms. This was without doubt a much larger number than anybody had ever been able to check. In order to make the test meaningful, 54 readings were used which, through research independent from von Soden, had proven themselves to be read by the majority of MSS belonging to one or more (but not all) known Byzantine groups.[29] These 54 readings included almost all important variant readings in Luke 1. Only "Neutral" readings without Byzantine group support and variants supported by less than a majority of any group were omitted.

Of the 54 test readings 53 were represented in von Soden's apparatus with either positive or negative evidence. A collation of von Soden's data on the 120 MSS against the TR in the 53 test readings formed the next step. Since the IGNTP makes all its collations of Greek MSS against the TR an accurate comparison could then be made. To draw this type of information from von Soden's apparatus is far from simple, since he only gives the support for the variant in his apparatus if that list is shorter than the support of his text. Frequently, therefore, one has to sift out all those MSS listed in the introductory pages which are not mentioned with the variant in the apparatus. It is legitimate to use this "negative" evidence since von Soden claims to use his MSS consistently when he uses them. An added complication is that all of von Soden's numbers must be converted to Gregory numbers. Altogether this is a long and treacherous task but not an impossible one.

One of the most shocking discoveries was that von Soden's introductory pages are untrustworthy. At least two MSS, Gregory's 230 and 473, he claims to have used but he clearly has not. On the other hand, MSS 495, 1354, and 1515 he uses without saying so. A third aberrant category is made up of MSS which are so often incorrectly cited that they must have been used only cursorily; MSS 16, 477, 482, and 1216 fall in this group. Proof of this is that these MSS are only used incorrectly when cited under the group symbol. If this explanation is correct, then von Soden failed to warn the reader.

Once the extent of error is seen, the word "inaccuracy" becomes a

[27]Hoskier, 307.
[28]Ibid., 326.
[29]The selection of these test readings will be discussed in detail in Chapter IV.

16

euphemism. Of the 99 checked MSS, 76 were missing one or more times when they should have been cited, or were listed when they should not have been. This breaks down into 59 MSS which were missing in von Soden's apparatus from 1 to 4 times, and 39 which were added incorrectly from 1 to 6 times. The comparison showed up mistakes at every stage. They can be roughly categorized as follows:

1. Mistaken collation. This is the only explanation for the many times a MS was specifically (by number) but incorrectly added or excepted.

2. Failure to make exceptions in group listings. This is the most frequent mistake. It is so common that it becomes impossible to reconstruct the text of a MS from von Soden's apparatus.

3. Differences between the list of MSS claimed to be used in the introduction to the text volume and the MSS which were actually used. Also, lacunae in MSS were not indicated.

4. Various typographical mistakes ranging from listing a MS with the wrong variant to scrambled numbers.

5. A host of mysterious mistakes which must have happened between the worksheets and the printer. Evidently, there was much less quality control in von Soden's offices than in a Byzantine scriptorium.

Kirsopp Lake once said that there never has been and never will be a perfect collation. Yet he did not deny that great accuracy is demanded. It was granted that for group study and classification of previously unclassified MSS no perfection was necessary. But von Soden's inaccuracies cannot be tolerated for any purpose. His apparatus is useless for a reconstruction of the text of the MSS he used. Not only does it involve a hazardous work process, but also the result will be untrustworthy. The situation is not better for group study. Exceptions of individual MSS to the majority of the group are frequently missing. What is worse for the classification of MSS is that there is not always a group majority where von Soden indicates it or vice versa.[30]

All of this may sound like a total condemnation of von Soden's *Die Schriften des Neuen Testaments*. It is certainly not meant to be that. Harsh as one must be on the quality of von Soden's end product and general procedure, one cannot ignore his achievement. More than 1200 minuscules were examined by von Soden in whole or in part. His classification is in the great majority of cases the only information we have about the text of MSS. Years of usage have shown that von Soden's classifications of MSS, although not always correct, are usually helpful.

The main drawback of von Soden's classifications is that for most MSS they are based on a very short selection of text. Thus a change in text-type, a very common phenomenon in Greek NT MSS, goes unnoticed. Consequently, a final judgment of the text of most MSS as to grouping cannot be made on von Soden's classification alone. The other drawback is that von Soden did not leave us a trustworthy tool to classify the many MSS which he was unable to examine.

[30]Recently, W. J. Elliott ("The Need for an Accurate and Comprehensive Collation of All Known Greek NT Manuscripts with their Individual Variants noted *in pleno*," *Studies in New Testament Language and Text* [George D. Kilpatrick Festschrift] [ed. W. J. Elliott; Leiden: Brill, 1976] 137-43) made a very negative evaluation of von Soden's accuracy after testing ten MSS used by von Soden in Acts. James R. Royse has shown that Elliott's interpretation of von Soden's apparatus is faulty and greatly exaggerates the degree of error ("Von Soden's Accuracy," *JTS* 30 [1979] 166-71).

Von Soden has given the student of groups a starting point, not a finished product or a classification tool. His legacy does not include a trustworthy method for discovering or studying groups. Rather, he gave a general picture of the mass of minuscules in terms of groups, and the promise that order can be brought into the chaotic world of Byzantine NT MSS.

CHAPTER III

# THE QUEST FOR
# TEXT CLASSIFICATION

## 1. HUTTON'S ATLAS OF TEXTUAL CRITICISM

The shadow of von Soden looms large in the classification of Greek NT MSS in terms of groups. The few Byzantine group studies prior to the publication of *Die Schriften des Neuen Testaments* soon dropped out of sight.[1] Since von Soden, the work on groups has consisted mainly in establishing the text of the archetype of some of the more important groups.[2] Yet the need for a simple and accurate classification tool was only heightened by von Soden's *magnum opus*. An interesting attempt to fill this pressing need had already been made by Edward Ardron Hutton in 1911, two years before the publication of von Soden's text and apparatus.[3] The timing could not have been worse.

Hutton's *Atlas* was in a sense already a reaction to von Soden. He was familiar with von Soden's introductory volumes and thoroughly frustrated by his way of presenting groups. Almost anticipating the Profile Method, he complained:

> Professor von Soden has given us list after list of readings of MSS. and groups. These lists are not only a weariness to the flesh but are based often upon the mere peculiarities of each group. Suppose one uniform set of readings had been chosen whereby to test all alike, I venture to think we should have obtained far more insight into the mutual relationship of documents. At present they are each divided into their groups, but the relationship of each group to the other documents is often all but impossible to determine.[4]

Hutton began a task left undone by Hort. He accepted with Hort the basic unity of the Byzantine text and its secondary nature. But Hort had realized that among the thousands of unexamined Byzantine minuscules some valuable MSS might lie hidden. Hutton wanted to discover these textual gems. He feared they might become mere museum curiosities, "like the lantern of Guy Fawkes, or that wonderful threepenny bit that 'Bodley' Coxe (may he rest in peace) once used as a touchstone to divide the sheep from the goats.''[5]

---

[1]E.g. Kirsopp Lake's model study, *Codex 1 of the Gospels and Its Allies* (TextsS 7/3; Cambridge: The University Press, 1902).

[2]See Chapter II.

[3]Edward Ardron Hutton, *An Atlas of Textual Criticism* (Cambridge: The University Press, 1911).

[4]Ibid., xi and xii.

[5]Ibid., x; the British are able to bring some life even into an Atlas of Textual Criticism.

Since Hutton was not interested in the Byzantine text, only in exceptions to that text, he did not concern himself with von Soden's Iota and Kappa groups. He considered it sufficient to distinguish between the three chief groups which had been the main staple of textual critics ever since Griesbach.[6]

Hutton's procedure stands out for its simplicity. Those NT passages were chosen where the Alexandrian, the Western, and the Byzantine texts offer mutually conflicting evidence. All the triple readings which showed some ambiguity, or where the evidence of the versions or Fathers could not be adduced with certainty, were eliminated.[7] The result was a total of 312 triple readings in the NT. The next step was to collate a MS in these 312 places (insofar as they are extant). Hutton provided separate charts of the triple readings in each of the Gospels, Acts, the Catholics, Paul, and the Apocalypse. On these charts Hutton included the readings of all MSS up to A.D. 1000 known to him, some additional important minuscules, many OL MSS, the versions, and at least sixteen Church Fathers. In this way, not only the affinity of a MS to a text-type could be determined, but also a comparison could be made with the main members of each text-type. In addition, mixed MSS would show up.

The value of Hutton's *Atlas* for a quick and general evaluation of the text of a MS is beyond question. Of course, Hutton's tool is not better than his definitions of the three major text-types. For the Alexandrian text he used especially ℵ and B. For the Byzantine text he seems to have used primarily E and V, and sometimes minuscules if the number of extant uncials was low. For the Western text he used some OL MSS in the Gospels; elsewhere he used a combination of factors which cannot be easily discerned from the charts.

One cannot help feeling that Hutton's definitions leave much to be desired. The three so-called text-types are by no means of a similar kind and quality. Few scholars today would call the "Western" text a text-type. It has been characterized as an uncontrolled and popular text.[8] As such it cannot be represented by a single reading. Hutton's use of versions as primary witnesses of the Western text shows the weakness of his definition.

The Byzantine text did not fare too well either in Hutton's hands. One can, of course, arbitrarily pick a few K[1] uncials or some closely related K[r] MSS and so produce an even text, but only by ignoring the limbs of other Byzantines scattered around this procrustean bed.

Hutton's 312 triple readings would have been satisfactory if they had been taken from three close-knit families of which the archetype could be reconstructed. But such was not the case. His selection procedure had a built-in bias against variety within the text-types. The result was artificial and disappointing. To be sure, the triple readings could spot the relation of P[75] to B in John, and Ω's relation to V, but most MSS do not have the ideal vital statistics of Hutton's text-types. As a result, far too many MSS appear unduly mixed. We need a much more accurate tool to measure, for example, the mutual relationships of the so-called Caesarean MSS.

[6]Ibid., 3.
[7]Ibid., 4-5.
[8]E. C. Colwell, "Hort Redivivus: A Plea and a Program," *Transitions in Biblical Studies* (ed. J. Coert Rylaarsdam; "Essays in Divinity" 6; Chicago: The University of Chicago, 1968) 149; repr. in *Studies in Methodology in Textual Criticism of the New Testament* (NTTS 9; Grand Rapids: Eerdmans, 1969) 166.

Hutton fell victim to the hundred-year-old hallowed tradition of three basic text-types. But Kirsopp Lake had begun to shake this tradition already in 1901. Von Soden and Streeter furthered its downfall until today the term text-type is limited to the Alexandrian and Byzantine texts, and then only with important qualifications.

## 2. ALAND'S THOUSAND READINGS

Hutton's approach has much in common with that of Kurt Aland.[9] Aland also is not interested in the Byzantine text as such, but only in MSS which significantly diverge from the Byzantine text. An improvement on Hutton is that Aland no longer works with a Western text-type. If we understand him correctly — the description of his "1000 cursives examined in 1000 passages with a view to evaluate their text" has not been published — Aland has selected his 1000 passages from places where the Byzantine text differs from non-Byzantine MSS. In the light of Hutton's problems of defining his triple readings, one would like to know how Aland determined what is a Byzantine reading and what is not. This crucial question awaits further word from Aland.

Also unanswered is the question whether Aland's thousand readings will determine only whether a MS is Byzantine, or perhaps also what it is if it is not Byzantine. Thus it is not certain whether we are dealing here with a tool for the classification of minuscules or with a rough selection instrument for MSS important enough, i.e. non-Byzantine enough, to be included in a future critical apparatus. It certainly is the latter, but hopefully it is a great deal more.

Regrettably, Aland did not think it necessary to select his 1000 readings from among all NT books. None was chosen from Matthew and Luke. In view of the very common change of text classification between Gospels, and even within a Gospel, we will remain uncertain about the classification of a MS in Matthew and Luke even if the 1000 readings indicate that other NT parts are Byzantine.

Most puzzling is Aland's announced treatment of the Byzantine text as a closed and distinct unit.[10] If he defines the Byzantine text in terms of von Soden's $K^1$, $K^x$, and $K^r$, what does he do when one or more of the important non-Byzantine groups read with the three main Kappa groups against the rest of the MS tradition? Actually, places where $K^1$, $K^x$, and $K^r$ have readings against all other groups are extremely rare. There is no such case in the three chapters of Luke analyzed in the Profile Method. Certainly agreement or disagreement with one "Byzantine reading" carries a great deal more weight than agreement or disagreement with another. Ultimately it is not so important how often a MS differs from the Byzantine text, but when and with what support. Statistical analysis (if this is what Aland has in mind?) will completely ignore this aspect.

Our argument with Aland centers on his contention that the Byzantine text has a tradition of its own.[11] For in contrast to the many unique readings of the "Neutral" and the "Caesarean" groups, the main Byzantine groups have practically none. This means either that the Byzantine text is almost completely derived

---

[9]See Chapter I, 3-4.
[10]Kurt Aland, "The Significance of the Papyri for New Testament Research," *The Bible in Modern Scholarship* (ed. J. Philip Hyatt; Nashville/New York: Abingdon, 1965) 342.
[11]Ibid.

from other text-types — something which many centuries of independent transmission cannot obscure — or that it has influenced non-Byzantine texts to such an extent that its unique features have been obliterated. In general, Hort took the former position and von Soden the latter. The truth is probably a combination of these two factors. Whatever the explanation, the consequence is that the Byzantine text does not have a clearly independent or distinct text tradition, although some of its subgroups have a very distinct transmission tradition. This fact must weigh heavily in any classification tool.

Due to its peculiar nature, the Byzantine text in many cases cannot be represented by a single reading, especially not if one wants to find non-Byzantine and mixed MSS as Aland does. It is too early to decide whether a $K^1$, $K^x$, or $K^r$ reading found in "Caesarean" MSS is due to Kappa influence, or whether the "Kappa" reading was derived from the "Caesarean" text. It is not necessary to decide between these two possibilities if the Byzantine text is represented in terms of its member groups instead of as a unity. For in that case one can determine whether a minuscule is a member of one of the main Byzantine groups quite apart from the value of its readings. But this would have necessitated the development of a profile method!

## 3. THE CAESAREAN TEXT

The 1920s brought a unique set of circumstances to the United States, reviving a demand for, and interest in, the classification of MSS in terms of groups. This was the time that many NT MSS were bought by American universities and collectors.[12] At the same time, lower criticism of the NT was practiced at the University of Chicago with a vigor and scope that has perhaps not been equaled elsewhere.[13] Of course, there was a connection between the large acquisition of ancient MSS and the blossoming of textual criticism at Chicago. Students enthusiastically collated the newly discovered MSS and tried to determine the value of their text.

A third factor ought to be mentioned. Kirsopp Lake, an outstanding British textual critic in the Hortian tradition, had come to teach at Harvard Divinity School in 1914. There he developed his hypothesis of the relationship between Family 1, Family 13, Θ, 565, 700, and 28 which later became known as the Caesarean text.[14] B. H. Streeter carried Lake's work another step forward by pinpointing Caesarea as the original location of what he called Family Θ. More important for our purposes was his discovery of "Caesarean" affinities in the other Iota groups of von Soden, especially Codices 157, 1071, and 1424 and its allies.[15]

All this ought not to have been surprising in view of von Soden's Iota

[12]Kenneth W. Clark, *A Descriptive Catalogue of Greek New Testament Manuscripts in America* (Chicago: The University of Chicago, 1937); Aland, *Studien zur Überlieferung*, 221, 226-29.

[13]The tradition of textual study at Chicago began with the brilliant textual critic Caspar René Gregory. His student Edgar J. Goodspeed produced a number of outstanding lower critics who have dominated the field in the United States.

[14]K. Lake and R. P. Blake, "The Text of the Gospels and the Koridethi Codex," *HTR* 16 (1923) 267-86.

[15]B. H. Streeter, *The Four Gospels: A Study of Origins* (New York: Macmillan, 1925) 572-81; idem, "Codices 157, 1071 and the Caesarean Text," *Quantulacumque* (ed. R. P. Casey, Silva Lake, and Agnes K. Lake; London: Christophers, 1937) 149-50.

recension. Lake and Streeter had merely revived an insight of von Soden which had been discredited a decade earlier. After von Soden's Iota groups were taken out of their questionable setting, and Codex Bezae had been left out of consideration, the Iota recension began to make some sense to scholars, though now under a different name.

## 4. GOODSPEED AND RIDDLE'S USE OF STATISTICAL ANALYSIS

The immediate result was a renewed interest in Byzantine groups with "Caesarean readings," especially in the United States. Published collations and MSS were searched for interesting readings. Unfortunately, no proper framework had been set up to do such research. The general procedure was the following:

A. The MS, or a part of it, was collated against the TR.

B. A section of the collation was selected, and support for the variants from the TR was added from Tischendorf's *editio octava maior*, Scrivener, and other editions and collections of collations.

C. Support for the variants was tabulated in order to find the MS or MSS which most often agree with the MS under study. This was frequently expressed in percentages of agreements with the major witnesses.

D. A classification was made in terms of the MS or MSS with which it showed the highest percentage of agreement.

A few examples of the usage of this procedure may prove instructive. In 1902 Edgar J. Goodspeed published a study and collation of the Newberry Gospels (Gregory's 1289).[16] He began with the selection of all significant variants from the TR. These he divided into Syrian, Pre-Syrian, and singular-subsingular readings. The last category he ignored since it was of no value for classification. Next he calculated the percentages of Syrian readings among the variants from the TR for each Gospel.[17] The resulting percentages had no significance in themselves. Therefore Goodspeed went through the same procedure with five other MSS (the Haskell Gospels, Uncials A and D, and Gregory's 61 and 892). He then observed that the MSS with the lowest number of divergences from the TR also had the highest percentage of Syrian readings. Although he claimed that this was precisely what he expected, one wonders whether he really knew the reason for this "coincidence," for if he did he would have seen the futility of his carefully calculated percentages.

Anyone using variants from the TR as a basis for classification must face the special character of Erasmus's text. When compared with a large number of late minuscules, the TR clearly is far from uniformly Byzantine.[18] There is no doubt about its affinities to the Kappa groups, but it departs too often to be called a good representative. Thus any Byzantine MS will have a certain number of variants from the TR that do not prove distance from but rather affinity to the Byzantine text. A

[16]Edgar J. Goodspeed, *The Newberry Gospels* (Chicago: The University of Chicago, 1902). It should be remembered that this publication came well before von Soden's *Die Schriften des Neuen Testaments*.

[17]For the Newberry Gospels, he gives 42.758962% as the Syrian element in Mark. The six decimals tell us, of course, more about Goodspeed than about the MS.

[18]E. C. Colwell, "The Complex Character of the late Byzantine Text of the Gospels," *JBL* 44 (1935) 213; and Kirsopp Lake, Robert P. Blake, and Silva New, "The Caesarean Text of the Gospel of Mark," *HTR* 21 (1928) 338.

"run of the mill" $K^x$ or $K^r$ MS will have at least 100 such variants in Luke alone. Hence of the total number of variants against the TR some will indicate affinity to, but others distance from, the Byzantine groups.

To use a hypothetical example, a certain MS may have 200 variants against the TR in a certain Gospel. In that Gospel the TR departs 100 times from the majority text of $K^x$ MSS. Following Goodspeed's procedure this MS could have as a maximum 50% Syrian (= Byzantine) readings. If that is the case it should be classified as a good member of the $K^x$ family with some surplus of non-Byzantine readings. All $K^x$ MSS have such surplus. Another MS may have only 100 variants from the TR of which 50 prove to be Syrian. Again Goodspeed would arrive at 50%, but this time he might well be wrong in calling the MS a member of the $K^x$ group. The 50 standard variants between the TR and the $K^x$ group which this MS lacked count against its membership in $K^x$. Thus, comparing the percentages of Syrian readings in variants from the TR among MSS can lead to false conclusions.

Goodspeed's observation that MSS with the lowest number of divergences from the TR have also the highest percentage of Syrian readings now stands in a different light. The great mass of Byzantine MSS, however divergent among themselves, share a high percentage of the readings which make the TR stand apart from the Byzantine groups. Since Goodspeed's Syrian readings among the variants from the TR will remain fairly constant for most MSS, any increase in variants will automatically lower the percentage of Syrian readings. It would have been much simpler and just as inaccurate if Goodspeed had used the numerical count of the divergences from the TR as an indication of distance from the Byzantine text. It would have saved him the hazardous job of deciding whether a reading was Syrian or non-Syrian.[19]

Von Soden had on the one hand simplified the work of classification by publishing a list of some 1200 NT MSS with their group affiliation, while on the other hand he had set a standard which necessitated much more detail in the study of an unclassified MS than had been necessary prior to his work. Donald W. Riddle's study of the Rockefeller McCormick NT (Gregory's 2400) is a good example of classification in the post-von Soden era.[20]

The classification of Codex 2400 could have been relatively simple. A study of the many outstanding illuminations of this MS showed a clear relationship to Codex 38 in iconography. In addition, both MSS were unquestionably written by the same scribe.[21] Some important information was derived from this identification. It established thirteenth-century Constantinople as the origin of Codex 2400, since this was specified in a colophon in Codex 38.

Although Riddle saw no obvious affinity in text between Codices 2400 and 38, he considered it worthwhile to look at von Soden's classification of Codex 38 and the MSS associated with it. Von Soden considered 38 a greatly weakened form of the $I^k$ group.[22] After checking 2400 with the $I^k$ readings in von Soden's ap-

---

[19]Goodspeed (*The Newberry Gospels,* 29) gives a table of the variants of the Newberry Gospels in Mark 1–3, indicating the MS support (taken from Tischendorf) and his assignment of Syrian, Neutral, or Western. Many of these assignments will not seem obvious to the reader today.

[20]Donald W. Riddle, *The Rockefeller McCormick New Testament, II: The Text* (Chicago: The University of Chicago, 1932).

[21]Ibid., 103.

paratus, Riddle concluded that 2400 was not a member of I$^\kappa$, and that its readings were of the Iota rather than the Kappa groups.[22]

After comparing the variant readings of 2400 with many published collations, Riddle hit on what he thought was a new little group of which 2400 was a leading member. Among these were Codices 489 and 482, which were also mentioned by von Soden in connection with Codex 38 as weak members of the I$^\kappa$ group. Riddle then was forced to conclude that 489 and 482 were incorrectly grouped by von Soden.[24]

This result did not end Riddle's tireless efforts to locate the text of 2400. He compared Codex 2400 with Kirsopp Lake's detailed study of more than 100 MSS in Mark 11.[25] Furthermore, he calculated how often the major uncials supported the variants of 2400. Although Π, K, and A (all members of I$^\kappa$!) had by far the highest percentages, and although Lake's list pointed at I$^\kappa$, Riddle still maintained that "2400 is not in the main in the K$^a$ [ = I$^\kappa$] family."[26]

Finally, Riddle, like most NT MS students of his time, went on a search for "Caesarean" readings. By using Lake's highly questionable method of calling Caesarean any reading against the TR that has the support of two group members, Riddle ended up with 167 Caesarean readings in Mark, or approximately 42% of the variants of Codex 2400. This was grounds enough for Riddle to call his codex weakened Caesarean with a mixture of I$^\kappa$ readings.

Of course, Riddle's haphazard procedure — though he was much more thorough than most of his contemporaries in classifying a MS — begs for a critique. Most glaring is the shocking ease with which Riddle dismissed von Soden's classification of Codices 38, 489, and 482. On the smallest bit of "independent" evidence MSS were reclassified as if von Soden had made only a rough guess. In this attitude toward von Soden Riddle does not stand alone. The legendary inaccuracy of von Soden's apparatus and the negative criticism of the Iota text-type had cast an air of suspicion over all von Soden's work. His classification of MSS was used only by default and discarded for the slightest reasons.[27]

Riddle's testing of von Soden's classification had been limited to the *pericope adulterae* and parts of his critical apparatus. But as has been argued before[28] — and as was partly admitted by von Soden himself — the *pericope adulterae* is an insufficient clue to the classification of a MS. Also, von Soden's apparatus may well be the place to test a core member of I$^\kappa$, but not a weak member, even aside from the gross inaccuracies of the apparatus. True, it is not Riddle's fault

---

[22]Von Soden, *Die Schriften* I/2, 855.

[23]Riddle, 107. Riddle did not seem to realize that as far as von Soden is concerned I$^\kappa$ stands out from the Kappa groups in its Iota readings.

[24]Ibid., 109.

[25] "Excursus I; the Ecclesiastical Text" in Lake, Blake, New, "The Caesarean Text," 338-57.

[26]Riddle, 126-27.

[27]So low has von Soden's stock fallen among some recent lower critics that it was possible for Russell Champlin to conclude, after some extremely limited and highly questionable statistical analysis, that von Soden's classification of Codex M as a member of I$^{\varphi r}$ and a weak member of Family 1424 could not be demonstrated (*Family E and Its Allies* [SD 27; Salt Lake City: University of Utah, 1966] 168). Such an erroneous judgment — Silva Lake and the Profile Method have proven von Soden's classification to be correct — can only be made out of ignorance of von Soden's groups and of the severe limitations of statistics in group study.

[28]See Chapter II, 10-12.

that one cannot use von Soden's volumes to test a weak I$^\kappa$ member, but Riddle had no excuse for drawing conclusions from a limited probe before he knew what a weak I$^\kappa$ member was supposed to look like.

As it is, Codices 2400 and 482 are weak but definite members of I$^\kappa$, and 489 is one of the leading members of that group.[29] The group has many weak members, i.e. "corrupted" toward K$^x$, but its features are so characteristic that even very weak members can be spotted with relative ease. Many of the weaker members show "block mixture" with K$^x$, a fact which is not always visible in von Soden's pages. Perhaps if Riddle had known these features he would have ceased his search earlier, when he was so close to an accurate classification.

An important element in Riddle's classification — and that of almost all others — was the use of statistical analysis. As we saw in the case of Goodspeed and Riddle, this statistical analysis is done on the basis of the variants from the TR. The reason for using the TR as a collation base is not entirely due to custom and availability. As a matter of fact, the Nestle-Aland text is much more accessible. More likely the use of the TR is due to the general repudiation of the Byzantine text since Hort.[30] The TR has become the "whipping boy" in lieu of the Byzantine text. It is considered the "absolute zero" in NT textual criticism. Departure from the TR automatically bestows favor on a variant.

The fallacy of this contention was brought out in connection with Goodspeed's classification of the Newberry Gospels. The TR is by no means the "absolute zero" of the Byzantine text. It departs from the common denominator more frequently than the mass of Byzantine minuscules. The irony is that when the TR departs from the main Byzantine groups, usually some members of Lake's Caesarean group will support the Byzantine groups. Thus what appears to be a good "Caesarean" reading is often an unquestionable part of the Byzantine text.[31] Statistical analysis can not discriminate between "Caesarean" readings with or without Byzantine group support. As a result percentages of "Caesarean" and non-Byzantine readings become grossly inflated.

The special character of the TR is only one challenge to the validity of statistical analysis. Much more serious is that if one uses the divergences from the TR as a base, this base will change with every MS. Riddle's Codex 2400 had 42% of its variants from the TR in Mark supported by at least two "Caesarean" MSS. This adds up to a total of 167 "Caesarean" readings in all of Mark. But the authors of *The Caesarean Text of Mark* give 392 "Caesarean" family readings in Mark 1, 6, and 11 alone! Compared with that the supposed "Caesarean" element in Codex 2400 appears insignificant.

Before Riddle could legitimately have called his MS "Caesarean," he would have had to do a great deal more work. Leaving Lake's loose and vulnerable definition of a "Caesarean" reading for a moment for what it is, one would have to

[29]This was confirmed by means of the Profile Method for Luke, and for Mark by Silva Lake, *Family* Π *and the Codex Alexandrinus: The Text According to Mark* (SD 5; London: Christophers, 1936) 15.

[30]E. C. Colwell, "The Significance of Grouping of New Testament Manuscripts," *NTS* (1958) 75 (repr. in *Studies in Methodology*, 4).

[31]The support collected for the variants is usually limited to the major non-Byzantine uncials. Thus a Byzantine departure from the TR can easily go undetected and end up in the list of "Caesarean" readings.

determine the total number of family readings in a passage or Gospel. Then a large number of MSS taken from all possible groups and text-types must be checked in these family readings. This will tell how often a $K^r$ MS, or an $I^\kappa$ MS, or a member of the "Neutral" group has a "Caesarean" reading. Only with all these figures as a background will the 167 "Caesarean" readings of Codex 2400 in Mark have any meaning at all. It is safe to predict that it will be hard to find a non-Caesarean MS with less than 100 so-called Caesarean readings in Mark, and that it is easy to equal Codex 2400.

E. C. Colwell noticed the meaninglessness of these statistical acrobatics years ago. When checking a collation of the Terrell Gospels (Gregory's 2322) with the TR, he noticed that it was easy to find "Caesarean" support for the great majority of the variants of this MS. How tempting with such a high percentage to call the MS "Caesarean!" "But," he reports, "the variants are few in number, the support is varied, and the MS has been shown to be a leading member of Von Soden's $K^r$ group." Thus he concludes, "Limitation of attention to variants from the Textus Receptus obscures the kinship of manuscripts."[32]

## 5. GEERLINGS'S USE OF STATISTICAL ANALYSIS

Incorrect use of statistical analysis has taken its toll in MS group studies as well. One such case, Jacob Geerlings's *Family E and Its Allies in Mark,* deserves some attention since it appeals to the Profile Method in its attempt to establish the unity of Family E in Mark and to show its relationship to members of well-defined text-types.[33] However, Geerlings's method, insofar as it can be reconstructed from his pages, resembles the Profile Method only remotely.

Geerlings begins with the definition of Family E as established by his former student R. Champlin for Matthew.[34] His purpose is mainly to establish that E is indeed a bona fide group in Mark. He claims that he can accomplish this by comparing in Mark 4 the uncial members of Family E, i.e. E, F, G, H, S, U, V, Ω, with MSS of well-defined text-types by means of the Profile Method. From the list of 89 variants and their support on pp. 3-4, it appears that these text-types are the well-known Alexandrian text-type (ℵ, B, C, 33), the Western (D) and Caesarean texts (Θ, W, Family 1, Family 13, 22, 157, 1071), Family Π (A, Π), two purple uncials (Φ, Σ), and the TR.

The method of selecting the 89 variants in Mark 4 is not stated but seems to involve those variants where at least 50% of the Family E uncials read together against one or more of the MSS used in the comparison. The resulting statistical tabulation was meant to demonstrate the unity of Family E and its relationship to well-known MSS or groups. However, Geerlings's tabulation demonstrates nothing as to the unity of his group. All that can be validly deduced from it is that those MSS

[32]Colwell, "The Significance," 76 (=*Studies in Methodology,* 5).

[33]Jacob Geerlings, *Family E and Its Allies in Mark* (SD 31; Salt Lake City: University of Utah, 1968) 2. *Family E and Its Allies in Luke* (SD 35; Salt Lake City: University of Utah, 1968) by the same author is based on the group analysis in the Mark volume. A detailed comparison of Geerlings's method and results with those of the Profile Method has been published by Frederik Wisse and Paul R. McReynolds in "Family E and the Profile Method," *Bib* 50 (1970) 67-75.

[34]Russell Champlin, *Family E and Its Allies in Matthew* (SD 28; Salt Lake City: University of Utah, 1966).

which agree less than 90% with the majority of the family E uncials are most likely not members of Family E. For most MSS used in the comparison, this was already well known.

On closer examination it becomes evident that Geerlings's statistical tabulation shows the opposite of what he intends. He assigns 100% to his Family E ($K^{1-i}$) but in reality its members range from 99% (E) to 94.5% (H and S) agreement with the majority of the group. This means that the TR with 94.5% falls within the range of the Family E definition.

Even more startling are the results of a test run with MS 1185, a collation of which has been published in *Family E and Its Allies in Luke*. When compared with the 89 variants in Mark 4, MS 1185 agrees with the majority of Family E 98% of the time. This makes 1185 a member of Family E second in quality only to E itself. However, as Geerlings knows, 1185 is a solid member of group $K^r$.

The implications of the entry of the TR and the $K^r$ MS 1185 into the E family are far-reaching, for they open the door to the bulk of Byzantine MSS. For if the TR and $K^r$, both clearly distinguishable entities among Byzantine MSS, fall into E's range, then certainly the more closely related mass of $K^x$ MSS will prove to be E members also. To put it conservatively, Geerlings's original thirteen family members have exploded into a teeming tribe of more than one thousand MSS in the Gospels. This colorful tribe already has a name; it is known as the Byzantine text-type.

In order to prove the unity of Family E, there was no need for Geerlings to show its distinctiveness from the "Neutral" text, the "Caesarean" text, or Codex Bezae. No one doubts this. The burden of proof is to show that Family E is clearly distinguishable from $K^x$, $K^r$, $K^1$, and other Byzantine groups. Geerlings was not able to do this.

Again the main culprit proved to be statistical analysis. Even if the test readings selected for classification are well chosen, statistical tabulation is quite capable of distorting them or rendering them useless. A statistical tabulation normally uses a mean against which all MSS are measured. If two MSS agree, for example, 88% of the time with the mean, it is most tempting to claim that they belong together. In reality, the two MSS involved may well be much farther removed from each other than each is from the mean. Statistics do not tell us where a MS departs from the mean, only how often. They are not capable of showing us with what it agrees when it disagrees with the mean. These are essential requirements for MS classification. Each test reading must be weighed and remain visible until the classification is made. Statistical tabulation can only lump variants together. Therefore this form of statistical tabulation for MS classification and group study ought to be abandoned.

## 6. COLWELL'S MULTIPLE READINGS

Dissatisfaction with the naive attempts at classification since von Soden led E. C. Colwell to develop a more reasoned approach to the problem. From the beginning his concern was speed and accuracy; speed, since the amount of unstudied textual material was so overwhelming; accuracy, since this was where his contemporaries had most dismally failed. These two factors seemed incompatible, however. Therefore Colwell conceived of three consecutive steps in the classification of a MS.[35]

The first step was an improvement on Hutton's triple readings. Instead of Hutton's three text-types, Colwell used any group reading as a factor. He also did not want to be limited by the arbitrary number three, and speaks instead of "Multiple Readings," which he defines as those readings

> in which the minimum support for each of at least three variant forms of the text is either one of the major strands of the tradition, or the support of a previously established group (such as Family 1, Family Π, the Ferrar Group, $K^l$, $K^i$, and $K^r$), or the support of some one of the ancient versions (such as af, it, $sy^s$, $sy^c$, bo, or sa), or the support of some single manuscript of an admittedly distinctive character (such as D).[36]

The advantages over Hutton's triple readings are obvious. First, Colwell works with established groups of which the main witnesses are known. In this way, Hutton's failure to define accurately the three major strands of text has been circumvented. Second, a passage of text produces significantly more multiple readings than triple readings. It is sufficient, therefore, to select some short passages of each part of the NT in order to obtain an overall view. At the same time, the multiple readings give much more detail than Hutton's tool. Hutton could distinguish at best between three types of MSS. As a result, most MSS must fall between these three types. Colwell has a much better range of existing textual groups, and hence will end up with much less ambiguous results.

Colwell's second step assumes that the multiple readings have provided a positive result. He then proposes to look at the MS in question in relation to the group or text-type to which it most often conformed in the multiple readings. This is both for confirmation of the result of step 1, and for locating a MS within a group. Unfortunately, he used the "Neutral" text-type as a test case. This group of MSS stands out from all other textual groups with its large number of distinctive readings, which led Colwell to an unnecessarily high standard:

> A group is not a group unless it has unique elements. Separate existence can be claimed only for groups with some readings "of their own." The newly-found manuscript cannot be related to a group without being related to the singular readings of the group.[37]

All this works for the "Neutral" text-type. The evidence of its leading MSS is readily available, and an acceptable list of unique readings can be compiled. The new MS which is related to this text-type can then be tested against the list of singular readings of the group. But to draw up such a list for any other group is quite another matter. Not only is the evidence harder to obtain, but the number of unique features diminishes dramatically the closer one gets to the Byzantine groups. Group

---

[35]E. C. Colwell, "Method in Locating a Newly-Discovered Manuscript within the Manuscript Tradition of the Greek New Testament," *SE* I (1959) 757-77 (repr. in *Studies in Methodology*, 26-44).

[36]Ibid., 759 ( = *Studies in Methodology*, 27-28).

[37]Ibid., 761 ( = *Studies in Methodology*, 30).

K$^r$ has only six unique readings in all of Luke,[38] and K$^x$, K$^i$, and K$^l$ certainly have less.[39]

The third step in Colwell's method is a determination of the quantity of agreement in the new MS with the MSS which seem most closely related to it. It forms a final confirmation of the classification of a MS, while at the same time it will pinpoint the MS which is nearest to it in the MS tradition.

Colwell's multiple-readings method has not progressed much beyond the samples used in the original article. To make it a complete tool, applicable to the whole NT, would involve an exorbitant amount of time and effort. Since he proposed the multiple-readings method Colwell himself has moved to a quantitative analysis of relationships that departs from the multiple readings at certain points.[40]

The starting point is again that, in order to establish relationships between MSS, the total amount of variation must be taken into account, not just the divergences from the TR.[41] Also all singular readings and those with a high probability of being of nongenetic origin are eliminated since they contribute nothing to the relationship of MSS. All those places of variation in the text were chosen where group division occurs. But in contrast to the multiple readings, Colwell now accepted places where the tradition separates into two strands.[42] He originally eliminated double readings from his multiple readings since they "do not yield easily their evidence for the location of a manuscript."[43] This addition increases the total number of variation units of a passage significantly. True variants with three or more forms are relatively rare. In most cases multiple readings involve both a transposition and one or more other elements. Such variation units with multiple factors of variation tend to scatter the evidence and obscure relationships. Thus the addition of "double readings" will improve the picture.

After the units of variation are selected for a passage, a large number of MSS representing all text-types and groups are collated. Then the percentages of agreement of any MS with all others can be tabulated. On the basis of a sample made in John 10, Colwell and Tune concluded that "the quantitative definition of a text-type is a group of manuscripts that agree more than 70 per cent of the time and is separated by a gap of about 10 per cent from its neighbors."[44]

If the variation units used by Colwell and Tune in John 10 were available, it would be possible to collate an unclassified MS in these places. Percentages could then be calculated and a classification could be made.

The quantitative analysis will work well with MSS belonging to the core of one of the established groups. Unfortunately, a large number of the minuscules have suffered mixture and their group affiliation has become blurred. Such MSS could

---

[38]David O. Voss, "Is Von Soden's K$^r$ a distinct type of Text?" *JBL* 57 (1938) 316.

[39]In Chapter IV, which deals with the Profile Method, it is argued that a group definition does not depend on unique readings but on a unique configuration of readings.

[40]E. C. Colwell and E. W. Tune, "The Quantitative Relationships between MS. Text-Types," *Biblical and Patristic Studies in Memory of Robert Pierce Casey* (ed. J. N. Birdsall and R. W. Thomson; Freiburg: Herder, 1963) 25-32 (repr. in *Studies in Methodology,* 56-62).

[41]Ibid., 25 (=*Studies in Methodology,* 56).

[42]Ibid., 26 (=*Studies in Methodology,* 57).

[43]Colwell, "Method," 758 (=*Studies in Methodology,* 27). This contention is only true if one wants to measure the amount of disagreement between MSS rather than agreements.

[44]Colwell-Tune, "Quantitative," 29 (=*Studies in Methodology,* 59).

never meet the Colwell-Tune standard of 70%.[45] Agreements expressed in percentages will tend to wash out the characteristics of the group to which the mixed MS belongs. Nothing can offset this drawback of statistical analysis. Only a method which will bring out the relative value of every reading in a test passage for group affiliation can spot the weak members of groups. But such a method cannot use statistics. Every detail of the characteristics of a group must be visible and remain visible until the classification has been made.

At the same time that the Profile Method was developed, Gordon D. Fee worked on a refinement of Colwell's method of locating a MS within the MS tradition. His concern was with major early witnesses such as P[66] and ℵ which do not, or not always, show a high quantitative agreement with any text-type, group, or MS. In an important study of the text of ℵ in the Gospel of John,[46] Fee argued that "peculiar agreements," which Colwell and Tune had eliminated because they may be accidental, should be included since they can confirm textual affinity in cases where the overall quantitative agreement is relatively low. Fee is trying to overcome the drawback of statistics by weighing the value of agreements. A second modification of Colwell's method would seem to limit the ability to weigh readings, however. Fee restricts the comparison to MSS up to the sixth century plus the TR, where Colwell had also taken later groups into account. Though this may give a clearer picture, it also eliminates the possibility for a MS to show close affinity to a MS or group represented only in the later tradition. In a later study Fee expands the "control" MSS again by including also the "secondary Neutrals," the "Caesarean" text, and the main Byzantine uncials.[47] As in the earlier study, he presupposes the traditional text-types. Fee's approach appears to work quite well for the early MSS and patristic citations, which it tries to locate in terms of the major text-types.

The quest for the classification of Greek NT MSS in the last fifty years has not been without direction. There has been a growing consciousness of the weaknesses of old methods and the difficulties involved. A demand for greater objectivity and accuracy was heard. The need for objectivity was felt in two ways, in the selection of readings and the selection of supporting MSS. Studies still appear in which the classification is attempted on the basis of variants from the TR, but only by ignoring the warnings of E. C. Colwell and others. The MS tradition must itself present the units of variation. Hundreds of collations are available now in some form or other that can be checked in selected passages to see where the tradition diverges significantly. Only this will present an objective basis on which MS and group relationships can be measured and evaluated.

Not less important is objectivity in supporting MS evidence. Great strides were made from Hutton to Fee. Ill-defined text-types have been disregarded and established groups have taken their place. But the ideal was far from realized.

[45] Jacob Geerlings and his former student, Russell Champlin, still using variations from the TR as a basis, demand at least 94 % agreement for familial relationship. See Jacob Geerlings, "Codex 1867," *Studies in the History and Text of the New Testament in Honor of Kenneth W. Clark* (ed. Boyd L. Daniels and M. Jack Suggs; SD 29; Salt Lake City: University of Utah, 1967) 58.

[46] "Codex Sinaiticus in the Gospel of John: A Contribution to Methodology in Establishing Textual Relationships," *NTS* 15 (1968-69) 23-44.

[47] "The Text of John in Origen and Cyril of Alexandria: A Contribution to Methodology in the Recovery and Analysis of Patristic Citations," *Bib* 52 (1971) 357-94. Fee uses the word "profile" and his criteria for choosing test readings are similar to those used for the Profile Method. A description of the Profile Method had been published at this time.

Several groups remained undiscovered. Only a few of the known groups have been studied and defined, and then usually in not more than one or two Gospels.

Finally, the limits of statistical evidence, long known to mathematicians, have now been recognized by at least some lower critics. Statistical analysis may have some value in expressing MS relationship, but its limitations for MS classification and group study must be clearly recognized.

Against the background of this quest for classification, its weaknesses and its lessons, the Profile Method was developed. Without the examples of past successes and failures it could not have been.

CHAPTER IV

# THE PROFILE METHOD

New approaches to old problems seldom come about in a vacuum. A unique set of circumstances is necessary to break through inadequate but familiar ways to a more promising procedure. Such was the case with the Profile Method. Its special circumstances are too integral a part of its development to be left unmentioned. We shall put them under two headings although they are unmistakably connected.

## 1. THE INTERNATIONAL GREEK NEW TESTAMENT PROJECT (IGNTP)

The most obvious requirement for the development of a new method is a need, preferably a clearly defined need. The IGNTP keenly felt such a need with respect to the selection of minuscules. The project had been gathering a large number of collations over the years for inclusion in a large and truly representative *apparatus criticus*. By the fall of 1966, the question was raised whether the available collations were sufficient to represent the whole MS tradition.

Representation at this point was put in terms of MS groups and mixed MSS. It was decided that, in any case, all known groups should be adequately represented, and also that a considerable number of divergent MSS, which up to the present had defied classification, should be included. "Divergence" was defined in terms of the TR, as it had been for many decades.

The ideal was clear and laudable, but no adequate procedure was available to reach it. As usual, what seemed such a simple and sensible policy on paper proved to be a Herculean task when applied to the actual MSS. A "makeshift" approach seemed inevitable. Von Soden was the most obvious person to turn to for group representation.

Von Soden lists seventeen Iota and Kappa groups in his text volume.[1] Of these groups, only $K^x$ and $K^r$ are not represented by specific MSS in his apparatus. Unfortunately, only 5 of the 17 groups have been studied in detail and confirmed by other scholars;[2] for others von Soden's word had to suffice. It was decided that one limited test would be made to check von Soden's groups. All the group members present among the collations of the IGNTP would be checked to see whether they tend to read together where variation occurs. By running this test it was hoped that

---

·[1]These are $I^\alpha$, $I^\eta$, $I^\iota$, $I^{\varphi a}$, $I^{\varphi b}$, $I^{\varphi c}$, $I^{\sigma r}$, $I^\beta$, $I^\sigma$, $I^o$, $I^r$, $I^\pi$, $I^\kappa$, $K^1$, $K^i$, $K^x$, and $K^r$.

[2]$I^\iota$ (The Ferrar group or Family 13) by Kirsopp and Silva Lake; $I^\eta$ (Family 1) by Kirsopp Lake; $I^\beta$ by E. C. Colwell; $I^\kappa$ (Family Π) by Silva Lake; and $K^r$ by David O. Voss.

33

also strategic members of a group, which could represent the range of a group, would show themselves.

As might have been predicted, the result of the test was very disappointing. Indeed, the old, well-established groups, such as Family 13, were visible, but the tests on other groups proved inconclusive. There was no way to tell how much divergence within a group could be allowed, or at what point a MS could no longer be called a group member, or a group no longer be called a group. Strategic group members were even harder to spot. It became clear that we were at the mercy of von Soden, not a pleasant prosect for a project which is trying to plot a new course in textual criticism.

There was no dependable way to assure that the collations of the IGNTP included enough group members and a sufficient range for adequate representation.[3] It was not even clear whether von Soden had represented his groups adequately in his apparatus. Critics would certainly and justifiably charge undue dependence on von Soden, an authority whose mistakes and inaccuracies are legendary.

The proud list of twice-checked collations suddenly looked haphazard and vulnerable. Even though this list might well include a fair representation of the total number of known minuscules, there was no way to assure the future user of the apparatus of this fact. No claim could be made about the collations beyond their number. This would condemn the proposed *apparatus criticus* to be nothing more than a collection of several hundred collations, accurate collations perhaps, but certainly not a cross section of the MS tradition.

In spite of the depressing results thus far, the different aspects of the problem had crystallized. To break the impasse, a method would have to be developed which could test all known groups and spot the members which could best represent the whole group. This method would have to be independent of von Soden in order to quiet the suspicions of friends and critics. The method should ideally be a rapid sampling tool so that many uncollated MSS could be checked for group membership and textual value. This would then drastically increase the number of MSS which the apparatus could claim to represent. Finally, the method should present an objective standard to evaluate the text of the considerable number of minuscules which do not fit readily into the known groups.


## 2. THE MASTER FILE OF COLLATIONS

In whatever way they are selected, a collection of 200 collations is bound to be a gold mine of textual evidence. Very few students of NT textual criticism have had the privilege of working with such a large amount of "raw material." The collations of the IGNTP of the Gospel of Luke presented the further advantage that all the MS evidence had been blended on a master file. Luke 1 was in an even more ideal form. All the existing variants, even the most minute changes and insignificant itacisms, had been typed out with the supporting MS evidence.

---

[3]At some point the IGNTP had tried to secure collations of all minuscules which had proved their importance in the past. For this purpose von Soden's groups had been taken into account but no scientific principle had guided this selection. Opportunity and chance played no small role in the selection of MSS for collation.

The 200 collations of Luke included 28 nonfragmentary uncials.[4] Only two major uncials, Gregory's N and V, had not yet been acquired by the Project. The 163 minuscules included almost all those which had proven their value in the history of the study of the NT text (the "Neutral" and "Caesarean" minuscules, members of Families 1 and 13, etc.). In addition, some attempt had been made to include members of less well-known groups. A large number, however, had been included not because of the known textual character of the MS, but because of availability. Most of these had been classified by von Soden but some had no classification at all. Thus, although the selection of minuscules could not claim to represent the whole cursive tradition, still it was a most impressive and useful collection.

## 3. THE IDEA OF PROFILE

The test of von Soden's groups in Luke 1 by means of the master file of collations, although its main purpose had not been realized, proved to have an invaluable side benefit. The search had initially been for the unique features of a group. Much of the group research in the past has been preoccupied with group readings not shared by any other group or text-type.[5] It seems that this approach is still a remnant of the old Lachmann principle that agreement in error shows familial relationship. As long as very distinctive groups, such as Families 1 and 13, were studied the principle worked reasonably well. These groups have a significant number of "single" group readings.[6] But it is like spotting identical twins by searching for hidden birthmarks instead of comparing the general features. Such unique group readings are not unlike errors, though they are usually sense readings. Most of these readings would strike medieval scribes and correctors as foreign and incorrect, with the result that they were often corrected. Weaker members of a group bear out this tendency, for they seem to lose the unique readings of a group before other features. Consequently, these weaker members no longer look like group members if only unique features are taken into account. This is enough to indict "single" group readings for the same reasons that Lachmann's agreement-in-error principle was rejected. One should not ignore the unique group features; they are important supporting material, but they cannot be the focus in group identification.

Where unique group readings in Families 1 and 13 were helpful, in some other groups they were completely absent. If unique readings were an essential criterion for finding familial relationship, few of von Soden's groups would have survived the test in Luke 1. Yet the search for the distinctive readings of groups in the master file of collations brought to light a remarkable pattern. When the group members, present on the master file, of von Soden's $I^{\varphi}$ groups were traced through

---

[4]The many fragmentary uncials in existence were included on the master file, but since their text seldom overlapped the test chapters (Luke 1, 10, and 20) they were not considered in the Profile Method. Neither were they included in the total of 200 collations. Also the papyri in Luke are too fragmentary to be of importance for classification.

[5]We find this emphasis on unique readings in E. C. Colwell, "Method in Locating a Newly-Discovered Manuscript within the Manuscript Tradition of the Greek New Testament," *SE* I (1959) 761 (repr. in *Studies in Methodology,* 30), and D. O. Voss, "Is Von Soden's $K^r$ a distinct type of Text?" *JBL* 57 (1938) 315-16.

[6]This is especially true if the "Neutral" group (von Soden's "H" text-type) is not taken into account.

Luke 1, it became evident that a majority of one of the groups would now combine with a majority of this group and later with another. Never would Gr M27 ($I^{\varphi r}$) read alone against the whole MS tradition, but the groups which would join it in support of variants from the TR would vary from reading to reading.

The implications of this phenomenon looked promising. It meant that even if a group could not be defined in terms of unique readings, it still might be possible to define it in terms of agreement and disagreement with other known groups. If all known groups could be taken into account, possibly enough contrasting combinations of agreements and disagreements between groups would appear that all groups could be defined in terms of each other in a relatively short sampling passage.

Another test was made with the Kappa groups. The difference between $K^1$, $K^x$, and $K^i$ had already been questioned long ago.[7] This doubt was supported by the profile of their readings against the TR. The differences were small and somewhat tenuous, no doubt partly due to the fact that $K^x$ is a very large group with blurred outlines. $K^r$ stood out clearly from the other Kappa groups, however.

## 4. THE TENTATIVE GROUP DEFINITIONS

From the queries made with the $I^{\varphi}$ and Kappa groups, it had become clear that the essential ingredients for group definition are all the variants in a passage which have the support of one or more groups. This immediately raised the problem of group support. How could one be certain that an alleged group supported a variant reading before the existence of the group had been proved and all the members of the group had been taken into account? No alternative presented itself apart from using tentative group definitions borrowed from the students of MS groups in the past.

There has been some criticism of the Profile Method at this point due to a basic misunderstanding.[8] The tentative group definitions have only a very limited function. They are needed to select the *test readings* which form the grid or screen on which the profiles of the individual MSS are projected. They do not determine what the *group readings* of a certain group are going to be. Group readings are established independently on the basis of the profiles of the qualifying members of the group. The tentative group definitions do no more than help determine which of the units of variations in a passage have a high probability of showing group affiliation.[9] It is necessary to limit the test readings to those which are meaningful in order to allow for easy profile comparison and classification. Variants of nongenetic origin or too large a number of test readings would unnecessarily complicate the process of classification.

---

[7]Kirsopp Lake, Robert P. Blake, and Silva New, "The Caesarean Text of the Gospel of Mark," *HTR* 21 (1928) 341 and 347-48.

[8]W. L. Richards, *The Classification of the Greek Manuscripts of the Johannine Epistles* (SBLDS 35; Missoula: Scholars, 1977) 208; idem, "A Critique of a New Testament Text-Critical Methodology — The Claremont Profile Method," *JBL* 96 (1977) 562-64. Richards echoes here a comment made by Klaus Junack that shows unfamiliarity with the principle and development of the Profile Method ("Zu den griechischen Lektionaren und ihrer Überlieferung der Katholischen Briefe," *Die alten Übersetzungen des Neuen Testaments, die Kirchenväterzitate und Lektionare* [ed. K. Aland; ANTF 5; Berlin: de Gruyter, 1972] 556). Richards' method of classification is discussed in Chapter VII.

[9]See below, § 6, "The Selection of the Test Readings."

A further restriction influenced the tentative group definitions. Only group members present in the files of the IGNTP could represent the groups.[10] This may seem like a severe handicap, but only if one loses sight of the alternatives. Starting from scratch would pose much greater problems. It would mean selecting variants with enough MS support that they could possibly include a majority of a group. Then would follow a long and treacherous process of trial and error to find the MSS which read together often enough to suggest group relationship.[11] Why not rather use the fruits of group studies in the past? Nothing would be lost and much could be gained. The tentative group definitions would have to prove themselves in any case! If the group as a whole, or an individual member, would not conform to the criteria of a distinctive and coherent profile it could always be rejected or adjusted. The tentative group definitions implied no final commitment. They formed a starting point and nothing more.[12]

The principal weakness of the tentative group definitions was that a unique group reading could have been overlooked. If the initial group was unbalanced it could have happened that a genuine, unique group reading did not have the support of a majority of the group and consequently was not taken up into the list of test readings. It was impossible after each group adjustment to go back to the master file and check whether some formerly rejected reading now deserved to be included. However, the groups with the most uncertain definition, or the weakest MS support, were also the ones least likely to have unique readings. Since almost all group readings of these groups with few, if any, unique readings are shared by at least one other group, their definition could be adjusted at a later time without having to change the list of test readings.

Setting up the tentative group definitions formed no special problem. Von Soden's classifications were used where no later group study was available. The unclassified MSS on file could, of course, not be taken into account. It was decided that two-thirds of the members would count as the majority of a group.[13]

## 5. THE TEXTUS RECEPTUS

All collations of the IGNTP are made against Scrivener's 1873 edition of the TR. In view of the special character of the TR,[14] the question arises whether the collation base could influence or invalidate the results of the Profile Method. But the problem concerning the TR in the past was the tendency to attach a positive value judgment to every departure from it. If a collation base is left completely neutral, it will be no more than a handy tool to compare the text of one MS with that of others. Any real or artificial text could fulfil this purpose. The TR happens to have been used for this

[10]The 163 minuscules on the master file were supplemented for this purpose by 83 collations which, for various reasons, had not been blended into the master file. Together with the uncials this gave a total of 282 MSS, including approximately 15% of the extant minuscules.

[11]This road was taken by W. L. Richards without reaching greater objectivity or more certain results but adding a great amount of work (see Chapter VII).

[12]See below, § 8, "The Principle of Self-Correction," and Chapter VII.

[13]Practical considerations and not principle are the guide here. One could argue for 50% or above, but a two-thirds majority gives a proper safeguard. Several groups were represented by relatively few members in the master file. If one member would have to be reclassified, or one would be added, the balance could easily be upset. D. O Voss, 317, used a two-thirds majority in his study of K[r].

[14]See Chapter III, 26.

purpose for more than a century, and has the distinct advantage of being close enough to the Byzantine groups to lighten the task of collation and lessen the chance of error with respect to the bulk of minuscules.

One could even argue that the TR as collation base is almost ideal for the Profile Method. If a text like Codex Vaticanus or Codex 1 had been used, the many Byzantine group members would have shown a large number of group readings that would encumber the task of classification. On the other hand, one would not want the collation basis to be identical to one of the Byzantine groups, for agreements against the collation basis lend themselves more easily for classification than agreements with the base. A MS much more often adds group readings other than its own than it misses a majority reading of the group to which it belongs. The TR caters to both requirements; it stands close to the Byzantine groups, yet keeps enough distance to enable every group to show at least some common elements at variance with the collation basis.[15]

## 6. THE SELECTION OF TEST READINGS

Not all places where variation occurs are useful for group study. By far the greatest number of variants are itacisms of one sort or another. Closely related group members often agree, even in itacisms, but on the whole itacisms depend on the habits of the scribe and not on the MS copied. The same is true for *nu*-movables, οὕτω-οὕτως, and abbreviations. Whenever one suspects that variation is due to scribal error or scribal convention, the reading ought to be rejected for group study.[16] Most of these cases can be categorized, but it is best to err on the side of caution. If enough MSS have been taken into account, the support of a variant will often give a clue. When the support is scattered over a few members of several known groups, one can safely guess that the variant is of nongenetic origin.

A second category of variants which have no value for the establishment of MS relationships involves singular and subsingular readings. Before this large group is omitted, a large number of MSS should be taken into account. The singulars among the variants of thirty MSS are reduced significantly if one hundred other MSS are added (of course, many new singulars would also turn up in that case), but if one begins with two hundred MSS the number of singulars is hardly affected by the addition of other collations. The reason is that singular and subsingular readings on a master file of two hundred collations are almost all misspellings and nonsense readings.[17] Such variants are the least likely to be copied by scribes. Only very seldom will a nonsense reading have the support of more than two MSS. If it happens, it is questionable whether real nonsense is involved.

The remaining variants in Luke 1, after the two above-mentioned categories had been deleted, were only a fraction of the original total. Of these, 54 proved

---

[15]At least four MSS (Gregory 525 and 2645 at the end of Luke, 1239 and 2708) have a text more or less identical with the TR. No doubt they were copied from the printed text. Most of the MSS dated in the sixteenth century or later were not profiled.

[16]See Colwell, "Method," 762 n. 2 ( = *Studies in Methodology*, 31 n. 2). W. L. Richards felt it necessary to prove this point through a laborious process involving the computer (*Classification*, 34-41).

[17]*Homoioteleuton* in the same passage happens frequently in a number of MSS of widely divergent age and textual tradition.

to be supported by the majority of the members of one or more of the traditional groups. In order to have some idea of the number involved, a count was made of the variants in Luke 1:1-26 apart from *nu*-movables, itacisms, abbreviations, obvious nonsense readings, and οὕτω-οὕτως variants. The remainder contained 169 singular or subsingular readings, of which only nine had the support of three MSS; all others had less. In none of the nine readings with the support of three MSS did all three MSS belong to the same known group.

Luke 1:1-26 contained seven "Neutral" readings with negligible minuscule support apart from the "Neutrals" among them. It was decided that these should not be used for the Profile Method. They would only inflate the number of test readings without making any contribution to the main purpose of the Profile Method: the classification and evaluation of the text of the minuscules. This does not mean that a newly-discovered "Neutral" MS cannot be identified. Even after all unique "Neutral" readings in Luke 1 had been eliminated, this text-type showed up clearly and distinctively in the test readings selected on the basis of the Iota and Kappa groups.[18] If the profiles of Kappa groups are distinctive without unique group readings, how much more the "Neutral" text-type!

A small group of variants — none in Luke 1:1-26 — has the support of the majority of all Iota and Kappa groups. This happens when the TR reads with the "Neutrals" against all others, or when it has a singular reading. Obviously, such readings with "universal" support have no value for the classification of minuscules.

Only 37 variants remained in Luke 1:26, of which 15 did not have the support of the majority of at least one of the known groups. These are listed in Table 1. A few of them clearly had minority support, but most of them showed by their nature and support that they were of nongenetic origin. The 22 remaining test readings in Luke 1:1-26 are listed in Appendix I, together with the other test readings in Luke 1, 10, and 20.

It is impossible to be certain that among the 15 rejected readings there may not be one or more majority readings of a hitherto unknown group or subgroup. This might have been a serious charge if the Profile Method were dependent on unique group readings. Since it is not, the Profile Method only has to surrender the claim that it contains a complete profile of a new group in the sampling chapters. As will be shown later,[19] this does in no way impair the ability of the Profile Method to discover new groups or subgroups. The profile of a group or MS is not an end in itself but only a tool; its value is not determined by its completeness but by its ability to provide a quick and accurate classification and evaluation of the text of a MS.

## 7. THE GROUP PROFILES

After the test readings have been selected, the available MSS can be profiled, i.e. their agreement with the chosen variants against the TR is listed in terms of the numbers assigned to the test readings. By putting the profiles of the alleged members of an established group in juxtaposition, if possible graphically, a group profile

---

[18]See Appendix III.
[19]See below, § 11, "The New Groups."

# TABLE 1

## VARIANTS IN LUKE 1:1-26 WITH THE SUPPORT OF MORE THAN THREE MSS BUT WITHOUT THE SUPPORT OF THE MAJORITY OF A GROUP

The reading before the bracket is the one found in the TR as well as in the third UBS edition of *The Greek New Testament*.

*Luke 1:*

| V E R S E | | |
|---|---|---|
| 1 | εν ] | omit |
| 2 | γενομενοι ] | omit |
| 7 | ταις ] | omit |
| 9 | ιερατειας ] | + αυτου |
| 12 | επεπεσεν ] | επεσεν |
| 13 | αγγελος ] | + κυριου |
| 13 | σοι ] | omit |
| 16 | αυτων ] | αυτου |
| 17 | προελευσεται ] | προςελευσεται[1] |
| 17 | επιστρεψαι ] | επιστρεψει |
| 21 | εν τω ναω ] | omit |
| 24 | συνελαβεν ] | + η |
| 24 | αυτου ] | ζαχαριου |
| 24 | εαυτην ] | αυτην |
| 26 | ο ] | omit |

[1]According to the UBS[3] edition of *The Greek New Testament* this reading is supported by Group 13. It was rejected as a test reading because it was read by less than a two-thirds majority of the members of this group.

emerges.[20] At this point those alleged group members of which the profile does not conform significantly to the others should be put aside for possible reclassification in terms of another group.[21] Those which do conform set the standard for the group profile. Test readings shared by about two-thirds of the members are primary readings; those with support of about one-third to two-thirds of the group members are secondary group readings. This high standard for primary group readings has the advantage that there will be less of a chance that primary readings change to secondary readings or vice versa when newly found group members are added. The secondary readings are valuable for spotting subgroups and studying the relationship between groups.

[20]See Table 2, which presents the profiles of the members of Gr 1216 in Luke 1.

[21]This does not necessarily mean that such MSS were incorrectly classified in former group studies. More likely their classification was based on test passages taken from a different biblical book with another group affiliation, or the MS is characterized by block mixture (see below, § 10, "The Sampling Chapters").

When the group profiles have been determined also for other established and newly discovered groups, the group profiles can be put in juxtaposition (see Appendix II). It should be remembered that, although groups often share some group readings, each bona fide group displays a distinctive pattern of agreement with and variation from the TR that distinguishes it from other groups. The relative value of each test reading for the identity of a group is now graphically visible. A unique group reading sets a group apart from all other groups. Most test readings, however, distinguish a group only from some other groups.

The qualifications for a bona fide group readily suggest themselves. First, a group profile requires a large degree of internal agreement among its members. Only when members of an alleged group show approximately the same profile of agreements and disagreements with the TR are they accepted as a genuine group. A MS does not need all group readings to qualify as a member. In some very distinctive groups, a large number of group characteristics may be missing before the classification of a member becomes questionable. Most MSS will have some test readings which are not shared by the majority of the group to which they belong. These "surplus" readings tend to increase when a MS misses some of the primary readings of its group. The reason for this is clear. Corruption or mixture would naturally involve the loss of some group characteristics and an increase of characteristics of other groups.

Five of von Soden's Iota groups — $I^{\alpha}$, $I^{\varphi b}$, $I^{\varphi c}$, $I^{\sigma}$, and $I^{o}$ — were disqualified because of lack of cohesion. Most of the members of von Soden's $I^{\varphi b}$ and $I^{\varphi c}$ were readily reclassified in terms of other groups. In the case of $I^{\alpha}$, $I^{\sigma}$, and $I^{o}$, von Soden had already admitted the special nature of these groups. They were made up, according to him, of MSS which showed great differences in the degree of corruption toward Kappa. The Profile Method makes no final judgment in this matter; ultimately von Soden may well be correct. The main purpose of the Profile Method is to locate MSS which agree significantly in text against the rest of the MS tradition. If what once was a genuine group has become so corrupted in its only extant members that only very few distinctive group characteristics remain, it cannot be called a group in terms of the Profile Method.[22]

The second group standard implied in the idea of profile is that a group profile must differ significantly from the profiles of other groups. All this means is that there must be sufficient reason to separate groups. The minimum difference was set at two group readings per sampling chapter. This meant that $K^1$ became a subgroup or cluster (Cl $\Omega$) of $K^x$, and $K^i$ disappeared entirely.[23] Group $\Pi^b$ and the $\Pi$ clusters are obviously descendants of group $\Pi^a$, which have been strongly influenced by $K^x$, but since $\Pi^b$ fulfils the requirements of a genuine group, it was accepted as an independent entity.

This policy is consistent with the original intent of the Profile Method. The Method wants to find groups of MSS that are close enough in text so that an entire group can be represented by a few of its members in an *apparatus criticus*. The relative value of a group ought not to play a role as yet. The main interest of the

[22]It is doubtful whether von Soden could defend the existence of such a "group" independent from his hypothesis of the fate of the Iota text-type.

[23]$K^i$ consists mainly of the uncials E, F, G, and H. It would have been of little importance for classification, even if it had qualified as an independent group.

Profile Method is to organize the mass of witnesses to a text into a manageable whole. It wants to bring out all the aspects of the MS tradition. Value judgments, such as good and bad, pure and corrupt, or important and secondary, should wait until all the evidence has been presented. Yet since the profiles show the relationship between groups and MSS, they would give a good basis for such judgments.

Since the group profiles carry along their own criteria, independence from previous group studies has been achieved. The starting point presented by former students of groups proved to be nothing more than a helpful beginning. The groups had to prove themselves independently. Thus the danger of a circular argument had been prevented.

## 8. THE PRINCIPLE OF SELF-CORRECTION

Some doubt could still remain that the selection of test readings was made on a much too small and uncertain basis. In several cases, only a fraction of the total number of MSS classified by von Soden as members of a group could be used for the selection of test readings. If more members had been available, some primary readings might well have become secondary readings, and some readings now rejected might have qualified. For this reason, 350 MSS, available on microfilm or as unrecorded collations, were added to the original 200 MSS on the master file.

The result was encouraging. Only a few test readings were dropped from the list. Some other readings shifted from secondary to primary readings, or vice versa, for a certain group. It also became possible to check back on readings which had been rejected because their support fell short of a two-thirds majority of one of the tentative groups. In no case did any of these qualify when further group members were taken into account.

Gradually, when more minuscules were profiled, some group profiles needed further small adjustments. The process of self-correction theoretically continues until the last minuscule is taken into account. The chances are against further changes, however. Of the group readings which hung in the balance when 200 MSS were taken into account, almost all became more definite in either direction when more MSS were added. There is actually little advantage in continuing to make these small adjustments in the group readings. Particularly with groups having a significant number of "weak" members there is a danger that too many primary readings become secondary readings when all members are taken into account. In such cases it is better to establish the group profile on the basis of the core members and to leave it unchanged when weak members are added. In some cases a new group or a subgroup can be formed from these weaker members. Practical considerations are here more important than principle.

## 9. THE CLASSIFICATION OF MANUSCRIPTS

The great majority of MSS profiled could be classified in terms of the groups confirmed or established by the Profile Method (see Chapter VI). Not surprisingly, a number of them defied classification. These have been marked in Chapter V as "Mix(ed)" or "Kmix(ed)." The "Mix" MSS have a relatively large number of non-Byzantine readings, while the "Kmix" MSS are basically Byzantine but not clearly members of one of the Byzantine groups. The difficulty in classifying the latter lies in the indefinite character of Group K$^x$. This large, amorphous group tends to function as the common denominator of the Byzantine "text." Its members often have a large number of "surplus" readings compared to the group readings. How much deviation from the group norm one should allow cannot be settled on objective grounds. Raising the K$^x$ group membership standards would sharply increase the number of "Kmix" MSS, and lowering the standards would endanger the group's distinctiveness.

The way the word "mixed" is used in profile classifications should be taken in a descriptive rather than genetic sense. It means nothing more than that the MS in question shares agreements with or variations from the TR with a number of groups, but these readings do not fall into a pattern which shows group membership nor are there other MSS with a similar profile with which it could form a group or cluster. The origin of such exceptional MSS needs further study, for which the profiles could be a starting point.

In order to classify a MS, it must be collated in the test readings of the three sampling chapters presented in Appendix II. A MS profile can then be drawn up and compared with the profiles of the groups presented in Appendix III. If the profile matches one of them the classification can be made. How much divergence from the group profile is allowed is indicated in Chapter VI for each group. Care must be taken to judge the value of each reading for the definition of a group.

After the initial classification has been made, the MS profile should, if possible, be compared with the profiles of the members of the group in question. Table 2 presents a chart with the profiles of the members of Group 1216 in Luke 1 as a sample.[24] This comparison both confirms the classification and locates the MS within the group. If the profile of a MS cannot be classified in terms of one of the groups, it should be compared with the profiles of the clusters and "Mix" MSS before it is assigned to the "Mix" or "Kmix" categories. Thus it is possible that new pairs or clusters can be distinguished among the mixed MSS.

## 10. THE SAMPLING CHAPTERS

After the test readings had been selected in Luke 1, it was decided to add two more sampling chapters for the following reasons.

1. The phenomenon of block mixture, i.e. one or more changes in group affiliation within a biblical book, necessitates several sampling passages.[25]

2. The character of the group membership of a MS often changes within one biblical book. Many MSS are weak group members in Luke 1, improve in Luke 10, and belong to the core of a group in Luke 20. Sometimes the situation is the reverse. Thus the classification in the other chapters becomes an important confirmation. In retrospect, the early chapters of a Gospel are not very well suited for group study. Scribes had the tendency to practice a little textual criticism at the beginning of a biblical book. As a result, group outlines are fussier, and more group

---

[24]It was not possible to publish the profiles of all the MSS used in this study. Those who want to consult any of them to check classifications or to engage in group studies should contact the author.

[25]Perhaps the most complex block mixture is found in the text of Codex 574 (E. C. Colwell, *The Four Gospels of Karahissar, I: History and Text* [Chicago: The University of Chicago, 1936] 216).

43

## TABLE 2

### THE PROFILES OF GROUP 1216 IN LUKE 1

| | 152 | 184 | 348 | 477 | 555 | 752 | 829 | 977 | 1216 | 1243 | 1279 | 1579 | 2174 | 2726 |
|---|---|---|---|---|---|---|---|---|---|---|---|---|---|---|
| 1 | | X | | | | | | | | | | | • | |
| 2 | | | | | | | | | | | | | • | |
| 3 | | | X | | | | | | | | | | • | X |
| 4 | | | | | | | | | | | | X | • | |
| 5 | | | | | | | | | | | | | • | |
| 6 | | | | | | | | | | | | | • | |
| 7 | | | | | | | | | | | | | | |
| 8 | | X | X | | | | X | | X | X | X | | X | |
| 9 | X | X | X | | X | X | X | | X | X | X | X | X | X |
| 10 | | | | | | | | | | | | | | |
| 11 | | | | | | | | | | | | | | |
| 12 | | | | | | | | | | | | | | |
| 13 | X | X | X | | X | X | X | | X | X | X | X | | X |
| 14 | | | | | | | | | | | | | | |
| 15 | | | | | | | | | | | | | | |
| 16 | X | X | X | | | X | X | | X | | X | X | | X |
| 17 | X | X | X | X | X | X | X | | X | X | X | X | X | X |
| 18 | | | | | | | | | | | | | | |
| 19 | | | | | | | | | | | | | | |
| 20 | | | | | | | | | | | | | | |
| 21 | | | | | | | | | | | | | | |
| 22 | X | X | X | | X | | X | | X | X | X | X | | |
| 23 | | | | | | | | D | | | | | | X |
| 24 | X | X | X | | X | X | X | E | X | X | X | X | | X |
| 25 | X | X | X | | X | X | X | F | X | X | X | X | | X |
| 26 | X | X | X | | X | X | X | E | X | X | X | X | | X |
| 27 | | | | | | | | C | | | | | | |
| 28 | | | | | | | | T | | | | | | X |
| 29 | | | | | | | | I | | | | | | |
| 30 | | | | | | | | V | | | | | | |
| 31 | | | | | | | | E | | | | | | |
| 32 | | | | | | | | | | | | | | |
| 33 | X | X | X | | X | X | | | X | | | | | |
| 34 | X | X | X | X | X | X | X | | X | X | X | X | X | X |
| 35 | | | | | | | | | | | | | | |

## TABLE 2

### THE PROFILES OF GROUP 1216 IN LUKE 1

|    | 152 | 184 | 348 | 477 | 555 | 752 | 829 | 977 | 1216 | 1243 | 1279 | 1579 | 2174 | 2726 |
|----|-----|-----|-----|-----|-----|-----|-----|-----|------|------|------|------|------|------|
| 36 | X | X | X | X | X | X | X |  | X | X | X |  |  | X |
| 37 | X | X | X |  | X | X | X |  | X | X | X | X |  | X |
| 38 |  |  |  |  |  |  |  |  |  |  |  |  |  |  |
| 39 |  |  |  |  |  |  |  |  |  |  |  |  |  |  |
| 40 |  |  |  |  |  |  |  |  |  |  |  |  |  |  |
| 41 |  |  |  |  |  |  |  |  |  |  |  |  |  |  |
| 42 |  | X | X |  |  | X | X |  | X |  | X |  |  | X |
| 43 | X | X | X |  | X | X | X |  | X | X | X | X |  | X |
| 44 |  |  |  |  |  |  |  |  |  |  |  |  |  |  |
| 45 |  |  | X |  |  |  |  |  |  |  |  |  |  |  |
| 46 |  |  |  |  |  |  |  |  |  |  |  |  |  |  |
| 47 |  |  |  |  |  |  |  |  |  |  |  |  |  |  |
| 48 |  |  |  |  |  |  | X |  |  |  |  |  |  |  |
| 49 |  |  |  |  |  |  |  |  |  |  |  |  |  |  |
| 50 |  |  |  |  |  |  |  |  |  |  |  |  |  |  |
| 51 |  |  |  |  |  |  |  |  |  |  |  |  |  |  |
| 52 |  |  |  |  |  |  |  |  |  | X | X | X |  |  |  |
| 53 |  |  |  |  |  |  | X |  |  |  |  |  |  |  |
| 54 |  |  |  |  |  |  |  |  |  |  |  |  |  |  |

members have suffered mixture here than elsewhere. This is evident in the fact that Luke 20 supplied 24 more test readings than Luke 1, while the latter has twice the amount of text.

    3. Some groups are much more distinct in one chapter than in another. In such cases, a confirmation of the classification is most welcome.

    4. Many MSS are defective, especially at the beginning of a Gospel. A number of sampling chapters assures classification of most fragmentary texts.

## 11. THE NEW GROUPS

There may still be a question whether the Profile Method is not limited to the groups used to select the test readings. Can it claim to expose all the groups present in the MS tradition of a text? Could not the charge be made that the net laid by the Profile Method can catch von Soden's type of fish, but who knows what escapes through the holes?

    To answer this charge, we do well to change images. The test readings are not really like a net with large holes, but much more like a grid or screen on which every MS and every group will project an image or profile. Thus the issue is not what escapes, but whether the image shows enough detail.

Enough data are available to state categorically that any unknown, bona fide group will project a clear profile against the background of the test readings. One could mention the fact that the "Neutral" group showed a very clear profile, though all of its distinctive group readings were left out of consideration in the initial selection of test readings. Furthermore, several new groups and many previously unknown clusters were found. But there are still better reasons. The real basis for the confidence that all new groups can be spotted lies in the details the Profile Method provides within groups. Much more is visible from a MS's profile than mere group affiliation. Subgroups were identified, and a large number of pairs, triplets, and clusters of closely related group members showed up. None of these involved enough MSS to warrant being treated as a separate group, but the additional information proved valuable for group representation in a critical apparatus.

Since the test readings are established already, a new group or cluster will not have unique group readings, but these are unnecessary for a distinctive profile. There is, of course, some merit in being able to see the complete profile of a group in a passage. The presence or absence of unique features tells us something about the nature of a group, but this information, valuable as it may be, does not affect the classification of MSS. The unique readings of a new group, if there are any, will become apparent when it is represented in a critical apparatus.

## 12. THE POTENTIAL OF THE PROFILE METHOD

Certain aspects and possibilities of the Profile Method remain unexplored. The first task was to profile all extant MSS in the sampling chapters. They form the basis for a final search for new groups and subgroups. With all group members visible in one comprehensive view, exhaustive intragroup studies become possible. In the process representatives can be selected for inclusion in a critical apparatus and, in some cases, the archetype of a group can be reconstructed. The comparisons which can be made with other groups in the same passage allow for a study of the development of each group, its corruption, and the way group and text-types have influenced each other. Finally, a new attempt should be made to draw all groups into an overall view of the history of the MS tradition. We cannot continue to criticize von Soden's reconstruction of the history of MS transmission without trying to do better ourselves. Hopefully, the Profile Method will contribute to the accomplishment of this task, which most lower critics claim is the essential element in the reconstruction of the best possible NT text, but which no one, except von Soden, has ever seriously begun.

CHAPTER V

# THE CLASSIFICATION OF 1385 LUCAN MANUSCRIPTS ON THE BASIS OF THE PROFILE METHOD

The first column of the list presented on the following pages gives the Gregory number of the MSS. In 1908 Caspar René Gregory changed to a new MS numeration for Greek MSS of the NT after consulting with a large number of interested scholars.[1] After Gregory's death in 1917 this list was updated and augmented, first by E. von Dobschütz,[2] then by Walther Eltester, and since 1949 by Kurt Aland.[3] In 1963 Aland replaced Gregory's outdated list and the six supplements by a new edition, the *Kurzgefasste Liste der griechischen Handschriften des Neuen Testaments*.[4] Already six years later a major supplement was necessary.[5] This supplement lists also the MSS of which the INTF in Münster, Germany, possesses microfilms or photographs. It reflects the holdings of the INTF during the profiling in Münster. The numbers preceded by a zero are uncials (majuscules);[6] the normal numbers are minuscules (cursives).

Of the MSS containing all or portions of the continuous Greek text of the Gospel of Luke the following could not or were chosen not to be profiled:
1. Fragmentary MSS which do not contain the text of at least one of the three test chapters in Luke. This eliminated the few papyri which contain a portion of Luke and many of the uncials.
2. MSS which can no longer be located or for which the INTF has not been able to acquire a complete microfilm. Many of these MSS are lost. Some of them reappear in Western libraries or private collections and receive a new number if they cannot readily be identified in terms of a lost MS. This list also includes commentaries

---

[1]*Die griechischen Handschriften des Neuen Testaments* (Leipzig: Hinrichs, 1908; repr. 1973) and somewhat expanded in *Textkritik des Neuen Testaments, III* (Leipzig: Hinrichs, 1909).

[2]"Zur Liste der Neutestamentlichen Handschriften," *ZNW* 23 (1924) 248-64; II in: *ZNW* 25 (1926) 299-306; III in: *ZNW* 27 (1928) 216-22; IV in: *ZNW* 32 (1933) 185-206.

[3]"Zur Liste der Neutestamentlichen Handschriften V," *ZNW* 45 (1954) 179-217; VI in: *ZNW* 48 (1957) 141-91.

[4]*Arbeiten zur neutestamentlichen Textforschung,* 1 (Berlin: de Gruyter, 1963); it includes some basic information about each MS.

[5]"Die griechischen Handschriften des Neuen Testaments: Ergänzungen zur 'Kurzgefasste Liste' (Fortsetzungsliste VII)," *Materialien zur neutestamentlichen Handschriftenkunde* (ANTF 3; Berlin: de Gruyter, 1969) 1-53.

[6]Many of the major uncials are also known by a Roman, Greek, or Hebrew capital letter which has been added in brackets.

and MSS dated after the fifteenth century which have generally been excluded from profiling. It is not always certain whether the MSS in this list actually contain Luke 1, 10, and 20. They are: 80, 241, 242, 252, 253, 258, 487, 488, 539, 542, 556, 646, 647, 648, 649, 650, 659, 661, 671, 676, 681, 682, 701, 712, 810, 813, 814, 907, 908, 922, 961, 981, 982, 985, 986, 990, 997, 1000, 1002, 1016, 1017, 1018, 1019, 1029, 1031, 1034, 1035, 1037, 1038, 1039, 1040, 1041, 1042, 1049, 1051, 1090, 1117, 1118, 1119, 1120, 1122, 1123, 1125, 1126, 1127, 1128, 1129, 1130, 1131, 1132, 1133, 1134, 1135, 1136, 1137, 1141, 1142, 1143, 1150, 1151, 1154, 1155, 1246, 1286, 1287, 1302, 1304, 1306, 1307, 1308, 1361, 1372, 1373, 1379, 1382, 1390, 1406, 1421, 1422, 1423, 1425, 1426, 1427, 1428, 1429, 1430, 1431, 1432, 1433, 1490, 1527, 1529, 1608, 1627, 1681, 1684, 1689, 1696, 1705, 1708, 1709, 1710, 1711, 1715, 1716, 1779, 1781, 1782, 1783, 1784, 1785, 1786, 1787, 1788, 1789, 1790, 1791, 1792, 1793, 1794, 1801, 1802, 1803, 1804, 1805, 1806, 1807, 1808, 1809, 1810, 1811, 1812, 1989, 1990, 2134, 2193, 2198, 2206, 2209, 2214, 2215, 2216, 2244, 2245, 2246, 2247, 2249, 2250, 2251, 2252, 2253, 2255, 2264, 2271, 2285, 2308, 2319, 2325, 2326, 2330, 2331, 2332, 2337, 2338, 2339, 2340, 2341, 2342, 2343, 2362, 2395, 2439, 2444, 2445, 2446, 2447, 2456, 2457, 2458, 2459, 2471, 2473, 2491, 2498, 2506, 2507, 2508, 2509, 2510, 2512, 2513, 2514, 2593, 2607, 2630, 2758.

3. MSS of which the microfilm at the INTF proved to be illegible.[7] These are: 57, 400, 417, 520, 1026, 1096, 1306, 1362, 1363, 1383, 1384, 1506, 1532, 1550, 1567, 1568, 1571, 1595, 1612 (palimpsest), 1688, 2113, 2211, 2309, 2310, 2385 (palimpsest), 2502 (too small), 2606, 2623, 2647, 2678, 2718, 2719.

4. MSS on microfilm at the INTF but dated after the fifteenth century. These generally postdate the first printed Greek text of the NT published by Erasmus on March 1, 1516. The chance of anything of textual value among them is rather small. Some of them are actually copies of Erasmus's printed text.[8] Late MSS available on microfilm, in collation or original in the U.S.A., were profiled. Not profiled were:[9] 61, 90, 289, 296, 335, 445, 522, 595, 724, 745, 755, 803, 956, 957, 963, 979, 988, 1044, 1063, 1064, 1065, 1068, 1086, 1088, 1139, 1367, 1414, 1591, 1615, 1620, 1629, 1639, 1640, 1644, 1652, 1680, 1700, 1702, 1704, 1901, 2136, 2137, 2301, 2422, 2477, 2488, 2497, 2703, 2711, 2714, 2715, 2721, 2737.

5. MSS on microfilm at the INTF of which the biblical text is accompanied by a commentary. In many cases the biblical text is interwoven and difficult to distinguish. In other cases only selected passages are commented on and thus the MS does not deserve to be included in the list of witnesses to the continuous Greek text. The main reason for excluding most of the commentaries from profiling was von Soden's claim that many have a unique textual tradition and thus deserve, like the lectionaries, to be treated separately. The Profile Method could be used to group and analyze the commentated text, but this awaits a future study.[10] The MSS excluded are: 055, 12,

---

[7]Many other microfilms are of insufficient quality to serve as basis for collation but could be read for profiling purposes.

[8]See above, vi.

[9]Excluding text with commentary (see below) and MSS of which the microfilm was illegible (see above).

[10]Those which were readily available on microfilm, in collation or the original in the U.S.A., were profiled if the text could be distinguished without difficulty from the commentary. These form about 25% of the total and include: 033, 040, 053, 127, 129, 137, 138, 139, 143, 151, 168, 301, 373, 374, 377, 391, 392, 427, 428, 569, 747, 841, 848, 854, 856, 884, 951, 989, 1021, 1078, 1080, 1177, 1178, 1230, 1252, 1253, 1255, 1312, 1313, 1327, 1337, 1392, 1424, 1533, 2148, 2346, 2414, 2452, 2470, 2604, 2637.

19, 20, 24, 25, 34, 36, 37, 39, 40, 48, 50, 63, 77, 95, 100, 108, 154, 186, 194,
195, 196, 210, 215, 222, 233, 237, 238, 239, 240, 243, 244, 259, 299, 300, 303, 305,
313, 316, 320, 329, 353, 357, 362, 370, 379, 381, 426, 434, 549, 589, 591, 598, 600,
684, 719, 720, 721, 722, 723, 727, 728, 729, 730, 731, 732, 733, 734, 735, 739, 740,
741, 744, 746, 749, 754, 771, 772, 773, 800, 807, 809, 817, 818, 819, 820, 833, 834,
835, 840, 846, 853, 855, 857, 858, 859, 861, 863, 868, 878, 879, 881, 886, 888,
889, 890, 891, 949, 964, 978, 1112, 1160, 1164, 1182, 1256, 1261, 1262, 1263,
1264, 1265, 1266, 1268, 1271, 1336, 1366, 1387, 1411, 1419, 1437, 1534, 1535,
1536, 1537, 1616, 1677, 1678, 1814, 1821, 1822, 2097, 2100, 2101, 2107, 2109,
2184, 2187, 2188, 2202, 2203, 2317, 2381, 2453, 2482, 2578, 2646, 2735.

6. Microfilms of ten MSS had been acquired by the INTF, but were at the time not available for profiling, were not known to contain Luke, or have since been dated earlier. They are: 2352, 2418, 2511, 2515, 2516, 2651, 2658, 2748, 2754, 2760.

This means that 468 Lucan MSS listed in 1969 remain to be profiled, though many of these are lost or inaccessible or too fragmentary.[11]

The second column of the list gives the date of the MS. When an exact year is given this means that the MS has a dated colophon. The Roman numerals represent paleographical estimates made by Gregory or other experts. Since the Byzantine book hand changed very little from the eleventh to the fifteenth century, dating for this period is difficult and the margin of error is large.[12]

The third column gives the group classification assigned by von Soden. When absent this means that the MS was not available to him. It should be remembered that von Soden based his classifications on only a few test passages and thus missed most of the cases of block mixture, i.e. the common phenomenon that the group or text-type affiliation changes between Gospels in the same MS or even within a Gospel. Thus a difference in classification between von Soden and the Profile Method means only that von Soden's classification proved to be invalid for the Gospel of Luke.

Von Soden used the following sigla:

A  The commentated text which presumably originated in Antioch. The commentary in Luke is by Titus of Bostra. None of the subdivisions of A proved to be a bona fide group, though some members form pairs or clusters. Von Soden did not use the A sigla in the apparatus to his text.

A[1]  Refers to 040 (Ξ).

A[3]  Refers to 033 (X).

A[4]  Refers to 053.

A[a]  Refers in Luke only to MSS 884 and 951 which are not related in Luke.

A[b]  Refers to four MSS in Luke of which 301 and 373 form a pair belonging to K[x].

A[c]  Refers to sixteen MSS in Luke which do not form a group. Only MSS 391 and 989 are closely related; they belong to Gr Π[a] in Luke 1 and 10, and to K[x] in Luke 20.

[11]MSS which are copied from another extant MS have the same Gregory number as their model with the exponent [abs] (= Abschrift). Aland lists for Luke: 9[abs], 30[abs], 205[abs], and 1160[abs]; they have not been taken into consideration, since they are of no interest for textual criticism. Many other candidates have been spotted by means of the Profile Method (see the pairs in Chapters V and VI).

[12]See E. C. Colwell, "A Chronology for the Letters E, H, Λ, Π, in the Byzantine Minuscule Book Hand," *Studies in Methodology in Textual Criticism of the New Testament* (NTTS 9; Grand Rapids: Eerdmans, 1969) 125-27.

49

| | |
|---|---|
| $A^k$ | Refers to 51 MSS in Luke which are, according to von Soden, related to the Antiochian commentated text; they do not form a group. However, MSS 53 and 902, 15 and 1163 form $K^x$ pairs, and a number of $A^k$ MSS belong to Grs 1167 and 1519. |
| H | Presumably the text established by Hesychius in Alexandria ca. A.D. 300. It is equivalent to Hort's Neutral and Alexandrian groups and my Gr B. |
| Hag | MSS written during the late thirteenth and early fourteenth century by Theodoros Hagiopetrites. Some form together with other MSS the large $K^x$ cluster 74. MSS 412 and 1394 form a $K^x$ pair. |
| I | Presumably the text established by Pamphilius in Caesarea ca. A.D. 300. |
| I′ | Refers to 29 miscellaneous Iota members which do not form a group. Von Soden did not use this siglum in the apparatus to his text. |
| $I^a$ | Refers in Luke only to MS 372. |
| $I^\alpha$ | Refers to twelve MSS in Luke which do not form a group. According to Streeter several of these, 038 ($\Theta$), 28, 544, and 700, form Family $\Theta$, which is better known as the Caesarean text. Von Soden was severely criticized for placing 05 (D) with these "Caesarean" MSS. |
| $I^\beta$ | Similar to Grs 1216 and 16. |
| $I^\eta$ | Similar to Grs 1, $22^a$, and $22^b$. |
| $I^\iota$ | Corresponds to Gr 13. |
| $I^\kappa$ | Similar to Grs $\Pi^a$, $\Pi^b$, and related clusters. |
| $I^o$ | Refers to ten MSS in Luke which do not form a group. |
| $I^r$ | Similar to Gr $\Lambda$. Cl 686 is made up of $I^r$ MSS. |
| $I^\sigma$ | Refers to nine MSS in Luke which do not form a group. |
| $I^\phi$ | Refers to six MSS in Luke which do not form a group. Von Soden did not use this siglum in the apparatus to his text. |
| $I^{\phi a}$ | Similar to Cl 1675. |
| $I^{\phi b}$ | Refers to 37 MSS in Luke which do not form a coherent group. Cl 7 and $K^x$ Cls 187 and 1084 are made up of $I^{\phi b}$ MSS. |
| $I^{\phi c}$ | Refers to twelve MSS which do not form a coherent group. Three of them form Cl 160 and five others form Cl $\Pi$1441. |
| $I^{\phi r}$ | Similar to the M groups and clusters. |
| K | Presumably the text established by Lucian in Antioch ca. A.D. 300. |
| $K^a$ | = $I^\kappa$ |
| $K^{ak}$ | Refers to 39 MSS which do not form a group. Von Soden did not use this siglum in the apparatus to his text. Some $K^{ak}$ MSS form small clusters and pairs which belong to $K^x$. |
| $K^1$ | Similar to Cl $\Omega$, a subgroup of $K^x$. |
| $K^i$ | Refers to six MSS which do not form a coherent group that can be distinguished from $K^x$. |
| $K^{ik}$ | Refers to four MSS in Luke which do not form a group. Von Soden did not use this siglum in the apparatus of his text. |
| $K^r$ | A Byzantine recension of the twelfth century which is characterized by a distinct lectionary equipment and careful scribal control. |
| $K^x$ | The dominant text from the ninth to the thirteenth century. It lacks scribal control and has unclear outlines. There can be little doubt that it exercised |

massive influence on other forms of the text current at the time. Von Soden did not study this group in detail.

Columns four, five, and six present the classifications made on the basis of the Profile Method. The groups (abbreviated Gr) and clusters (Cl) have in most cases been named for one of the leading members with a preference for the lowest number. Clusters generally refer to groups of less than ten members. Many clusters are actually subgroups belonging to one of the main groups. In addition to the group and cluster numbers the following abbreviations are used:

corr    text as corrected by a later hand.

def     defective.

fragm   fragmentary.

illeg   No profile could be made due to an illegible microfilm.

Kmix    Profiles which do not conform to any of the groups or clusters but which stand relatively close to $K^x$.

Mix     Profiles which do not conform to any of the groups or clusters and which diverge significantly from $K^x$.

NP      No profile was made for this chapter.

The seventh and final column states, if relevant, whether a MS is a weak (corrupted toward $K^x$), divergent (with a significant number of non-$K^x$ readings in surplus), or core (with a perfect or almost perfect profile) member of a group, and mentions the MS with which it forms a pair, or to which it is closely related, or the cluster to which it belongs. In relevant cases the nature and extent of the "surplus" readings has been specified. This column also lists the group to which a MS has been corrected if this can be determined.

## PROFILE CLASSIFICATION

| Gregory No. | Date | v. Soden Classif. | Luke 1 | Luke 10 | Luke 20 | Comments |
|---|---|---|---|---|---|---|
| 01 (ℵ) | IV | H | B | B | B | core member |
| 02 (A) | V | I$^{\kappa a}$ | Π$^a$ | Π$^a$ | Π$^a$ | diverging member |
| 03 (B) | IV | H | B | B | B | core member |
| 04 (C) | V | H | Mix | Mix | Mix | |
| 05 (D) | V/VI | I$^\alpha$ | B | B | B | diverging member |
| 07 (E) | VIII | K$^i$ | K$^x$ | K$^x$ | K$^x$ | Cl Ω |
| 09 (F) | IX | K$^i$ | Kmix | Def | Def | |
| 011 (G) | X | K$^i$ | K$^x$ | K$^x$ | K$^x$ | fragm in 10 |
| 013 (H) | IX/X | K$^i$ | K$^x$ | K$^x$ | K$^x$ | fragm in 10 |
| 017 (K) | IX/X | I$^{\kappa a}$ | Π$^a$ | Π$^a$ | Π$^a$ | core member |
| 019 (L) | VIII | H | B | B | B | core member |
| 021 (M) | IX | I$^{\phi r}$ | M27 | M27 | M27 | diverging member |
| 022 (N) | VI | I$^\pi$ | Def | Def | Mix | fragm in 20 |
| 024 (P) | VI | I$'$ | Def | Def | Mix | |
| 026 (Q) | V | I$'$ | Def | Def | Mix | |
| 027 (R) | VI | I$'$ | K$^x$ | K$^x$ | Mix | fragm in 10 |
| 028 (S) | 949 | K$^1$ | K$^x$ | K$^x$ | K$^x$ | Cl Ω |
| 030 (U) | IX | I$^o$ | Kmix | K$^x$ | Kmix | close to 974 and 1006 in 1 and 10 |
| 031 (V) | VIII/IX | K$^1$ | K$^x$ | K$^x$ | K$^x$ | Cl Ω |
| 032 (W) | V | H | B | K$^x$ | Mix | close to 1273 in 20 |
| 033 (X) | X | A$^3$ | Mix | Mix | Def | fragm in 10 some relationship to Gr B |
| 034 (Y) | IX | I$^\kappa$ | Π171 | Π171 | Π171 | Π$^a$ surplus in 1 |
| 036 (Γ) | X | I$'$ | K$^x$ | K$^x$ | K$^x$ | |
| 037 (Δ) | IX | H | Mix | K$^x$ | K$^x$ | |
| 038 (Θ) | IX | I$^\alpha$ | Mix | Mix | Mix | |
| 039 (Λ) | IX | I$^r$ | Λ | Λ | Λ | surplus in 10 |
| 040 (Ξ) | VII/VIII | A$^1$ | Kmix | B | Def | |
| 041 (Π) | IX | I$^{\kappa a}$ | Π$^a$ | Π$^a$ | Π$^a$ | core member |
| 044 (Ψ) | VIII/IX | H | B | Kmix | Mix | weak in 1 |
| 045 (Ω) | VIII/IX | K$^1$ | K$^x$ | K$^x$ | K$^x$ | Cl Ω; fragm in 1 |
| 047 | VIII/IX | I$'$ | K$^x$ | K$^x$ | K$^x$ | |
| 053 | IX | A$^4$ | K$^x$ | Def | Def | |
| 0130 | IX | I$'$ | Mix | Def | Def | |
| 0211 | VII | K$^1$ | K$^x$ | Kmix | Mix | Cl 1213 in 1; related to M groups in 10 and 20 |

# PROFILE CLASSIFICATION

| Gregory No. | Date | v. Soden Classif. | Luke 1 | Luke 10 | Luke 20 | Comments |
|---|---|---|---|---|---|---|
| 1 | XII | $I^{\eta a}$ | 1 | 1 | 1 | core member; close to 1582 |
| 2 | XII | $K^x$ | Kmix | $K^x$ | $K^x$ | |
| 3 | XII | $K^x$ | $K^x$ | NP | $K^x$ | |
| 4 | XIII | $I'$ | Kmix | $K^x$ | $K^x$ | |
| 5 | XIV | $A^k$ | Mix | Kmix | 1519 | |
| 6 | XIII | $I^\kappa$ | Π6 | Π6 | Π6 | |
| 7 | XII | $I^{\phi b}$ | Cl 7 | Cl 7 | Cl 7 | |
| 8 | XI | $K^x$ | $K^x$ | $K^x$ | $K^x$ | |
| 9 | 1167 | $I^{\phi b}$ | $K^x$ | Kmix | $K^x$ | |
| 10 | XIII | $I^{\phi r}$ | M10 | M10 | M10 | |
| 11 | XII | $K^{ak}$ | $Π^b$ | $K^x$ | $K^x$ | |
| 13 | XIII | $I^{\iota c}$ | 13 | 13 | 13 | core member |
| 14 | X | $K^x$ | $K^x$ | NP | $K^x$ | |
| 15 | XII | $A^k$ | $K^x$ | NP | $K^x$ | Cl 43; pair with 1163 |
| 16 | XIV | $I^{\beta b}$ | 16 | 16 | 16 | pair with 1528 |
| 17 | XV | $I^\beta$ | $K^x$ | NP | $K^x$ | Cl 17 |
| 18 | XIV | $K^r$ | $K^r$ | NP | $K^r$ | |
| 21 | XII | $I^\alpha$ | $K^x$ | $K^x$ | $K^x$ | |
| 22 | XII | $I^{\eta b}$ | 22b | 22b | 22b | core member |
| 23 | XI | $I^{\phi c}$ | Π1441 | $K^x$ | Π1441 | weak in 20 |
| 26 | XI | $I^\kappa$ | Kmix | $K^x$ | $K^x$ | |
| 27 | X | $I^{\phi r}$ | M27 | M27 | M27 | core member |
| 28 | XI | $I^\alpha$ | Mix | $K^x$ | $K^x$ | fragm in 20 |
| 29 | X | $K^{ak}$ | $K^x$ | NP | $K^x$ | corr to $Π^b$ |
| 30 | XV | $I^\beta$ | $K^x$ | NP | $K^x$ | Cl 17; pair with 288 |
| 31 | XIII | $I^\kappa$ | $K^x$ | NP | $K^x$ | Cl 1053 |
| 32 | XII | $A^k$ | 1519 | 1519 | 1519 | pair with 269 |
| 33 | IX | H | B | B | B | weak in 1 |
| 35 | XI | $K^r$ | $K^r$ | NP | $K^r$ | Subgroup 35 (first hand) |
| 38 | XIII | $I^\kappa$ | $K^x$ | $K^x$ | $K^x$ | Cl 1053 in 1 and 20 |
| 43 | XII | $K^x$ | $K^x$ | $K^x$ | $K^x$ | Cl 43; pair with 2420 |
| 44 | XII | $K^i$ | $K^x$ | $K^x$ | $K^x$ | pair with 1434 in 20 |
| 45 | XIV | $K^x$ | $K^x$ | NP | $K^x$ | |
| 46 | XII | $K^{ak}$ | $K^x$ | NP | $K^x$ | Cl 46 |
| 47 | XV | $K^x$ | Mix | $K^r$ | $K^r$ | Cl 56 in 10 and 20 |
| 49 | XII | $K^x$ | $K^x$ | $K^x$ | $Π^a$ | |

## PROFILE CLASSIFICATION

| Gregory No. | Date | v. Soden Classif. | Luke 1 | Luke 10 | Luke 20 | Comments |
|---|---|---|---|---|---|---|
| 51 | XIII | $K^x$ | $K^x$ | NP | $K^x$ | |
| 52 | 1286 | $K^{ak}$ | $K^x$ | NP | $K^x$ | Cl 46; pair with 1395 |
| 53 | XIV | $A^k$ | $K^x$ | NP | $K^x$ | pair with 902 |
| 54 | 1338 | $K^x$ | Kmix | Kmix | $K^x$ | related to Π groups |
| 55 | XIII | $K^r$ | $K^r$ | NP | $K^r$ | Cl 128 |
| 56 | XV | $K^x$ | $K^r$ | $K^r$ | $K^r$ | Cl 56 |
| 58 | XV | $K^x$ | $K^r$ | $K^r$ | $K^r$ | Cl 56 |
| 59 | XIII | $K^x$ | Kmix | $K^x$ | $K^x$ | |
| 60 | 1297 | $K^x$ | Cl 1685 | Cl 1685 | Cl 1685 | surplus in 1 |
| 64 | XII | | Cl 121 | Cl 121 | Cl 121 | |
| 65 | XI | $K^i$ | $K^x$ | NP | $K^x$ | Cl Ω |
| 66 | XIV | $K^r$ | $K^r$ | $K^r$ | $K^r$ | large surplus |
| 67 | XI | $I^\kappa$ | Mix | $K^x$ | Kmix | |
| 68 | XI | $I^\kappa$ | $\Pi^b$ | NP | $\Pi^b$ | |
| 69 | XV | $I^{tb}$ | 13 | 13 | 13 | |
| 70 | XV | $I^\beta$ | $K^x$ | NP | $K^x$ | Cl 17 |
| 71 | XII | $I^{\phi r}$ | M27 | M27 | M27 | core member |
| 72 | XI | $I^\kappa$ | $\Pi^a$ | $K^x$ | $K^x$ | |
| 73 | XII | $K^x$ | Mix | $K^x$ | $K^x$ | |
| 74 | 1292 | Hag | $K^x$ | NP | $K^x$ | Cl 74 |
| 75 | XI | $K^x$ | 1167 | 1167 | 1167 | pair with 2229 (corr) |
| 76 | XII | $K^x$ | Kmix | $K^x$ | Kmix | Cl 1193 |
| 78 | XII | $K^x$ | Cl 127 | NP | Cl 127 | close to 1052 |
| 79 | XV | $I^\alpha$ | $K^x$ | Mix | Mix | some relationship to Π groups |
| 83 | XI | $K^r$ | $K^r$ | $K^r$ | $K^r$ | perfect member |
| 89 | 1006 | $K^x$ | $K^x$ | $K^x$ | $K^x$ | Cl 74 |
| 98 | XI | $K^{ik}$ | $K^x$ | $K^x$ | Kmix | some relationship to M groups |
| 105 | XII | $K^x$ | $K^x$ | NP | $K^x$ | |
| 106 | X | | M106 | M106 | M106 | |
| 107 | XIII | $K^x$ | Mix | NP | $K^x$ | |
| 109 | 1326 | $K^x$ | $K^x$ | Kmix | Kmix | |
| 111 | XII | $I^{\phi b}$ | $K^x$ | NP | $K^x$ | Cl 281 |
| 112 | XI | $K^{ak}$ | $K^x$ | NP | $K^x$ | Cl 112 |
| 113 | XI | $I^\kappa$ | $K^x$ | Π473 | Π473 | Cl 1053 in 1 |
| 114 | XI | $I^\kappa$ | $\Pi^a$ | $\Pi^a$ | $\Pi^a$ | core member |
| 115 | X | $I^{\phi b}$ | Kmix | $K^x$ | Kmix | |

| Gregory No. | Date | v. Soden Classif. | Luke 1 | Luke 10 | Luke 20 | Comments |
|---|---|---|---|---|---|---|
| 116 | XII | $I^\kappa$ | Kmix | Kmix | 1167 | |
| 117 | XV | $I^{\phi b}$ | $K^x$ | NP | $K^x$ | |
| 118 | XIII | $I^{\eta b}$ | 1 | 1 | 1 | core member |
| 119 | XII | $I^\beta$ | 16 | 16 | 16 | |
| 120 | XII | $I^\beta$ | $K^x$ | $K^x$ | $K^x$ | Cl 17 |
| 121 | 1283 | $K^x$ | Cl 121 | Cl 121 | Cl 121 | |
| 122 | XII | $K^i$ | $K^x$ | $K^x$ | $K^x$ | Cl 122 |
| 123 | XI | $K^x$ | $K^x$ | $K^x$ | $K^x$ | Cl $\Omega$ |
| 124 | XI | $I^{\iota b}$ | 13 | 13 | 13 | weak member |
| 125 | XI | $K^{ak}$ | $K^x$ | NP | $K^x$ | |
| 126 | XI | $K^x$ | $K^x$ | $K^x$ | $K^x$ | |
| 127 | XI | $A^c$ | Cl 127 | Cl 127 | Cl 127 | close to 132 |
| 128 | XIII | $K^r$ | $K^r$ | $K^r$ | $K^r$ | Cl 128 |
| 129 | XII | $A^c$ | $K^x$ | NP | NP | |
| 130 | XV | $K^x$ | $K^x$ | NP | $K^x$ | fragm in 1 |
| 131 | XIV | $I^\eta$ | 1 | 1 | 1 | |
| 132 | XII | $K^x$ | Cl 127 | Cl 127 | Cl 127 | close to 127 |
| 133 | XI | $K^x$ | $\Pi$473 | $\Pi$473 | $\Pi$473 | surplus in 1 |
| 134 | XII | $K^x$ | 22b | 22b | 22b | weak member |
| 135 | X | $K^x$ | $K^x$ | $K^x$ | $K^x$ | |
| 137 | XI | $A^c$ | $K^x$ | $K^x$ | Kmix | Cl 137 |
| 138 | XII | $A^c$ | $K^x$ | NP | NP | |
| 139 | XII | $A^c$ | 291 | NP | NP | |
| 140 | XII | $K^x$ | $K^x$ | NP | $K^x$ | |
| 141 | XIII | $K^r$ | $K^r$ | NP | $K^r$ | Subgroup 35 |
| 142 | XI | $K^x$ | Kmix | $K^x$ | $K^x$ | |
| 143 | XI | $A^c$ | $K^x$ | $K^x$ | $K^x$ | Cl $\Omega$ |
| 144 | X | $K^x$ | $K^x$ | $K^x$ | $K^x$ | |
| 145 | XI | $K^x$ | $\Pi^a$ | $\Pi^a$ | Mix | weak in 1 and 10; pair with 2680 in 20, related to Gr 22 |
| 147 | XIII | $K^r$ | $K^r$ | NP | $K^r$ | Cl 147 |
| 148 | XI | $K^x$ | $K^x$ | $K^x$ | $K^x$ | |
| 149 | XV | $K^x$ | 22b | 22b | 22b | weak member |
| 150 | XI | $K^x$ | $K^x$ | $K^x$ | Kmix | related to $\Pi$200 in 20 |
| 151 | X | $A^c$ | $K^x$ | $K^x$ | $K^x$ | Cl $\Omega$ |
| 152 | XIII | $I^\beta$ | 1216 | 1216 | 1216 | pair with 555 |

## PROFILE CLASSIFICATION

| Gregory No. | Date | v. Soden Classif. | Luke 1 | Luke 10 | Luke 20 | Comments |
|---|---|---|---|---|---|---|
| 153 | XIV | I$^{\phi b}$ | K$^x$ | K$^x$ | K$^x$ | |
| 155 | XIV | K$^r$ | K$^r$ | NP | K$^r$ | surplus in 1 |
| 156 | XII | K$^x$ | Kmix | K$^x$ | K$^x$ | pair with 1320 in 1 |
| 157 | XII | I$^{\sigma}$ | K$^x$ | Mix | B | related to Gr B in 10 |
| 158 | XI | K$^x$ | K$^x$ | K$^x$ | $\Pi^a$ | |
| 159 | 1121? | K$^x$ | M159 | M159 | M159 | |
| 160 | 1123 | I$^{\phi c}$ | Mix | K$^x$ | K$^x$ | Cl 160 |
| 161 | X | I$^r$ | $\Lambda$ | $\Lambda$ | $\Lambda$ | fragm in 20 |
| 162 | 1153 | I | K$^x$ | Kmix | K$^x$ | |
| 163 | XI | I-K$^1$ | Cl 163 | Cl 163 | Cl 163 | pair with 345 |
| 164 | 1039 | I$^\phi$ or I$^r$ | $\Lambda$ | $\Lambda$ | $\Lambda$ | weak in 1 and 10; related to 1443 |
| 165 | 1291 | K$^x$ | Mix | K$^x$ | Kmix | pair with 176; related to Gr 22 |
| 166 | XIII | I$^r$ | Def | $\Lambda$ | $\Lambda$ | core member |
| 167 | XIII | K$^r$ | K$^r$ | NP | K$^r$ | Cl 167 |
| 168 | XIII | | Mix | Kmix | Def | some relationship to Cl 1675 in 1 and to Gr $\Lambda$ in 10 |
| 169 | XI | A$^k$ | K$^x$ | NP | K$^x$ | some relationship to Cl 1442 |
| 170 | XIII | K$^r$ | K$^r$ | NP | K$^r$ | Subgr 35 |
| 171 | XIV | I$^{\kappa}$ | $\Pi$171 | $\Pi$171 | $\Pi$171 | |
| 173 | XII | K$^x$ | Mix | Mix | $\Lambda$ | some relationship to Gr 1216 |
| 174 | 1052 | I$^{\iota b}$ | $\Lambda$ | $\Lambda$ | $\Lambda$ | |
| 175 | X | K$^x$ | $\Pi^a$ | $\Pi^a$ | $\Pi^a$ | weak member |
| 176 | XIII | K$^x$ | Mix | K$^x$ | Mix | pair with 165; related to Gr 22 |
| 178 | XII | I$^{\kappa}$ | $\Pi^a$ | $\Pi^a$ | K$^x$ | Cl 178 |
| 179 | XII | I$^{\phi b}$ | Mix | K$^x$ | K$^x$ | |
| 180 | XII | K$^x$ | K$^x$ | NP | K$^x$ | Cl 180 |
| 182 | XIV | I$^{\phi b}$ | K$^r$ | $\Pi^a$ | $\Pi^a$ | weak in 10 and 20 |
| 183 | XII | K$^x$ | K$^x$ | NP | K$^x$ | Cl 183 |
| 184 | XIII | I$^{\beta}$ | 1216 | 1216 | 1216 | core member |
| 185 | XIV | I$^{\phi b}$ | Cl 1531 | Cl 1531 | Cl 1531 | |
| 187 | XII | I$^{\phi b}$ | K$^x$ | K$^x$ | K$^x$ | Cl 187 |
| 188 | XII | K$^x$ | M106 | M106 | M106 | |
| 189 | XIV | K$^r$ | K$^r$ | NP | K$^r$ | Cl 189 |
| 190 | XIV | K$^x$ | Cl 190 | Cl 190 | Cl 190 | |
| 191 | XII | K$^x$ | M1326 | M349 | M349 | weak member |
| 192 | XIII | I$^{\phi b}$ | $\Pi$171 | $\Pi$171 | $\Pi$171 | |

| Gregory No. | Date | v. Soden Classif. | Luke 1 | Luke 10 | Luke 20 | Comments |
|---|---|---|---|---|---|---|
| 193 | XII | $K^x$ | $K^x$ | NP | $K^x$ | |
| 198 | XIII | $K^x$ | $K^x$ | NP | $K^x$ | Cl 74 |
| 199 | XII | $I^r$ | $\Lambda$ | $\Lambda$ | $\Lambda$ | core member |
| 200 | XI | $K^{ak}$ | $\Pi200$ | $\Pi200$ | $\Pi200$ | |
| 201 | 1357 | $K^r$ | $K^r$ | $K^r$ | $K^r$ | perfect member |
| 202 | XII | $K^x$ | $K^x$ | $K^x$ | $K^x$ | Cl 202 |
| 204 | XIII | $K^x$ | $K^r$ | NP | $K^r$ | Subgroup 35 |
| 205 | XV | $I^\eta$ | 1 | 1 | 1 | pair with 209 |
| 207 | XI | $K^x$ | $K^x$ | NP | $K^x$ | |
| 208 | XI | $K^x$ | $K^x$ | NP | $K^x$ | Cl 183 |
| 209 | XIV | $I^{\eta b}$ | 1 | 1 | 1 | pair with 205 |
| 211 | XII | $I^r$ | Def | $\Lambda$ | $\Lambda$ | weak in 10 |
| 212 | XI | $K^x$ | Kmix | $K^x$ | $K^x$ | |
| 213 | XI | $I^o$ | Mix | Mix | Mix | |
| 214 | XIV | $K^r$ | $K^r$ | $K^x$ | $K^x$ | weak in 1 |
| 217 | XII | $I^\beta$ | 16 | 16 | 16 | pair with 578 in 1 and 10 |
| 218 | XIII | $I^{\phi b}$ | $K^x$ | NP | $K^x$ | Cl 187 |
| 219 | XIII | $K^{ik}$ | $K^x$ | NP | $K^x$ | pair with 2217 |
| 220 | XIII | $I^\kappa$ | $\Pi^b$ | $\Pi^b$ | $\Pi^b$ | |
| 225 | 1192 | $A^k$ | Kmix | 1167 | 1167 | |
| 226 | XII | $K^x$ | $K^x$ | $K^x$ | $K^x$ | |
| 227 | XIII | $K^x$ | $K^x$ | $K^x$ | $K^x$ | |
| 228 | XIV | $K^x$ | $\Pi171$ | $\Pi171$ | $K^x$ | |
| 229 | 1140 | $I^{\kappa c}$ | $\Pi^a$ | $K^x$ | $K^x$ | |
| 230 | 1013 | $I^{\iota c}$ | $\Lambda$ | $\Lambda$ | $\Lambda$ | very weak in 20 |
| 231 | XII | $K^x$ | $K^x$ | $K^x$ | $K^x$ | |
| 232 | 1302 | $I^\beta$ | $K^x$ | $K^x$ | $K^x$ | |
| 234 | 1278 | Hag | $K^x$ | NP | $K^x$ | Cl 74 |
| 235 | 1314 | $I^\sigma$ | Kmix | $K^x$ | $K^x$ | |
| 236 | XI | $K^a$ | $\Pi171$ | $\Pi171$ | $\Pi171$ | |
| 245 | 1199 | $I^\sigma$ | Kmix | 1167 | 1167 | |
| 246 | XIV | $K^r$ | $K^r$ | NP | $K^r$ | perfect member |
| 247 | XII | $K^x$ | $K^x$ | $K^x$ | $K^x$ | Cl 1193 |
| 248 | 1275 | $I^{\kappa c}$ | Kmix | Kmix | M27 | weak in 20 |
| 251 | XII | $I'$ | Cl 1229 | Cl 1229 | Cl 1229 | |
| 260 | XIII | $K^x$ | $K^x$ | NP | $K^x$ | |

| Gregory No. | Date | v. Soden Classif. | Luke 1 | Luke 10 | Luke 20 | Comments |
|---|---|---|---|---|---|---|
| 261 | XII | $K^1$ | $K^x$ | NP | $K^x$ | |
| 262 | X | $I^r$ | $\Lambda$ | $\Lambda$ | $\Lambda$ | core member |
| 263 | XIII | $K^1$ | $K^x$ | NP | $K^x$ | |
| 264 | XII | $I^{\phi r}$ | $K^x$ | $\Pi^a$ | $K^x$ | weak in 10 (other hand) |
| 265 | XII | $I^{\kappa a}$ | $\Pi^a$ | $\Pi^a$ | $\Pi^a$ | core member |
| 266 | XIII | $I^\kappa$ | $\Pi$266 | NP | $\Pi$266 | |
| 267 | XII | $I^{\phi b}$ | Cl 7 | Cl 7 | Cl 7 | |
| 268 | XII | $I^\kappa$ | $\Pi$268 | NP | $\Pi$268 | pair with 787 |
| 269 | XII | $A^k$ | 1519 | 1519 | 1519 | pair with 32 |
| 270 | XII | $I^{\kappa b}$ | $\Pi^b$ | $\Pi^a$ | $\Pi^a$ | |
| 271 | XI | $A^k$ | $K^x$ | NP | $K^x$ | Cl $\Omega$ |
| 272 | XI | $K^1$ | $K^x$ | NP | $K^x$ | pair with 419 |
| 273 | XIII | $I'$ | Kmix | $K^x$ | Kmix | |
| 274 | X | $K^x$ | $K^x$ | NP | $K^x$ | |
| 275 | XII | $K^x$ | $K^x$ | NP | $K^x$ | |
| 276 | 1092 | $I^{\phi b}$ | Cl 276 | Cl 276 | Cl 276 | |
| 277 | XI | $K^1$ | $K^x$ | NP | $K^x$ | Cl $\Omega$ |
| 278 | 1072 | $I^\kappa$ | $\Pi$278 | $\Pi$278 | $\Pi$278 | |
| 279 | XII | $I^\alpha$ | $K^x$ | NP | Kmix | |
| 280 | XII | $I^{\kappa c}$ | $\Pi^a$ | $\Pi^a$ | $\Pi^a$ | core member |
| 281 | XII | $I'$? | $K^x$ | $K^x$ | $K^x$ | Cl 281 |
| 282 | 1176 | $K^x$ | Kmix | $K^x$ | $K^x$ | pair with 1714 in 1 |
| 283 | XIII | $K^x$ | Kmix | NP | $K^x$ | |
| 284 | XIII | $K^x$ | $K^x$ | NP | $K^x$ | |
| 285 | XV | $K^r$ | $K^r$ | NP | $K^r$ | weak in 20 |
| 286 | 1432 | | $K^x$ | $K^x$ | $K^x$ | |
| 287 | 1478 | $I^\beta$ | $K^x$ | NP | $K^x$ | Cl 17 |
| 288 | XV | $I^\beta$ | $K^x$ | NP | $K^x$ | CL 17; pair with 30 |
| 290 | XIV | $K^r$ | $K^r$ | NP | $K^r$ | pair with 363 |
| 291 | XIII | $I^\sigma$ | 291 | 291 | 291 | |
| 292 | XIII | $A^k$ | $K^x$ | $\Pi$473 | $\Pi$473 | |
| 293 | 1262 | $K^x$ | M1195 | M1195 | M1195 | weak member |
| 294 | 1291 | $K^x$ | $K^x$ | $K^x$ | $K^x$ | $\Pi^a$ in first part of 20 |
| 295 | XIII | $I^{\phi c}$ | $\Pi$1441 | NP | $\Pi$1441 | |
| 297 | XII | $A^k$ | $K^x$ | Kmix | Mix | |
| 298 | XII | $K^x$ | $K^x$ | $K^x$ | $K^x$ | Cl 1053 |

## PROFILE CLASSIFICATION

| Gregory No. | Date | v. Soden Classif. | Luke 1 | Luke 10 | Luke 20 | Comments |
|---|---|---|---|---|---|---|
| 301 | XI | A$^b$ | K$^x$ | K$^x$ | K$^x$ | pair with 373 |
| 324 | XIV | K$^x$ | K$^x$ | K$^x$ | K$^x$ | |
| 330 | XII | K$^x$ | 16 | 16 | 16 | |
| 331 | XI | I$^{\phi b}$ | Cl 585 | Cl 585 | Cl 585 | weak in 10 and 20 |
| 343 | XI | K$^x$ | Cl 343 | Cl 343 | Kmix | |
| 344 | X | K$^{ak}$ | K$^x$ | NP | K$^x$ | Cl Ω |
| 345 | XI | I-K$^1$ | Cl 163 | Cl 163 | Cl 163 | pair with 163; fragm in 20 |
| 346 | XII | I$^{\iota c}$ | 13 | 13 | 13 | core member |
| 347 | XII | K$^x$ | K$^x$ | NP | K$^x$ | |
| 348 | 1022 | I$^{\beta a}$ | 1216 | 1216 | 1216 | core member |
| 349 | 1322 | I$^{\phi a}$ | M349 | M349 | M349 | pair with 2388 |
| 350 | XI | K$^{ak}$ | M350 | M350 | M350 | |
| 351 | XII | K$^x$ | K$^x$ | NP | 22b | weak in 20 |
| 352 | XI | K$^x$ | K$^x$ | K$^x$ | K$^x$ | Cl 352 |
| 355 | XII | K$^1$ | K$^x$ | K$^x$ | K$^x$ | |
| 358 | XIV | K$^{ak}$ | K$^x$ | K$^x$ | K$^x$ | pair with 360 |
| 359 | XII | K$^x$ | K$^x$ | K$^x$ | K$^x$ | |
| 360 | XI | K$^{ak}$ | K$^x$ | K$^x$ | K$^x$ | pair with 358 |
| 361 | XIII | K$^r$ | K$^r$ | Def | K$^r$ | |
| 363 | XIV | K$^r$ | K$^r$ | K$^r$ | K$^r$ | pair with 290 |
| 364 | X | K$^x$ | K$^x$ | NP | K$^x$ | Cl Ω |
| 365 | XIII | I$^\kappa$ | Π$^b$ | NP | Π$^b$ | |
| 367 | 1331 | K$^x$ | K$^x$ | NP | K$^x$ | |
| 371 | X | K$^x$ | 291 | 291 | 291 | weak in 1 |
| 372 | XVI | I$^a$ | Mix | Mix | Mix | very strange text |
| 373 | XV | A$^b$ | K$^x$ | K$^x$ | K$^x$ | pair with 301 |
| 374 | XII | A$^c$ | Kmix | NP | NP | |
| 375 | XI | K$^x$ | K$^x$ | K$^x$ | K$^x$ | Cl 352 |
| 376 | XI | I$^r$ | K$^x$ | K$^x$ | K$^x$ | Cl 183; partly illeg in 1 |
| 377 | XV | A$^c$ | Mix | Kmix | Mix | |
| 380 | 1499 | K$^x$ | K$^x$ | K$^x$ | K$^x$ | corr towards Π groups |
| 382 | XIII | K$^1$ | Mix | Mix | Mix | some relationship to Cl 163 |
| 386 | XIV | K$^r$ | K$^r$ | NP | K$^r$ | Cl 167 |
| 387 | XII | K$^r$ | K$^r$ | NP | K$^r$ | pair with 1471 |
| 388 | XIII | K$^x$ | Π171 | Π171 | Π171 | weak in 1; pair with 2584 |
| 389 | XI | I$^\kappa$ | Π$^a$ | Π$^a$ | Π$^a$ | weak member |

| Gregory No. | Date | v. Soden Classif. | Luke 1 | Luke 10 | Luke 20 | Comments |
|---|---|---|---|---|---|---|
| 390 | 1282 | $K^x$ | $K^x$ | NP | $K^x$ | Cl 74 |
| 391 | XI | $A^c$ | $\Pi^a$ | $\Pi^a$ | $K^x$ | Cl 178; fragm and weak in 1 |
| 392 | XII | | Kmix | $K^x$ | $K^x$ | |
| 393 | XIV | K | Kmix | Kmix | Kmix | some relationship to $\Pi$ groups |
| 394 | 1330 | $K^r$ | $K^r$ | NP | $K^r$ | Subgroup 35 |
| 395 | XII | $I^r$ | Cl 490 | Cl 490 | Cl 490 | |
| 396 | XII | $K^x$ | $K^x$ | NP | $K^x$ | Cl $\Omega$ in 1 |
| 399 | IX/X | $K^1$ | Mix | $K^x$ | $K^x$ | |
| 401 | XII | $K^x$ | Mix | Kmix | Kmix | pair with 1013 in 10 and 20 |
| 402 | XIV | $K^r$ | $K^r$ | NP | $K^r$ | Subgroup 35 |
| 403 | XIII | $K^x$ | $K^x$ | NP | $K^x$ | |
| 405 | X | $K^x$ | Kmix | NP | $K^x$ | |
| 406 | XI | $I^\alpha$ | $K^x$ | NP | $K^x$ | |
| 407 | XII | $K^x$ | Def | $K^x$ | $K^x$ | Cl 1053 in 10 |
| 408 | XII | $K^1$ | $K^x$ | $K^x$ | $K^x$ | |
| 409 | XIV | $K^x$ | $K^x$ | NP | $K^x$ | |
| 410 | XIII | $K^x$ | M349 | M349 | M349 | |
| 411 | X | $K^x$ | Kmix | $K^x$ | $K^x$ | |
| 412 | 1301 | Hag | $K^x$ | $K^x$ | $K^x$ | pair with 1394 |
| 413 | 1302 | $K^x$ | $K^x$ | $K^x$ | $K^x$ | Cl 413 |
| 414 | XIV | $K^x$ | M349 | M349 | M349 | |
| 415 | 1356 | $K^r$ | $\Pi^b$ | NP | $\Pi^a$ | weak in 1 and 20 |
| 416 | XIV | $A^k$ | $K^x$ | Kmix | Kmix | |
| 419 | XII | $K^1$ | $K^x$ | $K^x$ | $K^x$ | pair with 272 |
| 422 | XI | $K^{ik}$ | Kmix | $K^x$ | $K^x$ | |
| 427 | XIII | | Mix | $K^x$ | Kmix | |
| 428 | XIII | | $K^x$ | $K^x$ | $K^x$ | Cl 1021 |
| 431 | XI | $A^k$ | 1167 | 1167 | 1167 | |
| 435 | X | $I^\kappa$ | $K^x$ | $K^x$ | $K^x$ | Cl 1053 |
| 438 | XII | $K^1$ | $K^x$ | NP | $K^x$ | |
| 439 | 1159 | $K^x$ | $K^x$ | NP | $K^x$ | pair with 877 |
| 440 | XII | $I'$ | $K^x$ | Kmix | $K^x$ | some relationship to $\Pi$ groups |
| 443 | XII | $I^o$ | M159 | M159 | M159 | |
| 444 | XV | $K^r$ | M1326 | NP | M1326 | $K^r$ equipment |
| 446 | XV | $K^{ak}$ | $K^x$ | $K^x$ | $K^x$ | Cl 1213; fragm in 1 |
| 447 | XV | $K^x$ | $K^x$ | M27 | M27 | close to 1014 in 10 and 20 |
| 448 | 1478 | $A^k$ | $K^x$ | NP | $K^x$ | Cl 183 |

| Gregory No. | Date | v. Soden Classif. | Luke 1 | Luke 10 | Luke 20 | Comments |
|---|---|---|---|---|---|---|
| 449 | XIII | $I^{\kappa}$ | 291 | 291 | 291 | pair with 2603 |
| 461 | 835 | $K^1$ | $K^x$ | $K^x$ | $K^x$ | Cl $\Omega$ |
| 470 | XI | $A^k$ | Cl 490 | Cl 490 | Cl 490 | |
| 471 | XII | $A^k$ | $K^x$ | $K^x$ | $K^x$ | Cl $\Omega$ |
| 472 | XIII | $I'$ | Mix | Kmix | Mix | pair with 1009; fragm in 20 |
| 473 | XIII | $I^{\kappa c}$ | $\Pi$473 | $\Pi$473 | $\Pi$473 | |
| 474 | XI | $I^{\kappa}$ | $K^x$ | $K^x$ | $K^x$ | |
| 475 | XI | $K^x$ | $K^x$ | Cl 475 | Cl 475 | |
| 476 | XI | $K^1$ | $K^x$ | $K^x$ | $K^x$ | |
| 477 | XIII | $I^{\beta a}$ | 1216 | 1216 | 1216 | weak in 1 and 10; pair with 2174 |
| 478 | X | $K^{ak}$ | $K^x$ | $K^x$ | $K^x$ | |
| 479 | XIII | $K^r$ | $K^r$ | $K^r$ | $K^r$ | Cl 479 |
| 480 | 1366 | $K^r$ | $K^r$ | $K^r$ | $K^r$ | perfect member |
| 481 | X | $I^{\kappa}$ | $\Pi^a$ | $K^x$ | $K^x$ | |
| 482 | 1285 | $I^{\kappa c}$ | $K^x$ | $\Pi^a$ | $\Pi^a$ | |
| 483 | 1295 | Hag | $K^x$ | $K^x$ | $K^x$ | Cl 74; corr to $K^r$ in 20 |
| 484 | 1292 | Hag | $K^x$ | $K^x$ | $K^x$ | Cl 74 |
| 485 | XII | $I'$ | $K^x$ | $K^x$ | $K^x$ | |
| 489 | 1316 | $I^{\kappa a}$ | $\Pi^a$ | $\Pi^a$ | $\Pi^a$ | core member; pair with 1219 |
| 490 | XI | $A^k$ | Cl 490 | Cl 490 | Cl 490 | |
| 491 | XI | $I^{\beta}$ | 16 | NP | 16 | |
| 492 | 1326 | $K^x$ | $K^x$ | NP | $K^x$ | |
| 493 | XV | $K^x$ | $K^x$ | $K^x$ | $K^x$ | |
| 494 | XIV | $K^x$ | Cl 343 | Cl 343 | Kmix | fragm in 20 |
| 495 | XII | $I'$ | Kmix | Kmix | Kmix | |
| 496 | XIII | $A^k$ | 1167 | 1167 | 1167 | |
| 497 | XI | $K^{ak}$ | $K^x$ | NP | $K^x$ | |
| 498 | XIV | $I^{\phi r}$ | M1386 | M1386 | M1386 | weak in 20 |
| 499 | XII | $A^k$ | $K^x$ | Kmix | $K^x$ | |
| 500 | XIII | $K^1$ | Illeg | Illeg | $K^x$ | |
| 501 | XIII | $K^x$ | $K^x$ | NP | $K^x$ | |
| 502 | XII | $K^x$ | $K^x$ | NP | $K^x$ | Cl 74 |
| 504 | 1033 | $K^x$ | $K^x$ | $K^x$ | $K^x$ | |
| 505 | XII | $K^x$ | $K^x$ | Kmix | $K^x$ | |
| 506 | XI | $K^x$ | Cl 276 | Cl 276 | Cl 276 | |
| 507 | XI | $K^x$ | $K^x$ | NP | $K^x$ | |

| Gregory No. | Date | v. Soden Classif. | Luke 1 | Luke 10 | Luke 20 | Comments |
|---|---|---|---|---|---|---|
| 508 | XIII | $I^{\kappa}$ | Mix | Kmix | $K^{x}$ | some relationship to M groups |
| 509 | XII | $K^{1}$ | $K^{x}$ | NP | $K^{x}$ | |
| 510 | XII | $K^{r}$ | $K^{r}$ | NP | $K^{r}$ | perfect member |
| 511 | XIII | $K^{r}$ | $K^{r}$ | Cl 1442 | Cl 1442 | Cl 147 in 1 |
| 512 | XIV | $K^{x}$ | $K^{r}$ | NP | $K^{r}$ | |
| 513 | 1130 | $I^{\beta}$ | Kmix | 1216 | 1216 | weak in 10 and 20; fragm in 1 |
| 514 | XII | $K^{x}$ | $K^{x}$ | NP | $K^{x}$ | |
| 515 | XI | $I^{\kappa}$ | Π473 | Π473 | Π6 | |
| 516 | XI | $K^{x}$ | $K^{x}$ | NP | $K^{x}$ | corr to $K^{r}$ (Subgroup 35) |
| 517 | XI/XII | $I^{\phi a}$ | Cl 1675 | Def. | Def. | core member |
| 518 | XII | $I^{\phi r}$ | $Π^{a}$ | M27 | M27 | weak in 20; not $Π^{a}$ at beginning of 1 |
| 519 | XIII | $K^{x}$ | $K^{x}$ | NP | $K^{x}$ | |
| 521 | 1322? | $K^{r}$ | $K^{r}$ | NP | $K^{r}$ | Subgroup 35 |
| 523 | XIV | $K^{x}$ | $K^{x}$ | NP | $K^{x}$ | |
| 524 | XII | $K^{1}$ | Kmix | $K^{x}$ | $K^{x}$ | |
| 525 | XV | $K^{x}$ | Kmix | $K^{x}$ | TR | almost identical to TR in 20 |
| 527 | XI | $K^{x}$ | $K^{x}$ | $K^{x}$ | $K^{x}$ | corr to Π268 |
| 528 | XI | $K^{x}$ | $K^{x}$ | NP | $K^{x}$ | |
| 529 | XII | $K^{x}$ | $K^{x}$ | $K^{x}$ | Kmix | pair with 2694 |
| 530 | XI | $K^{x}$ | $K^{x}$ | NP | $K^{x}$ | |
| 531 | XII | $K^{x}$ | $K^{x}$ | $K^{x}$ | Def. | |
| 532 | XI | $K^{x}$ | $K^{x}$ | $K^{x}$ | $K^{x}$ | Cl 532 |
| 533 | XIII | $K^{x}$ | Cl 121 | Cl 121 | Cl 121 | fragm in 1 |
| 534 | XIII | $A^{k}$ | $K^{x}$ | $K^{x}$ | $K^{x}$ | fragm in 1 and 20 |
| 536 | XIII | $K^{r}$ | Kmix | Π200 | $K^{x}$ | |
| 537 | XII | $I^{\kappa}$ | $Π^{a}$ | $K^{x}$ | $K^{x}$ | weak in 1; $Π^{a}$ at beginning of 10 |
| 538 | XII | $K^{x}$ | $K^{x}$ | Kmix | $K^{x}$ | |
| 543 | XII | $I^{\iota c}$ | 13 | 13 | 13 | core member |
| 544 | XIII | $I^{\alpha}$ | $Π^{a}$ | Kmix | $K^{x}$ | large surplus in 1 |
| 545 | 1430 | $I^{r}$ | Cl 585 | Cl 585 | Cl 585 | core member |
| 546 | XIII | $A^{k}$ | 1167 | 1167 | 1167 | |
| 547 | XI | $K^{r}$ | $K^{r}$ | $K^{r}$ | $K^{r}$ | Cl 147 |
| 548 | XI | $K^{x}$ | $K^{x}$ | NP | $K^{x}$ | |
| 550 | XII | $K^{x}$ | $K^{x}$ | NP | $K^{x}$ | Cl 550 |

## PROFILE CLASSIFICATION

| Gregory No. | Date | v. Soden Classif. | Luke 1 | Luke 10 | Luke 20 | Comments |
|---|---|---|---|---|---|---|
| 551 | XII | I$^{\phi b}$ | K$^x$ | K$^x$ | K$^x$ | |
| 552 | XII | I$^{\phi c}$ | K$^x$ | M106 | K$^x$ | Cl 1053 in 1 and 20 |
| 553 | XIII | K$^r$ | K$^r$ | NP | K$^r$ | Subgroup 35 (corr) |
| 554 | 1272 | K$^x$ | Kmix | K$^x$ | K$^x$ | fragm in 1 |
| 555 | XV | | 1216 | 1216 | 1216 | pair with 152 |
| 557 | XIII | I$^\phi$ | Π$^b$ | NP | Π$^b$ | |
| 558 | XIII | A$^k$ | K$^r$ | K$^r$ | 1519 | |
| 559 | XI | K$^x$ | K$^x$ | K$^x$ | Kmix | fragm in 1, 10, and 20 |
| 560 | XI | | K$^x$ | K$^x$ | K$^x$ | |
| 561 | XIII | K$^x$ | K$^x$ | K$^x$ | Kmix | Cl 74 in 1 |
| 563 | XI | K$^x$ | Mix | K$^x$ | Kmix | |
| 564 | X | K$^x$ | K$^x$ | NP | K$^x$ | |
| 565 | IX | I$^\alpha$ | B | K$^x$ | K$^x$ | core member in 1 |
| 568 | X | K$^{ak?}$ | K$^x$ | K$^x$ | K$^x$ | pair with 1452 |
| 569 | 1061 | A$^c$ | M27 | M27 | M27 | pair with 1170 |
| 570 | XII | K$^{ak}$ | K$^x$ | K$^x$ | K$^x$ | |
| 571 | XII | K$^x$ | Kmix | K$^x$ | K$^x$ | |
| 573 | XIII | A$^k$ | K$^x$ | NP | K$^x$ | |
| 574 | XIII | K$^x$ | Mix | K$^x$ | Cl 585 | Cl 281 in 10 |
| 575 | XV | K$^r$ | K$^r$ | NP | K$^r$ | |
| 577 | 1346 | K$^x$ | Kmix | Kmix | Kmix | close to Cl 545 in 1 and to Cl 1519 in 20 |
| 578 | 1361 | I$^\beta$ | 16 | 16 | 1167 | pair with 217 in 1 and 10 |
| 579 | XIII | H | B | B | B | weak in 10 and 20 |
| 580 | XII | K$^{ak?}$ | K$^x$ | K$^x$ | Π473 | |
| 581 | XIV | I$^\kappa$ | Π$^a$ | NP | Π$^a$ | pair with 2404; core member |
| 582 | 1334 | I$^{\phi c}$ | Π200 | Illeg | Π$^b$ | |
| 583 | XI | K$^{ak}$ | K$^x$ | NP | K$^x$ | Cl 112 |
| 584 | X | K$^{ak}$ | K$^x$ | K$^x$ | K$^x$ | Cl Ω |
| 585 | XI | K$^x$ | Cl 585 | Cl 585 | Cl 585 | core member |
| 586 | XIV | K$^r$ | K$^r$ | K$^r$ | K$^r$ | Cl 586 |
| 587 | XII | K$^x$ | K$^x$ | NP | K$^x$ | |
| 588 | 1321 | K$^r$ | K$^r$ | NP | K$^r$ | pair with 845 |
| 592 | 1289 | K$^{ak}$ | K$^x$ | NP | K$^x$ | |
| 593 | XIII | I$^\kappa$ | Π266 | Π266 | Π266 | |
| 594 | XIV | K$^r$ | K$^r$ | NP | K$^r$ | perfect member; partly illeg in 1 |

| Gregory No. | Date | v. Soden Classif. | Luke 1 | Luke 10 | Luke 20 | Comments |
|---|---|---|---|---|---|---|
| 597 | XIII | $K^x$ | 291 | 291 | 291 | |
| 609 | 1043 | $K^x$ | M609 | M609 | M609 | |
| 645 | 1305 | $K^r$ | $K^r$ | NP | $K^r$ | perfect member |
| 651 | XI | $K^x$ | M651 | M651 | M651 | |
| 652 | X | K | $\Pi^a$ | $K^x$ | $K^x$ | $\Pi^a$ at beginning of 20 |
| 655 | XI/XII | $K^1$ | Kmix | Kmix | $K^x$ | some relationship to $\Pi$ groups |
| 657 | XI/XII | $K^x$ | Kmix | $\Pi^a$ | $K^x$ | fragm in 1; weak in 10 |
| 660 | XI/XII | $I'$ | 22a | 22a | 22a | corr to $K^r$ (Subgroup 35) |
| 662 | XII | | Cl 121 | Cl 121 | Cl 121 | |
| 663 | XIII | $K^x$ | Cl 121 | Cl 121 | Cl 121 | |
| 664 | XV | $K^r$ | $K^r$ | $K^r$ | $K^r$ | large surplus in 1 |
| 666 | XIII | | $K^x$ | $K^x$ | $K^x$ | |
| 667 | XII | | $K^x$ | $K^x$ | $K^x$ | Cl $\Omega$ |
| 668 | XII | | $K^x$ | $K^x$ | $K^x$ | |
| 669 | X | $K^x$ | Def | $K^x$ | $K^x$ | |
| 672 | XI | $K^x$ | Def | $K^x$ | $K^x$ | |
| 673 | XII | $K^r$ | Def | $K^r$ | Def | |
| 677 | XIII | $K^x$ | $K^x$ | $K^x$ | $K^x$ | fragm in 1 |
| 679 | XIII | $I^\kappa$ | $\Pi^b$ | $\Pi^b$ | $\Pi^b$ | |
| 680 | XIV | $K^x$ | $K^x$ | $K^x$ | $K^x$ | Cl 43 |
| 683 | XIII | $I^\phi$ | Mix | $K^x$ | $K^x$ | |
| 685 | XIII | $K^r$ | $K^r$ | $K^r$ | $K^r$ | |
| 686 | 1338 | $I^r$ | Cl 686 | Cl 686 | Cl 686 | |
| 688 | 1179 | $K^1$ | $K^x$ | NP | $K^x$ | Cl $\Omega$ |
| 689 | XIII | $K^r$ | $K^r$ | NP | $K^r$ | Cl 1059 |
| 690 | XIV | $K^1$? | $K^x$ | NP | $K^x$ | partly illeg in 1 |
| 691 | XIII | $K^r$ | $K^r$ | NP | $K^r$ | |
| 692 | XII | $I^{\phi r}$ | M27 | M27 | M27 | |
| 693 | XIII | $I^\beta$ | 16 | 16 | 16 | |
| 694 | XV | $K^r$ | $K^r$ | $K^r$ | $K^x$ | |
| 695 | XIII | $I^{\phi b}$ | Mix | Kmix | $K^x$ | |
| 696 | XIII | $K^r$ | $K^r$ | NP | $K^r$ | perfect member |
| 697 | XIII | $I^\eta$ | 22a | 22a | 22a | |
| 698 | XIV | $K^x$ | $K^x$ | NP | $K^x$ | |
| 699 | XI | $K^1$ | $K^x$ | NP | $K^x$ | Cl $\Omega$ |
| 700 | XI | $I^\alpha$ | Mix | B | $K^x$ | core member in 10 |
| 702 | XII | | Kmix | $K^x$ | Kmix | |

| Gregory No. | Date | v. Soden Classif. | Luke 1 | Luke 10 | Luke 20 | Comments |
|---|---|---|---|---|---|---|
| 703 | XI | | $K^x$ | $K^x$ | $K^x$ | |
| 705 | XIII | $K^x$ | $K^x$ | NP | $K^x$ | |
| 706 | XIII | $I^\kappa$ | $\Pi^b$ | NP | $\Pi^b$ | related to $\Pi$200 in 20 |
| 707 | XI | $K^x$ | $K^x$ | NP | $K^x$ | |
| 708 | XI | $I^\kappa$ | Kmix | NP | $K^x$ | |
| 709 | XI | $I^\sigma$ | $\Lambda$ | $\Lambda$ | Def | |
| 710 | XIII | $K^x$ | Kmix | $K^x$ | $\Lambda$ | pair with 2465 in 20 |
| 711 | XI | $K^1$ | $K^x$ | $K^x$ | $K^x$ | |
| 713 | XII | $I^\sigma$ | Mix | Kmix | Mix | |
| 714 | XIII | $K^x$ | $K^x$ | NP | $K^x$ | |
| 715 | XIII | $A^k$ | $K^x$ | $K^x$ | Kmix | Cl 137 |
| 716 | XIV | $I'$ | Cl 343 | Cl 343 | Cl 686 | |
| 717 | XI | $K^x$ | $K^x$ | NP | $K^x$ | |
| 718 | XIV | $I^o$ | $K^x$ | $K^x$ | $\Pi^a$ | weak in 20 |
| 725 | XIII | $K^x$ | $K^x$ | NP | $K^x$ | |
| 726 | XIII | $I^{\kappa b}$ | $\Pi^b$ | $\Pi^b$ | $\Pi^b$ | |
| 747 | 1164 | $A^c$ | Kmix | $K^x$ | $K^x$ | |
| 748 | XII | $I^r$ | Cl 686 | Cl 686 | Cl 686 | |
| 750 | XII | $K^x$ | M27 | M27 | M27 | pair with 1222 |
| 752 | XII | $A^k$ | 1216 | NP | 1216 | core member |
| 756 | XI | K | $K^x$ | $K^x$ | $K^x$ | |
| 757 | XIII | $K^r$ | $K^r$ | NP | $K^r$ | pair with 1075 |
| 758 | XIV | $K^r$ | $K^r$ | NP | $K^r$ | Subgroup 35 (first hand) |
| 759 | XIII | $K^x$ | $K^x$ | NP | $K^x$ | |
| 760 | XII | $A^k$ | $K^x$ | $K^x$ | $\Pi^b$ | Cl 281 in 1 and 10 |
| 761 | XIV | $K^{ak}$ | $K^x$ | NP | $K^x$ | Cl 46; pair with 995 |
| 762 | XIV | $K^x$ | Kmix | $K^x$ | Kmix | |
| 763 | XIV | $K^r$ | $K^r$ | NP | $K^r$ | Cl 763 |
| 764 | XIV | $K^x$ | $K^x$ | NP | $K^x$ | |
| 765 | XII | $K^x$ | $K^x$ | NP | $K^x$ | Cl 550 |
| 766 | XIII | $I^{\phi b}$ | $K^x$ | NP | $K^x$ | |
| 768 | XII | $K^x$ | $K^x$ | NP | $K^x$ | |
| 769 | XIV | $K^r$ | $K^r$ | NP | $K^r$ | Subgroup 35 |
| 774 | XII | $K^x$ | $K^x$ | $K^x$ | $K^x$ | |
| 775 | XIII | $I^\kappa$ | $K^x$ | NP | $K^x$ | |
| 776 | XI | $I^\kappa$ | M106 | M106 | M106 | |

# PROFILE CLASSIFICATION

| Gregory No. | Date | v. Soden Classif. | Luke 1 | Luke 10 | Luke 20 | Comments |
|---|---|---|---|---|---|---|
| 777 | XII | $K^x$ | $K^x$ | NP | $K^x$ | |
| 778 | XII | $K^x$ | $K^x$ | NP | $K^x$ | |
| 779 | XII | $K^x$ | $K^x$ | Kmix | $K^x$ | related to Π groups |
| 780 | XI | $I^\sigma$ | Mix | $K^x$ | $K^x$ | |
| 781 | XIV | $K^r$ | $K^r$ | NP | $K^r$ | perfect member |
| 782 | XII | $K^x$ | Cl 1001 | Cl 1001 | Cl 1001 | |
| 783 | XIV | $K^x$ | $K^x$ | NP | $K^x$ | |
| 784 | XIV | $K^x$ | $K^x$ | $K^x$ | $K^x$ | fragm in 1 |
| 785 | XI | $K^x$ | $K^x$ | $K^x$ | $K^x$ | |
| 786 | XIV | $K^r$ | $K^r$ | $K^r$ | $K^x$ | surplus in 1 |
| 787 | XII | $I^\kappa$ | Π268 | NP | Π268 | pair with 268 |
| 788 | XI | $I^{\iota b}$ | 13 | 13 | 13 | core member |
| 789 | XIV | $K^r$ | $K^r$ | NP | $K^r$ | perfect member |
| 790 | XIV | $K^x$ | $K^x$ | Kmix | $K^x$ | fragm in 1 |
| 791 | XII | $K^{ak}$ | 22a | NP | 22a | |
| 792 | XIII | $K^{ak?}$ | Mix | Mix | Mix | pair with 2643 |
| 793 | XII | $K^x$ | $K^x$ | NP | $K^x$ | Cl 183 |
| 794 | XIV | $K^x$ | Kmix | NP | Kmix | |
| 795 | XIV | $K^x$ | $K^x$ | NP | $K^x$ | |
| 796 | XI | $I^\kappa$ | $K^x$ | $K^x$ | $K^x$ | |
| 797 | XIV | $K^x$ | $K^r$ | NP | $K^r$ | Subgroup 35; fragm in 20 |
| 799 | XII | $K^x$ | Mix | Kmix | $K^x$ | |
| 801 | XV | $K^x$ | Kmix | $K^x$ | $K^x$ | |
| 802 | XIV | $K^r$ | $K^r$ | Def | Def | |
| 804 | XII | $I^\kappa$ | $K^x$ | NP | Kmix | |
| 806 | XIV | $K^r$ | $K^r$ | $K^r$ | $K^x$ | |
| 808 | XII | $K^x$ | $K^x$ | NP | $K^x$ | Cl 1345 |
| 811 | XIII | | Kmix | NP | $K^x$ | related to Cl 1053 in 1 |
| 824 | XIV | $K^r$ | $K^r$ | $K^r$ | $K^r$ | perfect member |
| 825 | XIII | $K^x$ | $K^r$ | $K^r$ | $K^r$ | weak member of Cl 189 |
| 826 | XII | $I^{\iota c}$ | 13 | 13 | 13 | perfect member |
| 827 | XIII | $I^{\phi b}$ | Cl 827 | Cl 827 | Cl 827 | |
| 828 | XII | $I^{\iota c}$ | 13 | 13 | 13 | fragm in 10 |
| 829 | XII | $I^\beta$ | 1216 | 1216 | 1216 | |
| 830 | XIII | $K^x$ | $K^x$ | M27 | $K^x$ | |
| 831 | XI | $K^x$ | Def | Def | $K^x$ | |

## PROFILE CLASSIFICATION

| Gregory No. | Date | v. Soden Classif. | Luke 1 | Luke 10 | Luke 20 | Comments |
|---|---|---|---|---|---|---|
| 839 | XIV | $K^x$ | Cl 490 | Cl 490 | Cl 490 | pair with 1486 |
| 841 | XV | | Mix | Kmix | Kmix | |
| 843 | XII | $K^x$ | 1167 | NP | 1167 | |
| 844 | XV | $K^x$ | Mix | Kmix | 1519 | fragm in 1 |
| 845 | 1330 | $K^r$ | $K^r$ | NP | $K^r$ | pair with 588 |
| 848 | XIV | | Mix | $K^x$ | $K^x$ | pair with 1255 |
| 851 | XIV | $I^{\phi b}$ | Mix | Kmix | Mix | some relationship to Gr 7 in 20 |
| 852 | 1300 | $K^x$ | $K^x$ | $K^x$ | Def | fragm in 1 |
| 854 | 1287 | | Cl 2148 | Cl 2148 | $K^x$ | |
| 856 | 1280 | | Cl 2148 | Cl 2148 | Cl 2148 | weak in 20 |
| 860 | XII | $A^k$ | Mix | $K^x$ | $K^x$ | pair with 2108 |
| 864 | XIV | $K^x$ | $K^x$ | NP | $K^x$ | pair with 1609 |
| 867 | XIV | $K^r$ | $K^r$ | NP | $K^r$ | perfect member |
| 871 | XI | $K^x$ | 1519 | 1519 | 1519 | |
| 872 | XII | $I^{\eta b}$ | $K^x$ | $K^x$ | $K^x$ | |
| 873 | XI | $K^x$ | Kmix | NP | $K^x$ | |
| 875 | X | $K^x$ | $K^x$ | NP | $K^x$ | pair with 971 |
| 877 | 1197 | $K^x$ | $K^x$ | NP | $K^x$ | pair with 439 |
| 880 | XV | $I^{\beta}$ | $K^x$ | $K^x$ | $K^x$ | Cl 17 |
| 884 | XI | $A^a$ | Def | $K^x$ | 1 | weak in 20 |
| 892 | IX | H | B | B | B | core member |
| 895 | XIII | $K^x$ | M10 | NP | M10 | |
| 896 | XII | | 1167 | 1167 | 1167 | |
| 897 | XIII | $K^r$ | $K^r$ | NP | $K^r$ | perfect member |
| 898 | XIII | | Kmix | $K^x$ | Def | fragm in 1 and 10; some relationship to M groups |
| 899 | XI | $I^r$ | $\Lambda$ | NP | $\Lambda$ | core member |
| 900 | XIII | $K^x$ | $K^x$ | NP | $K^x$ | Cl 202 |
| 901 | XI | $I^{\phi b}$ | $K^x$ | NP | $K^x$ | corr to $\Pi$ groups in 20 |
| 902 | XII | $A^k$ | $K^x$ | NP | $K^x$ | pair with 53 |
| 903 | 1381 | $I^{\phi}$? | Mix | Mix | Mix | related to M groups |
| 904 | 1360 | $I^{\kappa}$ | $\Pi^a$ | $\Pi^a$ | $K^x$ | weak in 1 and 10 |
| 905 | XII/XIII | $K^{ak}$ | $K^x$ | NP | $K^x$ | Cl 1179 |
| 906 | XII/XIII | $K^x$ | $K^x$ | NP | $K^x$ | CL 281 |
| 923 | XII | $K^x$ | $K^x$ | NP | $K^x$ | Cl 281 |
| 924 | XII | $I^{\eta}$ | 22a | 22a | 22a | |

## PROFILE CLASSIFICATION

| Gregory No. | Date | v. Soden Classif. | Luke 1 | Luke 10 | Luke 20 | Comments |
|---|---|---|---|---|---|---|
| 925 | XIV | $K^x$ | $K^x$ | NP | $K^x$ | |
| 926 | XIII | $K^x$ | Cl 490 | Cl 490 | Cl 490 | |
| 927 | 1133 | $K^1$? | $K^x$ | $K^x$ | $K^x$ | |
| 928 | 1304 | $K^r$ | $K^r$ | $K^r$ | $K^r$ | Subgroup 35 |
| 929 | XIII | $K^x$ | $K^x$ | NP | $K^x$ | |
| 930 | XII | $K^x$ | $K^x$ | NP | $K^x$ | |
| 931 | XIII | $I^\kappa$ | $\Pi^b$ | NP | $\Pi^b$ | surplus in 1 |
| 932 | XIV | $K^x$ | $K^r$ | NP | $K^r$ | Cl 1323 |
| 933 | XII | $K^1$ | $K^x$ | NP | $K^x$ | |
| 934 | XIV | $K^x$ | $K^x$ | $K^x$ | $K^x$ | Cl 934 |
| 935 | XIV | $K^x$ | $K^x$ | NP | $K^x$ | |
| 937 | XI | $K^x$ | $K^x$ | $K^x$ | $K^x$ | fragm in 20 |
| 938 | 1318 | $K^r$ | $K^r$ | $K^r$ | $K^r$ | perfect member |
| 939 | XII | $K^x$ | Kmix | $K^x$ | Kmix | pair with 1693 |
| 940 | XIII | $K^r$ | $K^r$ | NP | $K^r$ | perfect member |
| 941 | XIII | $K^{ik}$ | $K^x$ | Illeg | Illeg | |
| 942 | XI | $K^{ak}$ | $K^x$ | $K^x$ | $K^x$ | |
| 943 | XI | $K^x$ | Kmix | $K^x$ | $K^x$ | |
| 944 | XI | $K^{ak}$ | $\Pi$473 | $\Pi$473 | $\Pi$473 | pair with 1207 |
| 945 | XI | $I^{\phi c}$ | Kmix | Kmix | $K^x$ | |
| 946 | XI | $A^k$ | $K^x$ | NP | $K^x$ | Cl 43 |
| 947 | XIII | $I^{\phi r}$ | M1386 | M1386 | M1386 | partly illeg |
| 948 | XII | $K^{ak}$? | Kmix | NP | $K^x$ | |
| 951 | 1317 | $A^a$ | 1167 | 1167 | 1167 | |
| 952 | XIV | $K^r$ | $K^r$ | NP | $K^r$ | perfect member |
| 953 | XIV | $K^r$ | $K^r$ | NP | $K^r$ | Cl 953 |
| 954 | XV | $I^{\phi a}$ | Cl 1675 | Cl 1675 | Cl 1675 | weak in 10 and 20 |
| 955 | XV | $K^r$ | $K^r$ | NP | $K^r$ | |
| 958 | XV | $K^r$ | $K^r$ | NP | $K^r$ | Cl 958 |
| 959 | 1331 | $K^r$ | $K^r$ | $K^r$ | $K^r$ | surplus in 20 |
| 960 | XIV | $K^r$ | $K^r$ | NP | $K^r$ | perfect member |
| 962 | 1498 | $K^r$ | $K^r$ | $K^r$ | $K^r$ | perfect member |
| 965 | XI | $I^\kappa$ | $\Pi$473 | $\Pi$473 | $\Pi$473 | pair with 1007 |
| 966 | XIII | $K^r$ | $K^r$ | NP | $K^r$ | pair with 1813 |
| 967 | XII | $K^x$ | Def | $K^x$ | $K^x$ | Cl 2592 |
| 968 | XII | $A^k$ | Cl 1012 | Cl 1012 | Cl 1012 | |

## PROFILE CLASSIFICATION

| Gregory No. | Date | v. Soden Classif. | Luke 1 | Luke 10 | Luke 20 | Comments |
|---|---|---|---|---|---|---|
| 969 | XIII | $I^\kappa$ | $K^x$ | $\Pi^b$ | $\Pi^b$ | Cl 281 in 1 |
| 971 | XII | $K^x$ | $K^x$ | NP | $K^x$ | pair with 875 |
| 972 | XI | $K^1$ | $K^x$ | NP | $K^x$ | |
| 973 | XII | $K^x$ | $K^x$ | NP | $K^x$ | corr to $K^r$; related to 1475 |
| 974 | XII | $K^1$ | Kmix | NP | Kmix | pair with 1006; close to 030 in 1 |
| 975 | XII | $K^1$ | $K^r$ | $K^r$ | $K^r$ | weak member |
| 976 | XII | $A^k$ | Kmix | NP | Kmix | |
| 977 | XIV | $K^x$ | Def | 1216 | 1216 | core member |
| 980 | 1129 | $I^o$ | Cl 490 | Cl 490 | Cl 490 | |
| 983 | XII | $I^{\iota a}$ | 13 | 13 | 13 | |
| 987 | XII | $A^k$ | Cl 1442 | NP | Cl 1442 | |
| 989 | XII | $A^c$ | $\Pi^a$ | $\Pi^a$ | $K^x$ | Cl 178 |
| 991 | XI | $K^x$ | $K^x$ | $K^x$ | $K^x$ | |
| 992 | XIII | $I^\kappa$ | $\Pi^a$ | $\Pi^a$ | $\Pi^a$ | weak member |
| 995 | XIV | $I^\kappa$ | $K^x$ | NP | $K^x$ | Cl 46; pair with 761 |
| 996 | XIV | $K^x$ | $K^x$ | Kmix | Kmix | pair with 1661 |
| 998 | XII | $I'$ | $K^x$ | $K^x$ | $K^x$ | Cl 180 |
| 999 | XIII | $K^x$ | Cl 1442 | Cl 1442 | Cl 1442 | |
| 1001 | XIII | $K^x$ | Cl 1001 | NP | Cl 1001 | |
| 1003 | XV | $K^r$ | $K^r$ | NP | $K^r$ | surplus in 1 |
| 1004 | 1291 | $I^\kappa$ | $K^x$ | $K^x$ | $K^x$ | |
| 1005 | XIV | $I^\eta$ | 22a | 22a | 22a | |
| 1006 | XI | $K^1$ | Kmix | Kmix | Kmix | pair with 974; close to 030 in 1 and 10 |
| 1007 | XII | $I^\kappa$ | $\Pi473$ | $\Pi473$ | $\Pi473$ | pair with 965 |
| 1008 | XIII | $I^\kappa$ | $K^x$ | $K^x$ | $K^x$ | |
| 1009 | XIII | $I^\kappa$ | Mix | Kmix | Mix | pair with 472 |
| 1010 | XII | $I^{\phi c}$ | Kmix | $K^x$ | $K^x$ | Cl 160 |
| 1011 | 1263 | $A^k$ | Cl 276 | Cl 276 | Cl 276 | |
| 1012 | XI | $I^\sigma$ | Cl 1012 | Cl 1012 | Cl 1012 | |
| 1013 | XI/XII | $K^x$ | Mix | $K^x$ | Kmix | pair with 401 in 10 and 20 |
| 1014 | XI | $I^\kappa$ | Kmix | M27 | M27 | close to 447 in 10 and 20 |
| 1015 | XIII | $A^k$ | 1167 | NP | 1167 | |
| 1020 | XIV | $K^r$ | $K^r$ | NP | $K^r$ | Cl 479 |
| 1021 | XIII | | Kmix | $K^x$ | $K^x$ | Cl 1021 |
| 1023 | 1338 | $K^r$ | $K^r$ | $K^r$ | $K^r$ | perfect member |

| Gregory No. | Date | v. Soden Classif. | Luke 1 | Luke 10 | Luke 20 | Comments |
|---|---|---|---|---|---|---|
| 1024 | XV | $I^{\phi r}$ | M1386 | M1386 | M1386 | |
| 1025 | XIV | $K^r$ | $K^r$ | NP | $K^r$ | |
| 1030 | 1518 | $K^r$ | $K^r$ | $K^r$ | $K^r$ | surplus in 1 |
| 1032 | XIV | $I^r$ | M27 | $K^x$ | $\Pi^a$ | weak in 1 and 20 |
| 1033 | XIV | $K^x$ | Mix | NP | $K^x$ | |
| 1036 | XIV | $K^x$ | 1519 | NP | 1519 | weak member |
| 1045 | XI | $K^1$ | $K^x$ | NP | $K^x$ | Cl Ω |
| 1046 | XII | $K^r$ | $K^r$ | NP | $K^r$ | perfect member |
| 1047 | XIII | $I'$ | M609 | M609 | M609 | |
| 1048 | XIII | $I^{\phi}$? | Mix | $\Pi^a$ | Mix | $K^x$ at beginning of 10 |
| 1050 | 1268 | $K^x$ | Cl 827 | Cl 827 | Cl 827 | |
| 1052 | XIII | $K^x$ | Cl 127 | NP | Cl 127 | close to 78 |
| 1053 | XIII | $K^x$ | $K^x$ | $K^x$ | $K^x$ | Cl 1053 |
| 1054 | XI | $K^x$ | Kmix | NP | $K^x$ | |
| 1055 | X | $K^x$ | $K^x$ | NP | $K^x$ | |
| 1056 | XI | $I^\kappa$ | $\Pi^b$ | NP | $\Pi^b$ | weak member |
| 1057 | XIII | $K^x$ | Cl 276 | Cl 276 | Cl 276 | |
| 1058 | 1145 | $A^k$ | M1402 | NP | M1402 | fragm in 1 |
| 1059 | XV | $K^r$ | $K^r$ | NP | $K^r$ | Cl 1059 |
| 1060 | XV | $K^x$ | Cl 121 | Cl 121 | Cl 121 | fragm in 10 |
| 1061 | 1362 | $I^r$ | Mix | Kmix | Kmix | related to 2747 |
| 1062 | XIV | $K^r$ | $K^r$ | NP | $K^r$ | perfect member |
| 1071 | XII | $I^o$ | Mix | Mix | Mix | some relationship to Gr B |
| 1072 | XIII | $K^r$ | $K^r$ | NP | $K^r$ | perfect member |
| 1073 | X/XI | $K^x$ | $K^x$ | $K^x$ | $K^x$ | |
| 1074 | XI | $K^x$ | $K^x$ | Kmix | $K^x$ | |
| 1075 | XIV | $K^r$ | $K^r$ | NP | $K^r$ | pair with 757 |
| 1076 | X | $K^x$ | Kmix | $K^x$ | $K^x$ | pair with 1417 |
| 1077 | X | $K^1$ | $K^x$ | $K^x$ | $K^x$ | Cl Ω |
| 1078 | X | $A^b$ | $K^x$ | $K^x$ | $K^x$ | |
| 1079 | X | $I^\kappa$ | $\Pi^a$ | $\Pi^a$ | $\Pi^a$ | core member; fragm in 20 |
| 1080 | IX | $A^b$ | $K^x$ | $K^x$ | $K^x$ | Cl Ω |
| 1081 | XII | $K^x$ | $K^x$ | NP | $K^x$ | |
| 1082 | XIV | $I^{\phi b}$ | $K^x$ | $K^r$ | $K^r$ | pair with 2135 in 10 and 20 |
| 1083 | XII | $K^x$ | $K^x$ | NP | $K^x$ | Cl Ω; fragm in 1 |
| 1084 | XIV | $I^{\phi b}$ | $K^x$ | NP | $K^x$ | Cl 1084 |

# PROFILE CLASSIFICATION

| Gregory No. | Date | v. Soden Classif. | Luke 1 | Luke 10 | Luke 20 | Comments |
|---|---|---|---|---|---|---|
| 1085 | XII | I$^{\phi c}$ | K$^x$ | Π1441 | Π1441 | |
| 1087 | XIII | K$^1$ | K$^x$ | Kmix | Mix | |
| 1089 | 1229 | K$^x$ | K$^x$ | NP | K$^x$ | |
| 1091 | XIII | A$^k$ | M10 | NP | M10 | |
| 1092 | XIV | K$^r$ | K$^r$ | NP | K$^r$ | weak in 1 |
| 1093 | 1302 | I' | Mix | Mix | Mix | |
| 1094 | XIII | K$^x$ | Π473 | Π473 | Π473 | |
| 1095 | XIV | K$^r$ | K$^r$ | NP | K$^r$ | Cl 167 |
| 1097 | XII | K$^x$ | Kmix | NP | K$^x$ | |
| 1110 | XI | K$^x$ | K$^x$ | K$^x$ | 1519 | Cl 2592 in 1 and 10 |
| 1111 | XIV | K$^r$ | K$^r$ | NP | K$^r$ | perfect member |
| 1113 | XIII | I$^\kappa$ | Π$^b$ | Π$^b$ | Π$^b$ | |
| 1114 | XIV | K$^x$ | Kmix | NP | K$^x$ | |
| 1116 | XV | | Def | K$^r$ | K$^r$ | weak in 10 |
| 1121 | 1304 | I$^\kappa$ | Kmix | K$^x$ | K$^x$ | Cl 202 in 10 and 20 |
| 1124 | XII | I$^{\phi b}$ | K$^x$ | K$^x$ | Def | fragm in 1 |
| 1138 | XII | K$^x$ | Π$^a$ | NP | Π$^a$ | weak in 1; pair with 1553 |
| 1144 | XII | | Π266 | Π266 | Π266 | partly illeg in 1 |
| 1145 | XII | K$^r$ | K$^r$ | NP | K$^r$ | perfect member |
| 1146 | XIV | | K$^r$ | K$^r$ | K$^r$ | perfect member |
| 1147 | 1370 | K$^r$ | K$^r$ | NP | K$^r$ | perfect member |
| 1148 | XIII | I$^{\phi b}$ | K$^x$ | NP | K$^x$ | Cl 281 |
| 1149 | XIII | K$^x$ | Kmix | NP | K$^x$ | |
| 1152 | 1133 | K$^x$ | K$^x$ | K$^x$ | K$^x$ | |
| 1157 | XI | K$^{ak}$ | K$^x$ | NP | K$^x$ | |
| 1158 | XV | K$^r$ | K$^r$ | NP | K$^r$ | perfect member |
| 1159 | XIV | I$^\kappa$ | Π$^a$ | NP | Π$^a$ | Cl 1272; fragm in 1 |
| 1163 | 1038 | A$^k$ | K$^x$ | K$^x$ | K$^x$ | Cl 43; pair with 15 |
| 1165 | 1335 | K$^r$ | K$^r$ | NP | K$^r$ | Cl 1323 |
| 1166 | X | I$^\kappa$ | Mix | K$^x$ | K$^x$ | |
| 1167 | XI | A$^k$ | 1167 | 1167 | 1167 | |
| 1168 | XI | K$^x$ | K$^x$ | K$^x$ | K$^x$ | |
| 1169 | XII | K$^x$ | Cl 1173 | K$^r$ | K$^x$ | K$^r$ Cl 1176 in 10 and 20 |
| 1170 | XI | I' | M27 | M27 | M27 | pair with 569 |
| 1171 | XIII | A$^k$ | Mix | K$^x$ | K$^x$ | |
| 1172 | X | K$^1$ | K$^x$ | K$^x$ | K$^x$ | |

# PROFILE CLASSIFICATION

| Gregory No. | Date | v. Soden Classif. | Luke 1 | Luke 10 | Luke 20 | Comments |
|---|---|---|---|---|---|---|
| 1173 | XIII | $K^x$ | Cl 1173 | Cl 1173 | Cl 1173 | |
| 1174 | XI | $K^x$ | $K^x$ | NP | $K^x$ | |
| 1176 | XII | $K^r$ | $K^r$ | $K^r$ | $K^x$ | $K^r$ Cl 1176 |
| 1177 | XIII | | Def | Def | $K^x$ | |
| 1178 | XIII | | $K^x$ | NP | NP | |
| 1179 | 1282 | $K^{ak}$ | $K^x$ | $K^x$ | $K^x$ | Cl 1179 |
| 1180 | XV | $K^r$ | $K^x$ | $K^x$ | $K^x$ | some relationship to $K^r$; largely illeg in 20 |
| 1181 | 1368 | $I^{\phi c}$ | Kmix | $K^x$ | $K^x$ | Cl 550 in 10 and 20 |
| 1185 | XIV | | $K^r$ | $K^r$ | $K^r$ | pair with 2635 |
| 1186 | XII | $K^x$ | $K^x$ | $K^x$ | $K^x$ | Cl 281 in 1 and 10; Cl 1053 in 20 |
| 1187 | XI | $I^r$ | $\Lambda$ | $\Lambda$ | $\Lambda$ | surplus in 10 |
| 1188 | XI/XII | $I^{\phi r}$ | Kmix | $K^x$ | $K^x$ | |
| 1189 | 1346 | $K^r$ | $K^r$ | $K^r$ | $K^r$ | surplus in 1 |
| 1190 | XII | $K^x$ | $K^r$ | $K^r$ | $K^x$ | $K^r$ Cl 1176 |
| 1191 | XI/XII | $K^1$ | $K^x$ | $K^x$ | $K^x$ | related to 272 and 419 in 1 |
| 1192 | XI | $I^{\eta b}$ | 22b | 22b | 22b | weak in 10 |
| 1193 | XII | $K^x$ | $K^x$ | $K^x$ | $K^x$ | Cl 1193 |
| 1194 | XI | $I^{\phi r}$ | M10 | M10 | M10 | |
| 1195 | 1123 | $K^x$ | M1195 | M1195 | M1195 | |
| 1196 | XIV | $I^\kappa$ | Π171 | Π171 | Π171 | |
| 1197 | XII | $K^x$ | Kmix | $K^x$ | Kmix | |
| 1198 | XII | $I^r$ | Cl 686 | Cl 686 | $K^x$ | |
| 1199 | XII | $K^r$ | $K^r$ | NP | $K^r$ | surplus in 1 |
| 1200 | XII | $I^{\kappa b}$ | $Π^b$ | $Π^b$ | $Π^b$ | |
| 1201 | 1250 | $K^x$ | $K^x$ | $K^x$ | $K^x$ | |
| 1202 | XV | $I^{\phi r}$ | M1386 | M1386 | M1386 | |
| 1203 | X | $K^x$ | $K^x$ | $K^x$ | $K^x$ | |
| 1204 | XII | $K^x$ | M1402 | M1402 | M1402 | |
| 1205 | XIII | $I^r$ | $\Lambda$ | $\Lambda$ | $\Lambda$ | |
| 1206 | 1247 | $K^x$ | Kmix | $K^x$ | $K^x$ | |
| 1207 | XI | $I^{\phi b}$ | Π473 | Π473 | Π473 | pair with 944 |
| 1208 | XIII | $K^x$ | M349 | M349 | M349 | weak in 10 and 20 |
| 1209 | 1067 | $I^\kappa$ | Π278 | Π278 | Π278 | |
| 1210 | XI | $I^{\eta b}$ | 22b | 22b | 22b | |
| 1211 | XI | $A^k$ | $K^x$ | $K^x$ | 1519 | surplus in 20 |

| Gregory No. | Date | v. Soden Classif. | Luke 1 | Luke 10 | Luke 20 | Comments |
|---|---|---|---|---|---|---|
| 1212 | XI | $K^{ak}$ | $K^x$ | $K^x$ | $K^x$ | Cl 1179 |
| 1213 | 1286 | $K^{ak}$ | $K^x$ | $K^x$ | $K^x$ | Cl 1213 |
| 1214 | XI | $K^{ak}$ | $K^x$ | $K^x$ | $K^x$ | |
| 1215 | XIII | $K^{ak}$ | Mix | $K^x$ | Kmix | Cl 2283 |
| 1216 | XI | $I^{\beta b}$ | 1216 | 1216 | 1216 | core member |
| 1217 | 1186 | $K^x$ | Mix | $K^x$ | $K^x$ | |
| 1218 | XII | $K^x$ | $K^x$ | $K^x$ | $K^x$ | |
| 1219 | XI | $I^{\kappa a}$ | $\Pi^a$ | $\Pi^a$ | $\Pi^a$ | core member; pair with 489 |
| 1220 | X | | M609 | M609 | M609 | fragm in 10 |
| 1221 | XI | $K^x$ | Kmix | $K^x$ | $K^x$ | |
| 1222 | XI | $I^{\phi r}$ | M27 | M27 | M27 | pair with 750 |
| 1223 | X | $I^{\phi c}$ | $\Pi$1441 | $\Pi$1441 | $\Pi$268 | |
| 1224 | XII | $K^r$ | $K^r$ | $K^r$ | $K^r$ | weak in 1 |
| 1225 | X | $K^{ak}$ | $K^x$ | $K^x$ | $K^x$ | |
| 1226 | XIII | $K^x$ | $K^x$ | $K^x$ | $K^x$ | |
| 1227 | XIII/XIV | $A^k$ | $K^x$ | $K^x$ | $K^x$ | |
| 1228 | XII | $K^x$ | Def | Kmix | M27 | |
| 1229 | XIII | $I'$ | Cl 1229 | Cl 1229 | Cl 1229 | |
| 1230 | 1124 | | Mix | Mix | Mix | related to Cl 163 |
| 1232 | XV | $K^x$ | $K^x$ | $K^x$ | $K^x$ | Cl 281 |
| 1233 | XV | $I^{\kappa}$ | $\Pi$171 | $\Pi$171 | $\Pi$171 | |
| 1234 | XIV | $K^r$ | $K^r$ | $K^r$ | $K^r$ | |
| 1235 | XIV | $K^x$ | 291 | 291 | 291 | |
| 1236 | XIV | $K^r$ | $K^r$ | $K^r$ | $K^r$ | Cl 189 |
| 1237 | XV | $I^{\phi r}$ | M1386 | M1386 | M1386 | weak member |
| 1238 | 1244 | $K^x$ | Def | $K^x$ | $K^x$ | |
| 1239 | XVI | | TR | TR | TR | copy of TR |
| 1240 | XII | $K^x$ | $K^x$ | $K^x$ | $K^x$ | |
| 1241 | XII | H | B | B | B | last part of 1 is not Gr B |
| 1242 | XIII | $I'$ | Kmix | Kmix | 1167 | |
| 1243 | XI | $I^{\beta}$ | 1216 | 1216 | 1216 | pair with 1579 |
| 1247 | XV | $K^x$ | $K^r$ | $K^r$ | $K^r$ | weak member |
| 1248 | XIV | $K^x$ | Kmix | $K^x$ | $K^x$ | |
| 1250 | XV | $K^r$ | $K^r$ | $K^r$ | $K^r$ | Subgroup 35 |
| 1251 | XIII | $K^r$ | $K^r$ | $K^r$ | $K^r$ | pair with 2367 |
| 1252 | 1306 | | Cl 1252 | Cl 1252 | Cl 1252 | |

| Gregory No. | Date | v. Soden Classif. | Luke 1 | Luke 10 | Luke 20 | Comments |
|---|---|---|---|---|---|---|
| 1253 | XV | | Mix | Mix | Mix | |
| 1255 | XIII | | Kmix | K$^x$ | K$^x$ | pair with 848 |
| 1269 | XIV | K$^x$ | Kmix | NP | K$^x$ | |
| 1272 | XV | I$^\kappa$ | Π$^a$ | NP | Π$^a$ | Cl 1272 |
| 1273 | 1128 | | K$^x$ | Π$^b$ | Mix | close to 032 in 20 |
| 1276 | XI | | K$^r$ | K$^r$ | K$^r$ | Cl 586 |
| 1278 | XII | I$^\eta$ | 22a | 22a | 22a | |
| 1279 | XI | I$^{\beta a}$ | 1216 | 1216 | 1216 | |
| 1280 | XV | K$^x$ | K$^x$ | NP | K$^x$ | |
| 1281 | X | I$^\kappa$ | K$^x$ | NP | K$^x$ | Cl Ω; fragm in 1 |
| 1282 | XII | | Mix | Kmix | K$^x$ | pair with 1443 |
| 1285 | XIII | K$^x$ | Kmix | K$^x$ | K$^x$ | |
| 1288 | XII | K$^x$ | K$^x$ | K$^x$ | K$^x$ | Cl 1053 in 1 and 10 |
| 1289 | XIII | | Mix | K$^x$ | K$^x$ | |
| 1290 | XV | | Def | K$^x$ | K$^x$ | |
| 1291 | XII | A$^k$ | K$^x$ | NP | K$^x$ | fragm in 1 |
| 1292 | XIII | I$^\kappa$ | Π$^b$ | NP | K$^x$ | weak in 1 |
| 1293 | XI | I$^{\phi c}$ | Kmix | K$^x$ | K$^x$ | Cl 160 |
| 1294 | XIII | K$^x$ | Kmix | NP | K$^x$ | |
| 1295 | IX | I$'$ | K$^x$ | K$^x$ | K$^x$ | Cl Ω |
| 1296 | XIII | K$^x$ | K$^x$ | NP | K$^x$ | |
| 1297 | 1290 | K$^x$ | Cl 121 | NP | Cl 121 | |
| 1298 | XIII | K$^x$ | Kmix | NP | K$^x$ | |
| 1299 | XIII | A$^k$ | Mix | NP | K$^x$ | |
| 1300 | XI | K$^x$ | K$^x$ | NP | K$^x$ | |
| 1301 | XII | I$^{\phi r}$ | Kmix | K$^x$ | Λ | |
| 1305 | 1244 | K$^x$ | K$^x$ | NP | K$^x$ | Cl 1547 |
| 1309 | XI/XII | K$^x$ | K$^x$ | K$^x$ | 1519 | pair with 2132 |
| 1310 | XII/XIII | K$^x$ | Π6 | Π6 | Π6 | |
| 1312 | XI | A$^c$ | K$^x$ | K$^x$ | K$^x$ | fragm in 1 |
| 1313 | XI | A$^c$ | Π$^a$ | Π$^a$ | Π$^a$ | weak in 20 |
| 1314 | XI | I$^\kappa$ | Kmix | K$^x$ | K$^x$ | some relationship to Π groups in 1 |
| 1315 | XII | K$^x$ | M106 | M106 | M106 | pair with 2590 |
| 1316 | XII | K$^x$ | K$^x$ | K$^x$ | K$^x$ | |
| 1317 | XI | K$^x$ | Kmix | K$^x$ | Kmix | fragm in 1 |

| Gregory No. | Date | v. Soden Classif. | Luke 1 | Luke 10 | Luke 20 | Comments |
|---|---|---|---|---|---|---|
| 1318 | XII | $K^x$ | $\Pi^b$ | Kmix | $K^x$ | surplus in 1 |
| 1319 | XII | $I^\kappa$ | $\Pi^b$ | $\Pi^b$ | $\Pi^b$ | |
| 1320 | XI | $K^x$ | Kmix | $K^x$ | $K^x$ | pair with 156 in 1 |
| 1321 | XI | $A^k$ | 1519 | 1519 | 1519 | surplus in 1; fragm in 20 |
| 1322 | XI | $K^x$ | $K^x$ | $K^x$ | $K^x$ | |
| 1323 | XII | $K^r$? | $K^r$ | $K^r$ | $K^r$ | Cl 1323 |
| 1324 | XI | $K^x$ | $\Pi200$ | $\Pi200$ | $\Pi200$ | |
| 1325 | 1724 | | Mix | Mix | Kmix | very strange text, perhaps influenced by TR |
| 1326 | XIV | $K^x$ | M1326 | M1326 | M1326 | |
| 1327 | XVIII | | $K^x$ | $K^x$ | Cl 1252 | partly illeg in 10 |
| 1328 | XIV | $K^x$ | $K^r$ | $K^r$ | $K^r$ | perfect member |
| 1329 | XII | $K^r$ | $K^r$ | $K^r$ | $K^r$ | Cl 1323 in 10 and 20 |
| 1330 | XIV | $K^r$ | Mix | $K^x$ | Def | |
| 1331 | XIV | $K^r$ | Mix | NP | $K^x$ | some relationship to M groups in 1 |
| 1333 | XI | $K^x$ | $K^x$ | Kmix | $K^x$ | |
| 1334 | XIII/XIV | $K^r$ | $K^r$ | $K^r$ | $K^r$ | pair with 2407; fragm in 10 |
| 1335 | XII/XIII | $K^x$ | Kmix | Kmix | $K^x$ | |
| 1337 | XIII | | Mix | Kmix | Mix | |
| 1338 | XII | $K^x$ | $K^x$ | $K^x$ | $K^x$ | Cl 281 |
| 1339 | XIII | $K^r$ | $K^r$ | $K^r$ | $K^r$ | perfect member |
| 1340 | XI | $K^x$ | 291 | 291 | 291 | fragm in 1 |
| 1341 | XII/XIII | $K^x$ | $K^x$ | $K^x$ | $K^x$ | Cl 550 |
| 1342 | XIII/XIV | $I'$?$I^\sigma$? | Mix | B | $K^x$ | weak in 10 |
| 1343 | XI | $K^x$ | $K^x$ | $K^x$ | $K^x$ | |
| 1344 | XII | $K^x$ | $K^x$ | Kmix | $K^x$ | |
| 1345 | XIV | $K^x$ | $K^x$ | $K^x$ | $K^x$ | Cl 1345 |
| 1346 | X/XI | $I^{\kappa a}$ | $\Pi^a$ | $\Pi^a$ | $\Pi^a$ | weak in 1 and 10 |
| 1347 | X | $I^{\phi r}$ | Kmix | $K^x$ | $K^x$ | |
| 1348 | XIV | $K^r$ | $K^x$ | $K^x$ | $K^r$ | weak in 20 |
| 1349 | XI/XII | $K^x$ | Cl 1675 | NP | NP | fragm in 1 |
| 1350 | XIV | $K^x$ | $K^x$ | $K^x$ | $K^x$ | Cl 43 |
| 1351 | X | $K^x$ | $K^x$ | $K^x$ | $K^x$ | Cl 2592 |
| 1352 | XIII | $K^x$ | $K^x$ | $K^x$ | $K^x$ | |
| 1353 | XII/XIII | $K^x$ | $K^x$ | $K^x$ | $K^x$ | Cl 934 |

| Gregory No. | Date | v. Soden Classif. | Luke 1 | Luke 10 | Luke 20 | Comments |
|---|---|---|---|---|---|---|
| 1354 | XIV | I$^{\kappa c}$ | Π$^a$ | K$^x$ | Π$^a$ | weak in 1 |
| 1355 | XII | I′ | Π$^a$ | Π$^a$ | Π$^a$ | weak in 10 |
| 1356 | XIV | K$^x$ | M106 | NP | M106 | weak in 1 |
| 1357 | X | K$^x$ | Mix | NP | K$^x$ | |
| 1358 | XI/XII | K$^x$ | K$^x$ | K$^x$ | Kmix | related to Cl 202 |
| 1359 | XII | K$^x$ | K$^x$ | K$^x$ | K$^x$ | Cl 281 |
| 1364 | XII | K$^x$ | K$^x$ | Mix | K$^x$ | Cl 43 |
| 1365 | XII | I′ | 22a | 22a | 22a | |
| 1375 | XII | I$^{\kappa b}$ | Π$^b$ | NP | Π$^b$ | |
| 1377 | XIV | | K$^x$ | K$^x$ | K$^x$ | |
| 1385 | XII | K$^x$ | Cl 1173 | NP | Cl 1173 | |
| 1386 | XII | I$^{\phi r}$ | M1386 | M1386 | M1386 | |
| 1388 | XV | | Kmix | Kmix | K$^x$ | |
| 1389 | XV | | K$^r$ | NP | K$^r$ | Cl 953 |
| 1391 | XIII | I$^{\phi b}$ | K$^x$ | NP | K$^x$ | |
| 1392 | X | A$^c$ | K$^x$ | K$^x$ | Π$^a$ | weak in 20 |
| 1393 | XII | K$^x$ | K$^x$ | K$^x$ | K$^x$ | related to K$^x$ Cl 532 in 20 |
| 1394 | 1301 | Hag | K$^x$ | K$^x$ | K$^x$ | pair with 412 |
| 1395 | 1366 | K$^x$ | K$^x$ | K$^x$ | K$^x$ | Cl 46; pair with 52 |
| 1396 | XIV | I′ | M1326 | Illeg | Illeg | |
| 1397 | XIV | K$^x$ | K$^x$ | NP | K$^x$ | Cl 74 |
| 1398 | XIII | I$^\kappa$ | Π$^a$ | NP | Π$^a$ | |
| 1399 | XIII | K$^x$ | K$^x$ | K$^x$ | Π$^a$ | partly illeg in 1 |
| 1400 | XIII | K$^r$ | K$^r$ | NP | K$^r$ | perfect member |
| 1401 | XII | K$^r$ | K$^r$ | NP | K$^r$ | partly illeg and weak in 1 |
| 1402 | XII | I$^{\phi b}$ | M1402 | M1402 | M1402 | |
| 1403 | 1300? | | K$^x$ | Kmix | K$^x$ | |
| 1404 | XIII | K$^x$ | K$^x$ | K$^x$ | K$^x$ | |
| 1407 | XIII | K$^{ak}$ | K$^x$ | NP | K$^x$ | Cl 1213 |
| 1408 | XII | I$^\kappa$ | K$^x$ | NP | K$^x$ | |
| 1409 | XIV | | K$^r$ | NP | K$^r$ | surplus in 1 |
| 1410 | XIV | K$^1$ or K$^{ak}$ | K$^x$ | NP | K$^x$ | |
| 1413 | XI | K$^x$ | M27 | NP | M27 | core member; fragm in 1 |
| 1415 | 1145 | K$^x$ | M27 | M27 | M27 | core member |
| 1416 | XII | K$^x$ | Kmix | NP | 1519 | |

| Gregory No. | Date | v. Soden Classif. | Luke 1 | Luke 10 | Luke 20 | Comments |
|---|---|---|---|---|---|---|
| 1417 | X | $K^x$ | Kmix | $K^x$ | Def | pair with 1076; fragm in 1 and 10 |
| 1418 | XII | $K^x$ | $K^x$ | NP | $K^x$ | |
| 1420 | XIII | | $\Pi^b$? | $\Pi^b$? | Def | fragm in 1 and 10 |
| 1424 | IX/X | $I^{\phi a}$ | Cl 1675 | Cl 1675 | Cl 1675 | diverging member |
| 1434 | XII | $I^\kappa$ | $\Pi^b$ | NP | $K^x$ | large surplus in 1; pair with 44 in 20 |
| 1435 | XIV | | $K^r$ | NP | $K^r$ | perfect member |
| 1436 | XIII | $K^x$ | Mix | NP | Kmix | |
| 1438 | XI | $K^x$ | 1167 | 1167 | 1167 | |
| 1439 | XI | $A^k$ | $K^x$ | $K^x$ | $K^x$ | |
| 1440 | XIII | $K^1$ | $K^x$ | NP | $K^x$ | |
| 1441 | XII | $I^{\phi c}$ | $\Pi$1441 | NP | $\Pi$1441 | |
| 1442 | XIII | $K^x$ | Cl 1442 | NP | Cl 1442 | |
| 1443 | 1047 | $I^{\phi r}$ | Mix | Kmix | $K^x$ | pair with 1282; related to 164 |
| 1444 | XI | $K^{ak}$ | $K^x$ | $K^x$ | $K^x$ | |
| 1445 | 1323 | $K^r$ | $K^r$ | $K^r$ | $K^r$ | perfect member |
| 1446 | XIII | $I^\kappa$ | Cl 827 | Cl 827 | Cl 827 | |
| 1447 | 1337 | $I^\kappa$ | $K^x$ | $\Pi$171 | $\Pi$171 | weak in 10 |
| 1448 | XI | $K^x$? | Cl 127 | Cl 127 | Cl 127 | |
| 1449 | XI | $K^{ak}$ | $K^x$ | $K^x$ | $K^x$ | Cl 1179 |
| 1450 | XII | $K^x$ | Cl 1442 | NP | Cl 1442 | |
| 1451 | XII/XIII | $I^\kappa$ | Cl 1012 | Cl 1012 | Cl 1012 | |
| 1452 | 992? | $K^x$ | $K^x$ | $K^x$ | $K^x$ | pair with 568 |
| 1453 | XII | $K^x$ | $K^r$ | NP | $K^r$ | Cl 958 |
| 1454 | XII | $I^r$ | Cl 1685 | NP | Cl 1685 | |
| 1455 | XI/XII | $I^\kappa$ | M106 | M106 | M106 | |
| 1456 | XIII | $K^x$ | $K^x$ | NP | $K^x$ | |
| 1457 | XII/XIII | $I^\kappa$ | Cl 827 | Cl 827 | Cl 827 | |
| 1458 | X | $K^x$ | M27 | M27 | M27 | core member |
| 1459 | XII | $K^x$ | $K^x$ | NP | $K^x$ | |
| 1460 | XII | $K^x$ | $K^x$ | NP | $K^x$ | |
| 1461 | XIII | $K^r$ | $K^r$ | NP | $K^r$ | Cl 763 |
| 1462 | XIV | $K^r$ | $K^r$ | NP | $K^r$ | Cl 1059 |
| 1463 | XIII | $I^\kappa$ | $\Pi^b$ | NP | $\Pi^b$ | |
| 1464 | XIII | $K^x$ | $K^x$ | NP | $K^x$ | |

# PROFILE CLASSIFICATION

| Gregory No. | Date | v. Soden Classif. | Luke 1 | Luke 10 | Luke 20 | Comments |
|---|---|---|---|---|---|---|
| 1465 | XIII | $K^r$ | $K^x$ | NP | $K^x$ | |
| 1466 | 1270 | $K^x$ | M349 | M349 | M349 | weak in 1 |
| 1467 | XIV | $K^x$ | $K^x$ | NP | $K^x$ | Cl 122 |
| 1468 | XII/XIII | $I^\kappa$ | Kmix | $\Pi$171 | $\Pi$171 | |
| 1469 | XIII | $I^\kappa$ | $\Pi$171 | $\Pi$171 | $\Pi$171 | |
| 1470 | XI | $K^1$ | $K^x$ | $K^x$ | $K^x$ | Cl $\Omega$ |
| 1471 | XIII | $K^x$ | $K^r$ | $K^r$ | $K^r$ | pair with 387 |
| 1472 | XIII/XIV | $K^x$ | Kmix | NP | Kmix | $K^x$ Cl 137 in 20 |
| 1473 | XII | $K^x$ | 1167 | 1167 | 1167 | |
| 1474 | XIII | $K^x$ | $K^x$ | NP | $K^x$ | pair with 2649 |
| 1475 | XII | $I^\kappa$ | $K^x$ | NP | $K^x$ | related to 973 |
| 1476 | 1333 | $K^x$ | $K^r$ | $K^r$ | $K^r$ | Cl 1323 |
| 1477 | XIII | $K^x$ | $K^x$ | NP | $K^x$ | |
| 1478 | XI/XII | $I^\kappa$ | $\Pi$268 | $\Pi$268 | $\Pi$268 | |
| 1479 | XII | $K^x$ | Mix | $K^x$ | 1167 | related to $K^x$ Cl 281 in 1 and 10 |
| 1480 | XIV | $K^r$ | $K^r$ | NP | $K^r$ | |
| 1481 | XII | $A^k$ | Kmix | $K^x$ | 1519 | |
| 1482 | 1404 | $K^r$ | $K^r$ | NP | $K^r$ | Subgroup 35 |
| 1483 | XI | $K^x$ | $K^x$ | $K^x$ | $K^x$ | |
| 1484 | XIII | $A^k$ | M350 | M350 | M350 | |
| 1485 | XII | $K^x$ | $K^x$ | $K^x$ | $K^x$ | Cl 532 |
| 1486 | 1098 | $K^x$ | Cl 490 | Cl 490 | Cl 490 | pair with 839 |
| 1487 | XIII | $K^r$ | $K^r$ | NP | $K^r$ | Subgroup 35 |
| 1488 | XIV | $K^r$ | $K^r$ | NP | $K^r$ | perfect member |
| 1489 | XII | $K^r$ | $K^r$ | NP | $K^r$ | Cl 1489 |
| 1491 | XII/XIII | $K^x$ | M106 | M106 | $K^x$ | |
| 1492 | 1342 | $K^x$ | $K^r$ | $K^r$ | $K^r$ | perfect member |
| 1493 | XIV | $K^r$ | $K^r$ | NP | $K^r$ | Subgroup 35 |
| 1494 | XIII | $K^x$ | $K^x$ | NP | $K^x$ | Cl 122 |
| 1495 | XIV | $I^{\phi b}$ | $K^x$ | NP | $K^x$ | Cl 1084 |
| 1496 | XIV | $K^r$ | $K^r$ | NP | $K^r$ | perfect member |
| 1497 | XIV | $K^x$ | Kmix | NP | $K^x$ | |
| 1498 | XIII | $A^k$ | $K^x$ | NP | $K^x$ | Cl 1021 |
| 1499 | XIV | $K^x$ | $K^r$ | NP | $K^r$ | surplus in 1 |
| 1501 | XIV | $K^r$ | $K^r$ | NP | $K^r$ | perfect member |
| 1502 | XIV | | Kmix | $K^x$ | $\Lambda$ | |

# PROFILE CLASSIFICATION

| Gregory No. | Date | v. Soden Classif. | Luke 1 | Luke 10 | Luke 20 | Comments |
|---|---|---|---|---|---|---|
| 1503 | 1317 | $K^r$ | $K^r$ | $K^r$ | $K^r$ | pair with 2323 |
| 1504 | XIV | $K^x$ | Def | Kmix | M1386 | |
| 1505 | 1084 | $K^x$ | Kmix | Kmix | $K^x$ | $K^x$ Cl 281 in 1 and 10; pair with 2495 |
| 1508 | XV | $K^r$ | $K^r$ | NP | $K^r$ | Cl 1059 |
| 1509 | XIV | $K^x$ | $K^x$ | NP | $K^x$ | |
| 1510 | XI | $I^\kappa$ | Kmix | $\Pi$278 | $\Pi$278 | |
| 1511 | XII/XIII | $K^1$ | $K^x$ | $K^x$ | 1167 | weak in 20 |
| 1512 | XIV | $I^\kappa$ | $K^x$ | NP | $K^x$ | |
| 1513 | XI | $K^x$ | Cl 127 | Cl 127 | Cl 127 | |
| 1514 | XI | $K^1$ | $K^x$ | $K^x$ | $K^x$ | |
| 1515 | XIII | $I'$ | Kmix | $\Pi$171 | $\Pi$171 | |
| 1517 | XI | $K^x$ | $K^x$ | $K^x$ | $K^x$ | corr to $K^r$ |
| 1519 | XI | $K^x$ | 1519 | 1519 | 1519 | |
| 1520 | XI | $K^x$ | Def | $K^x$ | $K^x$ | |
| 1521 | XI | $I^o$ | $K^x$ | $K^x$ | $K^x$ | |
| 1528 | 1136 | | 16 | 16 | 16 | pair with 16 |
| 1530 | XII/XIII | | $K^x$ | $K^x$ | $K^x$ | |
| 1531 | XI/XII | | Cl 1531 | Cl 1531 | Cl 1531 | |
| 1533 | 1236 | | Cl 1252 | Cl 1252 | Cl 1252 | |
| 1538 | XIV | $K^x$ | $K^x$ | $K^x$ | Kmix | |
| 1539 | XII | $K^x$ | $K^x$ | $K^x$ | $K^x$ | |
| 1540 | XI/XII | $K^x$ | $K^x$ | $K^x$ | $K^x$ | |
| 1541 | XIII | $K^x$ | $K^x$ | NP | $K^x$ | |
| 1542 | XII | $I^\alpha$ | Mix | $K^x$ | $K^x$ | |
| 1543 | 1355 | $K^r$ | $K^r$ | $K^r$ | $K^r$ | surplus in 1 and 20 |
| 1544 | XIV | $K^x$ | $K^r$ | NP | $K^r$ | weak member |
| 1545 | XI | $I^o$ | $K^x$ | $K^x$ | $K^x$ | |
| 1546 | XIII | $I^\kappa$ | $\Pi^a$ | $\Pi^a$ | $\Pi^a$ | |
| 1547 | 1339 | | $K^x$ | $K^x$ | $K^x$ | Cl 1547 |
| 1548 | 1359 | $K^r$ | $K^r$ | $K^r$ | $K^r$ | perfect member |
| 1549 | XIV | $K^x$ | M651 | NP | M651 | |
| 1551 | XIII | $K^r$ | $K^r$ | NP | $K^r$ | perfect member |
| 1552 | XIV | $K^r$ | $K^r$ | Illeg | Illeg | Cl 953 |
| 1553 | XIV | $K^x$ | $\Pi^a$ | NP | $\Pi^a$ | weak in 1; pair with 1138 |
| 1554 | XIV | $I^{\phi r}$ | Kmix | Kmix | $K^x$ | |

| Gregory No. | Date | v. Soden Classif. | Luke 1 | Luke 10 | Luke 20 | Comments |
|---|---|---|---|---|---|---|
| 1555 | XIII | $I^r$ | $\Lambda$ | $\Lambda$ | $\Lambda$ | not $\Lambda$ after Luke 20:31 |
| 1556 | 1068 | $K^1$ | $K^x$ | $K^x$ | $K^x$ | |
| 1557 | 1293 | $I^{\phi b}$ | M159 | M159 | $K^x$ | |
| 1558 | XIV | $K^x$ | Kmix | Kmix | Kmix | |
| 1559 | XIV | $K^r$ | $K^r$ | NP | $K^r$ | Subgroup 35 |
| 1560 | XIV | $K^r$ | $K^r$ | NP | $K^r$ | perfect member |
| 1561 | XII/XIII | $I^\kappa$ | $\Pi^a$ | $\Pi^a$ | $\Pi^a$ | weak in 1 and 10 |
| 1562 | XII | $I^\kappa$ | $\Pi$268 | $K^x$ | $K^x$ | |
| 1563 | XIII | $K^x$ | $K^x$ | M106 | M106 | Cl 413 in 1 |
| 1564 | 1300 | $K^x$ | $K^x$ | $K^x$ | Kmix | Cl 2592 in 1 and 10 |
| 1565 | XIII | $K^{ak}$ | $K^x$ | NP | $K^x$ | |
| 1566 | XI/XII | $A^k$ | 1519 | 1519 | 1519 | weak in 1 |
| 1569 | 1307 | $K^x$ | $K^x$ | Kmix | Kmix | pair with 2455 |
| 1570 | XI | | 1167 | 1167 | 1167 | |
| 1572 | 1304 | $K^r$ | $K^r$ | $K^r$ | $K^r$ | Subgroup 35 |
| 1573 | XII/XIII | $I^r$ | Mix | $\Lambda$ | $\Lambda$ | |
| 1574 | XIV | $I^o$ | Mix | Mix | Mix | |
| 1575 | XIII | $K^1$ | $K^x$ | NP | $K^x$ | |
| 1576 | XIII | $K^r$ | $K^r$ | NP | $K^r$ | perfect member |
| 1577 | 1303 | $K^x$ | Kmix | $K^x$ | $K^x$ | |
| 1578 | XIII | $I^\kappa$ | $K^x$ | NP | $\Pi^b$ | Cl 1053 in 1 |
| 1579 | XI | $I^{\phi b}$ | 1216 | 1216 | 1216 | core member; pair with 1243 |
| 1580 | XIV | $K^1$ | $K^x$ | NP | $K^x$ | Cl 180; fragm in 1 |
| 1581 | XIV | $K^x$ | $K^x$ | $\Pi$171 | $\Pi$171 | Cl $\Omega$ in 1 |
| 1582 | 949 | $I^{\eta a}$ | 1 | 1 | 1 | close to 1 |
| 1583 | XII | $K^{ak}$ | $K^x$ | $K^x$ | $K^x$ | |
| 1584 | XIV | $K^r$ | $K^r$ | NP | $K^r$ | perfect member |
| 1585 | XIII | $K^x$ | $K^x$ | NP | $K^x$ | |
| 1586 | XIII | $K^x$ | $K^x$ | NP | $K^x$ | Cl 1547 |
| 1587 | XV | $K^1$ | $K^x$ | NP | $K^x$ | |
| 1588 | XIV | $I^{\beta b}$ | 16 | 16 | 16 | |
| 1589 | XII | $K^x$ | M1195 | NP | M1195 | |
| 1590 | XII | $K^x$ | $K^x$ | NP | $K^x$ | Cl 281 |
| 1592 | 1445 | $K^x$ | $K^x$ | $K^x$ | $K^x$ | Cl 43 |
| 1593 | XIII | $I^\kappa$ | Cl 827 | NP | Cl 827 | |
| 1594 | 1284 | Hag | $K^x$ | $K^x$ | $K^x$ | Cl 74 |

| Gregory No. | Date | v. Soden Classif. | Luke 1 | Luke 10 | Luke 20 | Comments |
|---|---|---|---|---|---|---|
| 1596 | XV | $K^r$ | $K^r$ | $K^r$ | $K^r$ | Cl 1489; fragm in 1 |
| 1597 | 1289 | $K^x$ | $K^x$ | $K^x$ | $K^x$ | Cl 46 |
| 1598 | XIV | $K^x$ | $K^x$ | NP | $K^x$ | Cl 46 |
| 1599 | XIV | $K^r$ | $K^r$ | NP | $K^r$ | Cl 479 |
| 1600 | XIV | $K^r$ | $K^r$ | NP | $K^r$ | Subgroup 35; no $K^r$ equipment |
| 1601 | XIII | $K^r$ | $K^r$ | NP | $K^r$ | Cl 1601 |
| 1602 | XIV | $I^\kappa$ | Kmix | $K^x$ | $K^x$ | |
| 1603 | XII | $K^x$ | $K^x$ | NP | $K^x$ | |
| 1604 | XIII | $I'$ | Mix | Kmix | Mix | pair with 2546 in 10 and 20 |
| 1605 | 1342 | $I^\kappa$ | Π171 | Π171 | Π171 | |
| 1606 | XIII | $I^{\phi b}$ | $K^x$ | $K^x$ | $K^x$ | Cl 187; partly illeg in 1 and 10 |
| 1607 | XI | | $K^x$ | $K^x$ | $K^x$ | |
| 1609 | XIV | $K^r$ | $K^x$ | NP | $K^x$ | pair with 864; $K^r$ equipment |
| 1614 | 1324 | $K^r$ | $K^r$ | $K^r$ | $K^r$ | surplus in 1 |
| 1617 | XV | $K^r$ | $K^r$ | NP | $K^r$ | perfect member |
| 1619 | XV | $K^r$ | $K^r$ | NP | $K^r$ | Cl 763 |
| 1621 | XV | $K^r$ | $K^r$ | NP | $K^r$ | Cl 479 |
| 1622 | XIII | $K^r$ | $K^r$ | NP | NP | Cl 1622; 10 and 20 by late hand |
| 1623 | XIV | $K^x$ | $K^x$ | $K^x$ | $K^x$ | Cl 532 |
| 1624 | XV | $K^r$ | $K^x$ | NP | $K^x$ | |
| 1625 | XIV | $K^r$ | $K^r$ | NP | $K^r$ | Cl 189 |
| 1626 | XV | $K^x$ | M27 | M27 | M27 | pair with 2705 |
| 1628 | 1400 | $K^r$ | $K^r$ | $K^r$ | $K^r$ | perfect member |
| 1630 | 1314 | $K^r$ | M349 | M349 | M349 | unusual surplus in 10 |
| 1632 | XIV | $K^x$ | $K^x$ | NP | $K^x$ | Cl 122 |
| 1633 | XIV | $K^r$ | $K^r$ | NP | $K^r$ | Cl 1601 |
| 1634 | XIV | $K^r$ | $K^x$ | $K^x$ | $K^r$ | Cl 1059 in 20 |
| 1635 | XV | $K^x$ | $K^x$ | NP | $K^x$ | Cl 74 |
| 1636 | XV | $K^r$ | $K^r$ | NP | $K^r$ | perfect member |
| 1637 | 1328 | $K^r$ | $K^r$ | $K^r$ | $K^r$ | perfect member |
| 1638 | XIV | $K^r$ | $K^r$ | NP | $K^r$ | surplus in 1 |
| 1641 | XV | $K^x$ | Mix | NP | Kmix | |
| 1642 | 1278 | $K^x$ | $K^x$ | Cl 121 | Cl 121 | |
| 1643 | XIV | $K^x$ | $K^x$ | $K^x$ | Kmix | fragm in 1 |
| 1645 | 1303 | $K^x$ | $K^x$ | $K^x$ | $K^x$ | |
| 1646 | 1172 | $K^1$? | Cl 163 | Cl 163 | Cl 163 | close to 1695 |

## PROFILE CLASSIFICATION

| Gregory No. | Date | v. Soden Classif. | Luke 1 | Luke 10 | Luke 20 | Comments |
|---|---|---|---|---|---|---|
| 1647 | 1274 | $K^x$ | Mix | Mix | Kmix | |
| 1648 | XV | $K^x$ | $K^r$ | NP | $K^r$ | Cl 763 |
| 1649 | XV | $K^r$ | $K^r$ | NP | $K^r$ | perfect member |
| 1650 | XV | $K^r$ | $K^r$ | NP | $K^r$ | perfect member |
| 1651 | XV | $K^x$ | Cl 7 | NP | Cl 7 | surplus in 1 |
| 1653 | XV | $K^x$ | $K^x$ | NP | $K^x$ | |
| 1654 | 1326 | $I^\alpha$ | Cl 7 | Cl 7 | Cl 7 | weak in 1 and 10 |
| 1655 | XIV | $K^x$ | $K^x$ | NP | $K^x$ | |
| 1656 | XV | $K^r$ | $K^r$ | NP | $K^r$ | perfect member |
| 1657 | XIV | | $K^x$ | $K^x$ | $K^x$ | Cl 122 |
| 1658 | XV | $K^r$? | $K^r$ | NP | $K^r$ | Cl 1059; fragm in 1 |
| 1659 | XV | $K^r$ | $K^r$ | NP | $K^r$ | Cl 1489 |
| 1660 | XIV | $K^x$ | Kmix | NP | $K^x$ | |
| 1661 | XV | $K^x$ | Kmix | Kmix | Kmix | pair with 996 |
| 1662 | X | $K^x$ | $K^x$ | $K^x$ | Def | fragm in 1 |
| 1663 | X | $I^\kappa$ | $\Pi^a$ | M27 | M27 | surplus in 1 |
| 1664 | XIII | $K^x$ | $K^r$ | $K^x$ | $K^x$ | Cl 479 in 1 |
| 1665 | XII | $K^x$ | Cl 121 | NP | Cl 121 | |
| 1666 | XIII | $K^x$ | Cl 276 | Cl 276 | Cl 276 | |
| 1667 | 1309 | $K^r$ | $K^r$ | NP | $K^r$ | |
| 1668 | XI | $K^x$ | $K^x$ | NP | $K^x$ | |
| 1669 | XIII | $K^x$ | $K^x$ | Kmix | Def | fragm in 1 |
| 1670 | XIII | $K^x$ | Mix | $K^x$ | $K^x$ | |
| 1671 | XIII | $K^x$ | $K^x$ | NP | $K^x$ | pair with 2112 |
| 1672 | XI | $K^1$ | $K^x$ | NP | $K^x$ | |
| 1673 | XII | | Def | Def | $K^x$ | fragm in 20 |
| 1675 | XIV | $I^{\phi a}$ | Cl 1675 | Cl 1675 | Cl 1675 | core member |
| 1676 | 1354 | $K^x$ | $K^x$ | NP | $K^x$ | Cl 1213 in 1 |
| 1679 | XV | $K^x$ | $K^x$ | NP | $K^x$ | Cl 74 |
| 1682 | XVI | $I^r$ | Mix | $K^x$ | $K^x$ | |
| 1683 | XII | $K^x$ | Def | $\Pi^b$ | Def | fragm in 10 |
| 1685 | 1292 | $I^{\phi b}$ | Cl 1685 | Cl 1685 | Cl 1685 | |
| 1686 | 1418 | $K^r$ | $K^r$ | NP | $K^r$ | perfect member |
| 1687 | XII | $K^x$ | $K^x$ | NP | $K^x$ | |
| 1690 | XV | $I^\kappa$ | $\Pi^a$ | NP | $\Pi^a$ | |
| 1691 | XI | $K^1$ | $K^x$ | $K^x$ | $K^x$ | Cl $\Omega$ |

# PROFILE CLASSIFICATION

| Gregory No. | Date | v. Soden Classif. | Luke 1 | Luke 10 | Luke 20 | Comments |
|---|---|---|---|---|---|---|
| 1692 | XII | $I^{\phi}$ | Mix | Kmix | Kmix | |
| 1693 | XI | $K^x$ | $K^x$ | NP | Kmix | pair with 939 |
| 1694 | XIII | $K^r$ | $K^r$ | NP | $K^r$ | Subgroup 35 (first hand) |
| 1695 | 1311 | $I^{\phi b}$ | Cl 163 | Cl 163 | Cl 163 | close to 1646 |
| 1697 | XIII | $K^x$ | Kmix | $K^x$ | Mix | |
| 1698 | XIV | $K^r$ | $K^r$ | NP | NP | fragm in 1 |
| 1699 | 1359 | $I^{\kappa}$ | $K^r$ | $K^r$ | $\Pi^a$ | Cl 167 in 1 and 10; Cl 1272 in 20 |
| 1703 | XIV | | $K^r$ | NP | $K^r$ | perfect member |
| 1712 | XV | $K^x$ | $K^x$ | NP | $K^x$ | fragm in 1 |
| 1713 | XV | $K^r$ | $K^r$ | NP | $K^r$ | perfect member |
| 1714 | XII | $K^x$ | Mix | $K^x$ | Def | pair with 282 in 1 |
| 1780 | XIII | | Kmix | $K^x$ | $K^x$ | |
| 1797 | 1226 | | Mix | Kmix | $K^x$ | |
| 1800 | XII | $A^k$ | $K^x$ | $K^x$ | $K^x$ | fragm in 1 |
| 1813 | XII | | $K^r$ | NP | $K^r$ | pair with 966 |
| 1816 | X | $I^{\kappa}$ | $\Pi^a$ | $\Pi^a$ | $\Pi^a$ | weak member |
| 1823 | XV | $K^x$ | Mix | $K^x$ | $K^x$ | |
| 1966 | XI | $K^x$ | $K^x$ | NP | $K^x$ | Cl 413 |
| 2095 | XIII | $K^x$ | Mix | NP | 1167 | |
| 2096 | XII | | Cl 1012 | Cl 1012 | Cl 1012 | |
| 2098 | XI | | M609 | $\Pi$200 | $\Pi$200 | fragm in 10 and 20 |
| 2099 | XIII | $K^x$ | $K^x$ | NP | $K^x$ | |
| 2108 | XII | | Kmix | $K^x$ | Def | pair with 860; fragm in 1 |
| 2112 | XIII | $K^x$ | $K^x$ | NP | $K^x$ | pair with 1671 |
| 2117 | XII | $K^x$ | Kmix | NP | $K^x$ | |
| 2118 | XII | $K^x$ | $K^x$ | $K^x$ | Kmix | Cl 1193 |
| 2120 | XII | $K^x$ | $K^x$ | NP | $K^x$ | |
| 2121 | XI | $I^{\phi r}$ | M350 | NP | M350 | fragm in 1 |
| 2122 | XII | $K^r$ | $K^r$ | NP | $K^r$ | perfect member |
| 2123 | XIII | $I^{\phi b}$ | $K^x$ | $K^x$ | $K^x$ | Cl 1084; fragm in 1 |
| 2126 | XII | $K^x$ | 1519 | 1519 | 1519 | |
| 2127 | XII | $I^{\beta}$ | $\Pi$473 | $\Pi$473 | $\Pi$473 | |
| 2131 | XIV | | Kmix | $K^x$ | $K^x$ | fragm in 10 |
| 2132 | XI | | $K^x$ | $K^x$ | 1519 | pair with 1309 |
| 2133 | XI | $K^x$ | $K^x$ | NP | $K^x$ | |
| 2135 | XII | $I^{\kappa}$ | $K^r$ | $K^r$ | $K^r$ | pair with 1082 |

| Gregory No. | Date | v. Soden Classif. | Luke 1 | Luke 10 | Luke 20 | Comments |
|---|---|---|---|---|---|---|
| 2139 | XII | $K^x$ | $K^x$ | NP | $K^x$ | |
| 2140 | XIII | $K^x$ | $K^x$ | NP | $K^x$ | Cl 281 |
| 2141 | XIII | $K^x$ | $K^x$ | M349 | M349 | Cl 1053 in 1 |
| 2142 | IX | $A^k$ | $K^x$ | $K^x$ | $K^x$ | Cl Ω |
| 2144 | XI | $I^{\phi b}$ | $K^x$ | $K^x$ | $K^x$ | fragm in 1 |
| 2145 | 1144/5 | $I^o$ | M1195 | M1195 | $K^x$ | |
| 2146 | XII | $K^x$ | M651 | M651 | M651 | |
| 2147 | XI | $K^x$ | $K^x$ | $K^x$ | Def | |
| 2148 | 1337 | | Cl 2148 | Cl 2148 | Cl 2148 | |
| 2159 | 1281 | | $K^x$ | $K^x$ | $K^x$ | |
| 2172 | XI | $K^1$ | Def | Def | $K^x$ | |
| 2173 | XII | $I^{\phi b}$ | $K^x$ | NP | $K^x$ | |
| 2174 | XIV | $I^\beta$ | 1216 | 1216 | 1216 | pair with 477; weak in 1 and 10; fragm in 1 |
| 2175 | XV | $K^r$ | $K^x$ | $K^x$ | $K^x$ | fragm in 20; $K^r$ equipment |
| 2176 | XI | $A^k$ | $K^x$ | $K^x$ | $K^x$ | Cl Ω |
| 2177 | XII | $K^1$ | $K^x$ | $K^x$ | $K^x$ | |
| 2178 | XV | $K^x$ | Mix | $K^x$ | $K^x$ | |
| 2181 | 1054 | $K^x$ | $K^x$ | NP | $K^x$ | |
| 2182 | XII | | $K^x$ | $K^x$ | $K^x$ | |
| 2191 | XII | $I^{\phi b}$ | $K^x$ | Kmix | $K^x$ | |
| 2195 | X | | $K^x$ | $K^x$ | $K^x$ | Cl 43 in 10 |
| 2200 | XIV | $K^x$ | M1195 | $K^x$ | $K^x$ | |
| 2201 | XV | $K^x$ | $K^x$ | NP | $K^x$ | fragm in 1 |
| 2204 | XV | $K^r$ | $K^r$ | NP | $K^r$ | Subgroup 35 |
| 2213 | XV | $K^r$ | $K^x$ | Illeg | $K^x$ | partly illeg in 1 |
| 2217 | XII | $K^{ak}$ | $K^x$ | NP | $K^x$ | pair with 219 |
| 2220 | XII | $K^x$ | $K^x$ | Kmix | $K^x$ | |
| 2221 | 1432 | $K^r$ | $K^r$ | NP | $K^r$ | |
| 2222 | XIV | | $K^x$ | $K^x$ | $K^x$ | fragm |
| 2223 | 1281 | | Π? | Illeg | M? | largely illeg |
| 2224 | IX | $K^x$ | $K^x$ | $K^x$ | $K^x$ | |
| 2229 | XI | $K^x$ | 1167 | 1167 | 1167 | pair with 75 |
| 2238 | XIII | | $\Pi^b$ | $\Pi^a$ | $\Pi^b$ | weak in 10 and 20 |
| 2260 | XII | | $K^r$ | NP | $K^r$ | Cl 479 |
| 2261 | XIV | | $K^r$ | NP | $K^r$ | Subgroup 35 |

| Gregory No. | Date | v. Soden Classif. | Luke 1 | Luke 10 | Luke 20 | Comments |
|---|---|---|---|---|---|---|
| 2263 | XII | $K^x$ | Kmix | Kmix | Kmix | |
| 2265 | XIV | | Mix | $K^x$ | $K^x$ | |
| 2266 | XIV | $K^x$ | $K^x$ | $K^x$ | $K^x$ | Cl 74 |
| 2273 | XIV | | $K^r$ | NP | $K^r$ | perfect member |
| 2277 | XI | | $K^x$ | $K^x$ | 1519 | Cl 2592 in 1 and 10 |
| 2278 | 1314 | | $\Pi^b$ | $\Pi^b$ | $\Pi^b$ | |
| 2280 | XII | | $\Pi$268 | $\Pi$268 | $\Pi$268 | fragm in 1 |
| 2281 | XI | $K^1$ | $K^x$ | $K^x$ | $K^x$ | |
| 2282 | XI | $K^x$ | $K^x$ | $K^x$ | Def | |
| 2283 | XIII | | Kmix | $K^x$ | $K^x$ | Cl 2283 |
| 2284 | XIII | | $K^r$ | $K^r$ | $K^r$ | surplus in 1 |
| 2287 | XI | | $K^x$ | NP | $K^x$ | Cl $\Omega$; fragm in 20 |
| 2290 | X | | M349 | M349 | M349 | weak in 10 |
| 2291 | XIII | | Cl 1531 | Cl 1531 | Cl 1531 | |
| 2292 | 1283 | $K^x$ | $K^x$ | NP | $K^x$ | |
| 2295 | XI | $K^x$ | $K^x$ | $K^x$ | $K^x$ | fragm in 1 |
| 2296 | XII | $K^r$ | $K^r$ | NP | $K^r$ | perfect member |
| 2297 | XI | $K^x$ | $K^x$ | $K^x$ | Def | fragm in 10 |
| 2300 | XIII | | Def | Kmix | Def | |
| 2304 | XIII | | $K^x$ | NP | $K^x$ | |
| 2311 | XII/XIII | | Def | Def | $K^x$ | Cl 413 |
| 2314 | XII | | $K^x$ | $K^x$ | $K^x$ | |
| 2315 | XII | | M1402 | M1402 | M1402 | |
| 2316 | XIV | | Kmix | $K^x$ | $K^x$ | fragm in 20 |
| 2321 | XI | | Cl 490 | Cl 490 | Cl 490 | |
| 2322 | XII/XIII | | $K^r$ | $K^r$ | $K^r$ | perfect member |
| 2323 | XII/XIII | | $K^r$ | NP | $K^r$ | pair with 1503 |
| 2324 | X | | $\Pi^a$ | $\Pi^a$ | $\Pi^a$ | weak in 10 |
| 2328 | XII | | Cl 276 | Cl 276 | Cl 276 | |
| 2346 | XII | | 291 | 291 | 291 | |
| 2354 | 1287 | | $K^x$ | $K^x$ | $K^x$ | Cl 352 in 10 and 20 |
| 2355 | XIV | | $K^r$ | $K^r$ | $K^r$ | |
| 2356 | XIV | | $K^x$ | $K^x$ | $K^x$ | Cl 352 in 10 and 20 |
| 2358 | XII | | $K^x$ | $K^x$ | $K^x$ | |
| 2364 | XII/XIII | | $K^r$ | $K^x$ | $K^x$ | |
| 2367 | XII | | $K^r$ | NP | $K^r$ | pair with 1251 |

| Gregory No. | Date | v. Soden Classif. | Luke 1 | Luke 10 | Luke 20 | Comments |
|---|---|---|---|---|---|---|
| 2368 | XII | | Def | $K^x$ | Def | Cl 2592 |
| 2369 | X | | Kmix | $K^x$ | $K^x$ | |
| 2370 | XII | | $K^r$ | $K^x$ | $K^x$ | Cl 1323 in 1 |
| 2371 | XIII | | $\Pi473$ | $\Pi473$ | $\Pi473$ | |
| 2372 | XIII | | 22a | 22a | 22a | |
| 2373 | X | | $K^x$ | Cl 475 | Cl 475 | |
| 2374 | XIII | | $K^x$ | $K^x$ | $K^x$ | |
| 2375 | XIV | | Cl 585 | Cl 585 | Cl 585 | surplus in 1 and 20 |
| 2376 | XIII | | $K^x$ | $K^x$ | $K^x$ | Cl 202; fragm in 1 and 20 |
| 2382 | XII | | $K^r$ | $K^r$ | $K^r$ | Cl 586 |
| 2383 | XIII/XIV | | $K^x$ | $K^x$ | $K^x$ | |
| 2386 | XI | | Kmix | $K^x$ | $K^x$ | |
| 2387 | XIV | | Cl 1531 | Cl 1531 | Cl 1531 | |
| 2388 | XII | | M349 | M349 | M349 | pair with 349 |
| 2389 | XI/XII | | $K^x$ | $K^x$ | $K^x$ | |
| 2390 | XIII | | Def | $K^x$ | $K^x$ | fragm in 10 and 20 |
| 2394 | XIII | | M106 | M106 | M106 | weak in 1 |
| 2396 | XIII | | Def | $K^x$ | $K^x$ | fragm in 20 |
| 2397 | 1303 | | Cl 1001 | Cl 1001 | Cl 1001 | |
| 2398 | XIV | | $\Pi^a$ | Def | $K^x$ | fragm in 1 |
| 2399 | XIV | | $K^r$ | $K^r$ | $K^r$ | Cl 1059; fragm in 1 |
| 2400 | XIII | | $\Pi^a$ | $\Pi^a$ | $\Pi^a$ | weak member |
| 2404 | XIII | | $\Pi^a$ | $\Pi^a$ | $\Pi^a$ | core member; pair with 581 |
| 2405 | XIII | | Mix | $\Pi^a$ | $\Pi^a$ | |
| 2406 | XIV | | $K^x$ | $K^x$ | $K^x$ | Cl 46 |
| 2407 | 1332 | | $K^r$ | $K^r$ | $K^r$ | pair with 1334 |
| 2411 | XII | | $\Pi^a$ | $\Pi^a$ | $\Pi^a$ | |
| 2414 | X | | $K^x$ | $K^x$ | $K^x$ | fragm in 1 |
| 2415 | XI/XII | | $K^x$ | $K^x$ | $K^x$ | fragm in 1 |
| 2420 | 1296? | | $K^x$ | $K^x$ | $K^x$ | Cl 43; pair with 43; seems to be corr toward TR |
| 2426 | XII | | Kmix | $K^x$ | $K^x$ | |
| 2430 | XI | | Mix | $\Pi171$ | Kmix | |
| 2437 | XII | | 1519 | 1519 | 1519 | surplus in 10 |
| 2442 | XI | | $K^x$ | $K^x$ | $K^x$ | Cl $\Omega$ |
| 2451 | XI | | $K^x$ | $K^x$ | Def | partly illeg in 1 |

| Gregory No. | Date | v. Soden Classif. | Luke 1 | Luke 10 | Luke 20 | Comments |
|---|---|---|---|---|---|---|
| 2452 | XV | | K$^r$ | NP | K$^r$ | pair with 2454 |
| 2454 | XIV | | K$^r$ | NP | K$^r$ | pair with 2452 |
| 2455 | XV | | K$^x$ | Kmix | Kmix | pair with 1569 |
| 2459 | XII | | Cl 1252 | Cl 1252 | Cl 1252 | fragm in 1 |
| 2460 | XII | | K$^r$ | NP | K$^r$ | perfect member |
| 2462 | XIV/XV | | Kmix | NP | K$^x$ | |
| 2463 | 1354 | | Π$^a$ | NP | Π$^a$ | Cl 1272 |
| 2465 | XIII | | Λ | Λ | Λ | pair with 710 in 20 |
| 2466 | 1329 | | K$^r$ | NP | K$^r$ | Cl 1059 |
| 2467 | 1421 | | M1386 | M1386 | M1386 | |
| 2470 | ? | | K$^x$ | K$^x$ | K$^x$ | Cl 1021 |
| 2472 | XIV | | Cl 190 | Cl 190 | Cl 190 | |
| 2475 | XI | | K$^x$ | K$^x$ | K$^x$ | partly illeg in 10 and 20 |
| 2476 | XIV | | K$^x$ | K$^x$ | K$^x$ | Cl 281 |
| 2478 | XII/XIII | | Π$^b$ | NP | Π$^b$ | |
| 2479 | XIII | | K$^x$ | NP | K$^x$ | |
| 2483 | XIII | | K$^r$ | K$^r$ | K$^x$ | Cl 586 in 1 and 10 |
| 2487 | XI | | Cl 1229 | Cl 1229 | Cl 1229 | |
| 2492 | XIII | | Π$^b$ | Π$^b$ | Π$^b$ | weak member |
| 2494 | 1316 | | K$^x$ | K$^x$ | K$^x$ | Cl 1345 |
| 2495 | XIV/XV | | Kmix | K$^x$ | K$^x$ | Cl 281 in 1 and 10; pair with 1505 |
| 2496 | 1555 | | K$^r$ | K$^r$ | K$^r$ | Cl 1323 |
| 2499 | XIII/XIV | | K$^x$ | K$^x$ | K$^x$ | |
| 2500 | 891 | | Def | K$^x$ | K$^x$ | Cl 2592 |
| 2503 | XIV | | K$^r$ | K$^r$ | K$^r$ | perfect member |
| 2517 | X | | Def | Π$^a$ | Def | fragm in 10 |
| 2518 | XIV | | Kmix | K$^x$ | K$^x$ | |
| 2520 | XIV | | K$^r$ | NP | K$^r$ | Cl 128 |
| 2521 | XVII | | M1326 | NP | NP | fragm in 1 |
| 2522 | XIII/XIV | | Kmix | Kmix | Mix | pair with 2561; fragm in 1 |
| 2523 | 1453 | | K$^x$ | Mix | K$^x$ | |
| 2524 | XIV | | K$^x$ | NP | Kmix | fragm in 1 |
| 2525 | XIII/XIV | | Mix | Π$^a$ | K$^x$ | Cl 178 in 10 and 20 |
| 2526 | XIV/XV | | K$^x$ | Kmix | K$^x$ | fragm in 1 and 10 |
| 2528 | XIII/XIV | | Cl 1012 | Cl 1012 | Cl 1012 | |

| Gregory No. | Date | v. Soden Classif. | Luke 1 | Luke 10 | Luke 20 | Comments |
|---|---|---|---|---|---|---|
| 2529 | XII/XIII | | $K^x$ | $K^x$ | $K^x$ | |
| 2530 | 1321 | | Cl 127 | Cl 127 | Cl 127 | weak in 1 |
| 2533 | 1271 | | Mix | Kmix | $K^x$ | |
| 2535 | XIII | | $K^x$ | $K^x$ | $K^x$ | fragm in 1 and 10 |
| 2539 | XII | | $K^x$ | $K^x$ | $K^x$ | Cl 43 |
| 2542 | XIII | | Mix | 1 | 1 | weak member |
| 2545 | 999 | | $K^x$ | $K^x$ | $K^x$ | |
| 2546 | XII | | Kmix | Mix | Mix | pair with 1604 in 10 and 20 |
| 2549 | XII | | M1195 | $K^x$ | M1195 | fragm in 1 |
| 2550 | XII | | $K^x$ | $K^x$ | $K^x$ | |
| 2554 | 1434 | | $K^r$ | NP | $K^r$ | Subgroup 35 |
| 2557 | XII | | $K^x$ | $K^x$ | $K^x$ | Cl 352; fragm in 20 |
| 2559 | XII | | $K^r$ | NP | $K^r$ | Cl 958; fragm in 1 |
| 2561 | XI | | Kmix | Kmix | Mix | pair with 2522; fragm in 1 |
| 2562 | XII | | $K^x$ | NP | $K^x$ | |
| 2563 | X | | $K^x$ | $K^x$ | $K^x$ | Cl Ω |
| 2567 | XI | | M106 | NP | M106 | weak in 20 |
| 2571 | XI | | $K^x$ | $K^x$ | $K^x$ | Cl Ω |
| 2584 | XIII | | Π171 | Π171 | Π171 | weak in 1; pair with 388 |
| 2585 | XI | | Λ | $K^x$ | Λ | weak in 1 and 20 |
| 2586 | XI | | Λ | NP | Λ | |
| 2590 | 1225? | | M106 | M106 | M106 | pair with 1315 |
| 2591 | XV | | $K^x$ | $K^x$ | $K^x$ | |
| 2592 | XI | | $K^x$ | $K^x$ | $K^x$ | Cl 2592 |
| 2600 | XIII | | Def | Def | $K^x$ | fragm in 20 |
| 2603 | XII | | 291 | 291 | 291 | pair with 449 |
| 2604 | XII | | 1167 | 1167 | 1167 | largely illeg in 10 |
| 2605 | XIII | | Kmix | Kmix | $K^x$ | Cl 2283 |
| 2608 | XIII | | Kmix | $K^x$ | $K^x$ | |
| 2609 | XI | | $K^x$ | Cl 475 | Cl 475 | fragm in 1 and 10 |
| 2610 | XIII | | $K^x$ | $K^x$ | Def | |
| 2611 | XIII | | $K^x$ | $K^x$ | $K^x$ | fragm in 1 |
| 2612 | XIII | | $K^x$ | Def | $K^x$ | |
| 2613 | XI | | M106 | M106 | M106 | |
| 2614 | XIII | | $K^x$ | Π171 | Π171 | |
| 2615 | XII | | $\Pi^a$ | $\Pi^a$ | $\Pi^a$ | |

| Gregory No. | Date | v. Soden Classif. | Luke 1 | Luke 10 | Luke 20 | Comments |
|---|---|---|---|---|---|---|
| 2616 | XII | | $K^x$ | Kmix | $K^x$ | |
| 2620 | XIII | | $K^x$ | $K^x$ | $K^x$ | |
| 2621 | 1380 | | Def | $K^r$ | $K^r$ | perfect member |
| 2622 | 1109 | | Cl 276 | Cl 276 | Cl 276 | |
| 2624 | XIII | | $\Pi^b$ | NP | $\Pi^b$ | |
| 2633 | XIII | | Kmix | Def | Def | |
| 2634 | XIV | | $K^x$ | $K^x$ | Kmix | partly illeg in 1 and 20 |
| 2635 | 1568 | | $K^r$ | NP | NP | pair with 1185 |
| 2637 | XI | | $K^x$ | $K^x$ | $K^x$ | Cl $\Omega$; fragm in 10 |
| 2641 | XIV | | $K^x$ | $K^x$ | $K^x$ | |
| 2642 | XI | | $K^x$ | $K^x$ | $K^x$ | |
| 2643 | 1289 | | Mix | Mix | Mix | pair with 792 |
| 2644 | XIII | | $K^x$ | $K^x$ | $K^x$ | Cl 112 |
| 2645 | XI | | $K^x$ | $K^x$ | $K^x$ | fragm in 1; last part of 20 is copy of TR |
| 2649 | XI | | $K^x$ | $K^x$ | $K^x$ | pair with 1474 |
| 2650 | 1154 | | $K^x$ | $K^x$ | $K^x$ | fragm in 1 |
| 2653 | XIV | | Kmix | $K^x$ | $K^x$ | related to 401 and 1013 in 20 |
| 2656 | 1650 | | Kmix | $K^x$ | Kmix | |
| 2660 | XIII | | $K^x$ | $K^x$ | $K^x$ | Cl 934 |
| 2661 | XI | | M609 | M609 | M609 | |
| 2665 | 1274 | | Mix | $K^x$ | $K^x$ | |
| 2670 | XIII | | Kmix | 22a | 22a | |
| 2673 | XV | | $K^r$ | NP | $K^r$ | Cl 1323 |
| 2676 | XIII | | M10 | M10 | M10 | |
| 2677 | XII | | Def | Def | $K^x$ | fragm in 20 |
| 2679 | XIV | | $K^x$ | $K^x$ | $K^x$ | most of 1 by later hand |
| 2680 | XIII | | Mix | Kmix | Mix | pair with 145 in 20 |
| 2683 | XI | | $K^x$ | $K^x$ | $K^x$ | partly illeg in 20 |
| 2684 | XI | | Kmix | $K^x$ | $K^x$ | |
| 2685 | XV | | $\Pi$268 | NP | $\Pi$268 | weak in 1 |
| 2686 | XV | | $K^x$ | $K^x$ | $\Pi^a$ | fragm in 1; weak in 20 |
| 2687 | XII | | Cl 276 | Cl 276 | Cl 276 | weak in 1 |
| 2688 | XIII | | Cl 276 | Illeg | Cl 276 | |
| 2689 | XIV | | $K^r$ | NP | $K^r$ | Cl 1059 |
| 2691 | XV | | Kmix | Def | $K^x$ | |

| Gregory No. | Date | v. Soden Classif. | Luke 1 | Luke 10 | Luke 20 | Comments |
|---|---|---|---|---|---|---|
| 2692 | XV | | K$^r$ | NP | K$^r$ | surplus in 1 |
| 2693 | XI | | Cl 686 | K$^x$ | K$^x$ | |
| 2694 | XII | | K$^x$ | K$^x$ | Kmix | pair with 529 |
| 2695 | XII | | Cl 190 | Cl 190 | Cl 190 | |
| 2697 | XIII | | K$^x$ | Def | Def | fragm in 1 |
| 2701 | 1302 | | K$^x$ | K$^x$ | K$^x$ | |
| 2702 | XII | | K$^x$ | K$^x$ | K$^x$ | Cl Ω |
| 2705 | XIV | | M27 | M27 | M27 | pair with 1626 |
| 2706 | 1480 | | K$^x$ | K$^x$ | K$^x$ | |
| 2707 | 1297 | | K$^x$ | K$^x$ | K$^x$ | Cl 74 |
| 2708 | XVI | | TR | NP | TR | copy of TR |
| 2709 | 1377 | | K$^r$ | NP | K$^r$ | perfect member |
| 2710 | XIV | | K$^x$ | K$^x$ | K$^x$ | |
| 2713 | XV | | K$^x$ | Cl 2148 | Cl 2148 | |
| 2722 | X | | K$^x$ | Illeg | Illeg | Cl Ω |
| 2724 | XIII | | Cl 190 | Cl 190 | K$^x$ | Cl 1053 in 20 |
| 2725 | XII | | Π$^b$ | K$^x$ | Λ | weak in 20 |
| 2726 | XIII | | 1216 | 1216 | 1216 | |
| 2727 | XII | | K$^x$ | K$^x$ | K$^x$ | |
| 2728 | XV | | 291 | 291 | 291 | |
| 2729 | XV | | K$^x$ | K$^x$ | Def | |
| 2730 | 1357 | | Π171 | Π171 | Π171 | |
| 2732 | 1294 | | Def | K$^x$ | K$^x$ | |
| 2734 | 1397 | | K$^x$ | Illeg | Illeg | |
| 2747 | XV | | Mix | K$^x$ | K$^x$ | related to 1061 |
| 2749 | XII | | K$^x$ | K$^x$ | K$^x$ | Cl 74 |
| 2750 | XIII | | Illeg | K$^x$ | K$^x$ | partly illeg in 20 |
| 2751 | XIII | | Def | Cl 276 | Cl 276 | |
| 2752 | XI/XII | | K$^x$ | K$^x$ | K$^x$ | |
| 2756 | XIII | | Π$^b$ | NP | Π$^b$ | |
| 2757 | XII/XIII | | Mix | Kmix | K$^x$ | |
| 2765 | XIV | | K$^r$ | NP | K$^r$ | perfect member |
| 2766 | XIII | | Kmix | Cl 827 | Cl 827 | |
| 2767 | XIV | | K$^r$ | NP | K$^r$ | |
| 2771 | ? | | Cl 1531 | Cl 1531 | Cl 1531 | |
| 2773 | XIV/XV | | K$^x$ | NP | K$^x$ | Cl 122; K$^r$ equipment |

CHAPTER VI

# THE MANUSCRIPT GROUPS AND CLUSTERS

The main groups are presented in the order of the Latin alphabet, then the Greek alphabet, and finally the numbers. The clusters are in numerical order, the pairs in the order of the member with the lowest number. The test readings in brackets are secondary readings for the group or cluster in question. The group descriptions present only basic information. More exhaustive group studies are being prepared by Paul R. McReynolds in a separate study.

## 1. GROUP B

This group involving 15 MSS has traditionally been known as the Neutral or Alexandrian text-type; von Soden called it H for Hesychius. There is no clear reason why it should be treated differently from other MS groups. Most of its members are well known and the group is well represented in the critical apparatus of modern editions of the Greek NT. In the last hundred years this group has taken the place of the TR in that its text is assumed to be relatively pure and the closest approximation to the originals. As a group it is grossly overrepresented in the critical apparatus published during the last hundred years. This is partly due to the fact that it counts a number of famous early uncials among its members. The text of this distinct group could, however, be represented by MSS 01 (‎‫א‬) and 03 (B); any further witnesses would be redundant and give the false impression of wide support over against non-B readings for which generally little MS support is presented. Ideally the group should be represented in an *apparatus criticus* by a siglum supplemented by the nongroup readings of its oldest members.

MS 04 (C), which is often associated with group B, is not a member in Luke. It may be surprising that 05 (D) is clearly related to Gr B in Luke though it is an exceptional member. That the unique group readings of B and the unique features of D were not taken into account in the selection of test readings has, no doubt, accentuated the relationship between D and Gr B. The relationship of MSS 565, 700, and 1342 to Gr B in part of Luke had also escaped notice, though 565 and 700 are often included in critical apparatus.

The group profiles of B are:
Luke 1: 2, 6, 8, (9), 20, 24, 25, 26, (28), 32, (36), 39, 41, (42), 47, 48, (49), 50, (51), 52. Test Readings 5, 14, 19, and 33 can be expected to be found in surplus.
Luke 10: 7, 11, 13, 15, 18, 20, 22, 23, 26, 29, 37, 45, 46, 49, 51, 52, (56), 57, 58, 64. Readings 3, 21, 36, 48, and 62 can be expected to be found in surplus.

Luke 20: 1, (6), (7), 10, 13, 14, 19, 25, 27, 37, 38, 41, 42, 43, 45, 46, (47), 48, 50, 51, 55, 60, 62, 65, 72, (74), 76. Readings 33, 49, and 58 can be expected to be found in surplus.

The following MSS are members of Gr B in at least part of Luke: 01, 03, 05, 019, 032 (Luke 1), 040 (Luke 10), 044 (Luke 1), 33, 157 (Luke 20), 565 (Luke 1), 579, 700 (Luke 10), 892, 1241, 1342 (Luke 10).


## GROUP K$^r$

This large group consisting of more than two hundred MSS was discovered by von Soden.[1] The group is the result of an early twelfth-century attempt to create a unified NT text. The copying was carefully controlled and the accuracy is unequalled in the history of the transmission of the NT text. K$^r$ slowly gained in popularity and became the most copied Greek text of the late Middle Ages. On the basis of the present location of most of the members of the K$^r$ recension, it appears to have originated in the area of Constantinople or Mount Athos. The great majority of the K$^r$ members can be recognized by the distinctive marginal lectionary equipment which differs from the traditional Eusebian canons. Von Soden used this to identify K$^r$ members and consequently included some non-K$^r$ MSS which had a K$^r$ equipment and missed some K$^r$ members which lacked the distinctive equipment. The text of K$^r$ is also distinct and easily identified, however. David O. Voss confirmed the distinctiveness of the K$^r$ group.[2]

The group readings of K$^r$ are:
Luke 1: 34, 37, 43.
Luke 10: 11, 23, 57, 60, 63.
Luke 20: 4, 13, 19, 30, 35, 52, 55, 62, 65.

The following MSS are members of K$^r$ in at least part of Luke: 18, 35, 47, 55, 56, 58, 66, 83, 128, 141, 147, 155, 167, 170, 182 (Luke 1), 189, 201, 204, 214 (Luke 1), 246, 285, 290, 361, 363, 386, 387, 394, 402, 479, 480, 483 (Luke 20 corr), 510, 511 (Luke 1), 512, 516 (corr), 521, 547, 553, 558, 575, 586, 588, 594, 645, 660 (corr), 664, 673, 685, 689, 691, 694 (Luke 1 and 10), 696, 757, 758, 763, 769, 781, 786 (Luke 1 and 10), 789, 797, 802, 806 (Luke 1 and 10), 824, 825, 845, 867, 897, 928, 932, 938, 940, 952, 953, 955, 958, 959, 960, 962, 966, 973 (corr), 975, 1003, 1020, 1023, 1025, 1030, 1046, 1059, 1062, 1072, 1075, 1082 (Luke 10 and 20), 1092, 1095, 1111, 1116, 1145, 1146, 1147, 1158, 1165, 1169 (Luke 10), 1176 (Luke 1 and 10), 1185, 1189, 1190 (Luke 1 and 10), 1199, 1224, 1234, 1236, 1247, 1250, 1251, 1276, 1323, 1328, 1329, 1334, 1339, 1348 (Luke 20), 1389, 1400, 1401, 1409, 1435, 1445, 1453, 1461, 1462, 1471, 1476, 1480, 1482, 1487, 1488, 1489, 1492, 1493, 1496, 1499, 1501, 1503, 1508, 1517 (corr), 1543, 1544, 1548, 1551, 1552, 1559, 1560, 1572, 1576, 1584, 1596, 1599, 1600, 1601, 1614, 1617, 1619, 1621, 1622, 1625, 1628, 1633, 1634 (Luke 20), 1636, 1637, 1638, 1648, 1649, 1650, 1656, 1658, 1659, 1664 (Luke 1), 1667, 1686, 1694, 1698, 1699 (Luke 1 and 10), 1703, 1713, 1813, 2122, 2135, 2204,

---

[1] *Die Schriften* I/2, 757-65, 780-81, 799-805.
[2] "Is von Soden's K$^r$ a distinct type of Text?" *JBL* 57 (1938) 311-18.

2221, 2260, 2261, 2273, 2284, 2296, 2322, 2323, 2355, 2364 (Luke 1), 2367, 2370 (Luke 1), 2382, 2399, 2407, 2452, 2454, 2460, 2466, 2483 (Luke 1 and 10), 2496, 2503, 2520, 2554, 2559, 2621, 2635, 2673, 2689, 2692, 2709, 2765, 2767.

Of these 221 MSS, 59 have a perfect profile (see Chapter V). Sixteen subgroups or clusters can be distinguished among the $K^r$ members. Most of them diverge only slightly from the group profile.

$K^r$ subgroup 35 lacks reading 37 in Luke 1. It consists of MSS 35 (first hand), 141, 170, 204, 394, 402, 516 (corr), 521, 553, 660 (corr), 758 (first hand), 769, 797, 928, 1250, 1482, 1487, 1493, 1559, 1572, 1600, 1694 (first hand), 2204, 2261, and 2554.

$K^r$ Cl 56, consisting of MSS 47 (Luke 10 and 20), 56, and 58, is related to $K^r$ Cl 1323 and has the following profile:

Luke  1: 9, 34, 36, 37, 43.
Luke 10: 4, 11, 21, 23, 57, 60, 62.
Luke 20: 1, 4, 11, 13, 19, 30, 35, 43, 44, 52, 62.

$K^r$ Cl 128, consisting of MSS 55, 128, and 2520, adds reading 4 in Luke 1 and lacks readings 60 and 63 in Luke 20.

$K^r$ Cl 147, consisting of MSS 147, 511 (Luke 1), and 547, adds readings 21 and 36 in Luke 1.

$K^r$ Cl 167, consisting of MSS 167, 386, 1699 (Luke 1 and 10), and 1095, adds reading 36 in Luke 1.

$K^r$ Cl 189, consisting of MSS 189, 1236, 1625, and, at some distance, 825, is related to $K^r$ Cls 56 and 1323 and has the following profile:

Luke  1: 9, 34, 36, 37, 43.
Luke 10: 11, 23, 57.
Luke 20: 2, 4, 12, 19, 30, 35, 52, 55, 61, 62, 76.

$K^r$ Cl 479, consisting of MSS 479, 1020, 1599, 1621, 1664 (Luke 1), and 2260, adds reading 48 in Luke 1.

$K^r$ Cl 586, consisting of MSS 586, 1276, 2382, and 2483 (Luke 1 and 10), lacks reading 63 in Luke 10.

$K^r$ Cl 763, consisting of MSS 763, 1461, 1619, and 1648, lacks reading 35 in Luke 20.

$K^r$ Cl 953, consisting of MSS 953, 1389, and 1552, adds readings 27 and 48 in Luke 1 and lacks readings 30 and 65 in Luke 20.

$K^r$ Cl 958, consisting of MSS 958, 1453, and 2559, adds readings 9 and 28 in Luke 1.

$K^r$ Cl 1059, consisting of MSS 689, 1059, 1462, 1508, 1634, 1658, 2399, and 2689, adds reading 8 in Luke 20.

$K^r$ Cl 1176 consists of the three Patmos MSS 1169 (Luke 10 and 20), 1176, and 1190. It belongs to $K^x$ in Luke 20. MS 1169 belongs in Luke 1 to another Patmos cluster together with MSS 1173 and 1385. The cluster has the following profile:

Luke  1: 3, 34, 37, 43.
Luke 10: 11, 23, 57.
Luke 20: 4, 13, 19, 35, 55, 60, 62.

$K^r$ Cl 1323, consisting of MSS 932, 1165, 1323, 1329 (Luke 10 and 20), 1476, 2370 (Luke 1), 2496, and 2673, is related to $K^r$ Cls 56 and 189. It has the following profile:

Luke  1:  9, 34, 36, 37, 43.
Luke 10:  4, 11, 23, 57, 60.
Luke 20:  4, 19, 30, 35, 52, 55, 62, 65.

K$^r$ Cl 1489, consisting of the Athos MSS 1489, 1596, and 1659, adds reading 28 in Luke 1.

K$^r$ Cl 1601, consisting of the Athos MSS 1601, 1622, and 1633, adds reading 9 in Luke 1.

In addition to the clusters eleven pairs can be distinguished among the K$^r$ members.

MSS 1334 and 2407 lack readings 37 and 43 in Luke 1 and 65 in Luke 20.
MSS 1082 and 2135 add reading 60 and lack 30 and 65 in Luke 20.
MSS 1185 and 2635 add reading 1 in Luke 1.
MSS 757 and 1075 lack reading 30 in Luke 20.
MSS 1503 and 2323 add reading 64 in Luke 20.
MSS 290 and 363 add readings 10 and 36 in Luke 1 and 74 in Luke 20.
MSS 588 and 845 add reading 39 in Luke 20.
MSS 2452 and 2454 add readings 3, 9, and 40 in Luke 1.
MSS 966 and 1813 add reading 27 in Luke 1 and lack 30 in Luke 20.
MSS 387 and 1471 add readings 4, 6, 16, and 23 in Luke 1.
MSS 1251 and 2367 add reading 21 in Luke 1.

### 3. GROUP K$^x$

A total of 734 MSS of the 1385 profiled belong to K$^x$ in at least part of the Gospel of Luke (see Chapter V). Due to the overwhelming numbers, any attempt to represent the Byzantine minuscules by a single siglum will result in the obliteration by K$^x$ of all other Byzantine groups.

Gr K$^x$ was discovered by Hermann von Soden, who defined it as those Kappa MSS which are neither K$^1$ nor K$^r$.[3] He did not study the group in detail and considered it possible that the group could be further subdivided.[4] For most MSS he collated in Luke only chs. 7 and 8 to determine whether they belonged to Kappa.[5] The only distinction he made among K$^x$ members was according to the presence and type of the *pericope adulterae*.[6]

Due to the massive influence of K$^x$ on other groups and its lack of control, the group's boundaries remain blurred. Thus von Soden's Grs K$^i$ and K$^{ik}$ are not distinguishable from K$^x$, and K$^1$ could not maintain itself as an independent group and is treated here as a K$^x$ Cl. More problematic is the question, how many K$^x$ readings can be missing and how many surplus readings can be added before a MS no longer deserves to be classified as K$^x$? Somewhat arbitrarily it was decided to allow a tolerance for K$^x$ of four test readings variance with the group profile in a chapter. MSS which did not belong to a group other than K$^x$ and which read five or six times against the group profile in a chapter were designated as "Kmix." A MS

---

[3] *Die Schriften* I/2, 713.
[4] Ibid.
[5] Ibid., I/2, 717 and 775.
[6] Ibid., I/2, 734-57.

94

which is classified $K^x$ in at least one test chapter and Kmix in the other(s) can still be called $K^x$ as a whole. MSS which read at least seven times against the $K^x$ group profile in a chapter were designated as "Mix(ed)."

The group profiles of $K^x$ are:

Luke  1: 6, 34.
Luke 10: (3), 15, 18, 23, (44), 57, (60).
Luke 20: 4, 13, 19, 35, 50, 54, 55, 57, 62, (65).

Among the $K^x$ members a total of twenty-nine subgroups or clusters could be distinguished and seventeen pairs.[7]

$K^x$ Cl $\Omega$ is related to von Soden's Gr $K^1$. He considered it the oldest form of Kappa from which in the tenth century Gr $K^x$ evolved.[8] It stands so close to $K^x$, however, especially in Luke 10 and 20, that it could not be maintained as an independent group. Further doubt about von Soden's $K^1$ derives from the fact that only 11 of the 29 Cl $\Omega$ members classified by von Soden were designated by him as $K^1$. In any case it is correct to call this large cluster of 37 MSS an early form of $K^x$, though not necessarily the one from which the other forms of $K^x$ evolved.

Profile:

Luke  1: 6, 8, 22, 34, 52.
Luke 10: 3, 15, 18, (23), 44, 57, (60), (62).
Luke 20: 4, 13, 19, 35, 50, 54, 55, 57, 62, (65).
Members: MSS 07 (E), 028 (S), 031 (V), 045 ($\Omega$), 65, 123, 143, 151, 271, 277, 344, 364, 396 (Luke 1), 461, 471, 584, 667, 688, 699, 1045, 1077, 1080, 1083, 1281, 1295, 1470, 1581 (Luke 1), 1691, 2142, 2176, 2287, 2442, 2563, 2571, 2637, 2702, 2722.

$K^x$ Cl 17 consists of seven MSS classified by von Soden as the weak branch of $I^\beta$.

Profile:

Luke  1: 3, 4, 6, 9, 34, 36.
Luke 10: 15, 18, 23, 44, 57.
Luke 20: 4, 13, 19, 35, 50, 54, 55, 57, 62, 65.
Members: MSS 17, 30, 70, 120, 287, 288, and 880. Among these MSS 30 and 288 form a pair.

$K^x$ Cl 43 consists of MSS 15, 43, 680, 1163, 1350, 1364, 1592, 2195 (Luke 10), 2420, and 2539. Among these MSS 43 and 2420, and 15 and 1163 form pairs.

Profile:

Luke  1: 4, 6, 22 (omit), 34, 36.
Luke 10: 3, 15, 16, 18, 35, (60).
Luke 20: 4, 13, 19, 35, 50, 54, 55, 62, (64), 65, (70).

$K^x$ Cl 46 consists of MSS 46, 52, 761, 995, 1395, 1597, 1598, and 2406. Among these MSS 52 and 1395 form a pair (add reading 21 in Luke 1 and 74 in Luke 20) as well as MSS 761 and 995 (add readings 9 and 37 in Luke 1 and 76 in Luke 20).

---

[7]It is possible that an exhaustive search could distinguish even more $K^x$ clusters and pairs.
[8]Ibid., I/2, 713 and 718.

Profile:

Luke  1:  4, 6, 28, 34, 46 (omit).

Luke 10:  14, 15, 18, 23, 44, 52, 55, 57, 62.

Luke 20:  4, 13, 35, 54, 55, 57, 62.

$K^x$ Cl 74 consists of MSS 74, 89, 198, 234, 390, 483, 484, 502, 561 (Luke 1), 1397, 1594, 1635, 1679, 2266, 2707, and 2749. Of these MSS 74, 234, 483, 484, 1594, and perhaps some others were written by the calligraphist Theodoros Hagiopetrites in the late thirteenth century.

Profile:

Luke  1:  6, 9, 27, 34.

Luke 10:  15, 18, 23, 44, 57, 60.

Luke 20:  4, 13, 19, 35, 50, 54, 62.

$K^x$ Cl 112 consists of MSS 112, 583, and 2644. The profile in Luke 10 is rather uncertain.

Profile:

Luke  1:  6, 16, 34, 41.

Luke 10:  18, 19, 23, 24, 57, 62.

Luke 20:  4, 13, 19, 35, 54, 55, 57, 62.

$K^x$ Cl 122 consists of MSS 122, 1467, 1494, 1632, and 1657.

Profile:

Luke  1:  4, 6, 34, 43.

Luke 10:  1, 15, 18, 23, 44, 57.

Luke 20:  4, 9, 19, 50, 54, 55, 57, 62, 65, 66 (εδηλωσεν), (77).

$K^x$ Cl 137 consists of MSS 137, 715, and 1472 (Luke 20).

Profile:

Luke  1:  6, 8, 34.

Luke 10:  15, 18, 22, 23, 57, 60.

Luke 20:  19, 23, 26, 50, 54, 55, 60, 62, 74.

$K^x$ Cl 160 consists of MSS 160, 1010, and 1293; all three MSS were classified $I^{\varphi c}$ by von Soden.

Profile:

Luke  1:  2, 6, 8, 21, 22, 34, 52.

Luke 10:  3, 15, 18, 23, 44, 57.

Luke 20:  4, 13, 19, 39, 50, 54, 55, 57, 62.

$K^x$ Cl 180 consists of MSS 180, 998, and 1580.

Profile:

Luke  1:  4 (εναντι] omit), 6, 9, 34, 53.

Luke 10:  3, 9, 15, 18, 23, 44, 57.

Luke 20:  4, 13, 19, 30, 35, 50, 54, 55, 57, 65, 78.

$K^x$ Cl 183 consists of MSS 183, 208, 376, 448, and 793.

Profile:

Luke  1:  4, 6, 9, 34, 36.

Luke 10:  7, 15, 18, 23, 44, 57.

Luke 20:  4, 13, 19, 35, 50, 54, 55, 57, 62.

$K^x$ Cl 187 consists of MSS 187, 218, and 1606; all three MSS were classified $I^{\varphi b}$ by von Soden.

Profile:

Luke  1:  4, 6, 33, 34, 37.

Luke 10:  3, 15, 18, 22, 23, (35), 42, 50, (51), 57, 64.

Luke 20:  4, 13, 39, 50, 54, 55, 57, 61, 62.

K$^x$ Cl 202 consists of MSS 202, 900, 1121 (Luke 10 and 20), and 2376.

Profile:

Luke  1:  4, 6, 9, (28), 34.

Luke 10:  15, 18, 23, 34, 57, (62).

Luke 20:  4, 13, 19, 35, 39, 43, 50, 55, 62.

K$^x$ Cl 281 consists of MSS 111, 281, 574 (Luke 10), 760 (Luke 1 and 10), 906, 923, 969 (Luke 1), 1148, 1186 (Luke 1 and 10), 1232, 1338, 1359, 1505 (Luke 1 and 10), 1590, 2140, 2476, and 2495 (Luke 1 and 10). MSS 1505 and 2495 form a pair.

Profile:

Luke  1:  5, 6, 28, 33, 34, 37.

Luke 10:  3, 7, 15, 23, 57, 62.

Luke 20:  4, 13, 19, 41 (+ υποκριται), 50, 54, 55, 57, 62.

K$^x$ Cl 352 consists of MSS 352, 375, 2354 (Luke 10 and 20), 2356 (Luke 10 and 20), and 2557.

Profile:

Luke  1:  6, 8, 34, 52.

Luke 10:  3, 15, 18, 23, 25, 57, 60, (62), 63.

Luke 20:  4, 8, (13), 19, 35, (43), 54, 55.

K$^x$ Cl 413 consists of MSS 413, 1563 (Luke 1), 1966, and 2311.

Profile:

Luke  1:  5, 11, 28, 34, 36, (37).

Luke 10:  3, 15, 18, 57, 62.

Luke 20:  4, 8, 13, 19, 35, 61, 62, 73.

K$^x$ Cl 532 consists of MSS 532, 1485, and 1623.

Profile:

Luke  1:  4, 6, 34, 36.

Luke 10:  3, 15, 18, 25, 57.

Luke 20:  4, 19, 35, 54, 55, 60, 64, 65, 68.

K$^x$ Cl 550 consists of MSS 550, 765, 1181 (Luke 10 and 20), and 1341.

Profile:

Luke  1:  6, 17, 28, 34, 52.

Luke 10:  3, 15, 18, 19, 23, 44, 57, 62.

Luke 20:  4, 13, 50, 54, 55, 57, 60, 62.

K$^x$ Cl 934 consists of MSS 934, 1353, and 2660.

Profile:

Luke  1:  6, 9, 23, 28, 34, 36, 37, 42.

Luke 10:  15, 18, 21, 23, 44, 57, 60.

Luke 20:  4, 13, 39, 50, 54, 55, 57, 60, 61, 62, 65.

K$^x$ Cl 1021 consists of MSS 428, 1021, 1498, and 2470; all four MSS are commentated texts.

Profile:

Luke  1: 6, 9, 33, 34, 36, 37, 52.

Luke 10: 15, 18, 24 (εν τη ημερα εκεινη] omit), 48, 57, 60, 62.

Luke 20: 4, 8, 13, 23, 35, 49, 50, 55, 57.

K^x Cl 1053 consists of MSS 31, 38 (Luke 1 and 20), 113 (Luke 1), 298, 407 (Luke 10), 435, 552 (Luke 1 and 20), 1053, 1186 (Luke 20), 1288 (Luke 1 and 10), 1578 (Luke 1), 2141 (Luke 1), and 2724 (Luke 20).

Profile:

Luke  1: 28, 30 (εν δε ταις ημεραις ταυταις αναστασα Μαριαμ), 34.

Luke 10: 8 (οπως ] ινα), 15, 23, (25), 44, 57, 63.

Luke 20: 2, 13, 19, 31, 33, 35, 42, 50, 54, 55, 62, 65.

K^x Cl 1084 consists of MSS 1084, 1495, and 2123; all three MSS were classified I^{φb} by von Soden and are related to Cl 7.

Profile:

Luke  1: 6, 9, 16, 28, 33, 34.

Luke 10: 15, 18, 23, 50, 57, 62.

Luke 20: 4, 13, 21, 35, 50, 54, 62.

K^x Cl 1179 consists of MSS 905, 1179, 1212, and 1449; all four MSS were classified K^{ak} by von Soden.

Profile:

Luke  1: 4, 6, 33, 34, (37), (42).

Luke 10: 18, 23, 57, 60.

Luke 20: 4, 13, 19, 35, 54, 55, 57, 62.

K^x Cl 1193 consists of MSS 76, 247, 1193, and 2118.

Profile:

Luke  1: 4, 6, (9), 28, 34.

Luke 10: 3, 15, 18, 35, 57, 60.

Luke 20: 4, (13), (19), 31 (τουτους] omit), 36, 50, 54, 55, 61, 62, (70), 73.

K^x Cl 1213 consists of MSS 0211 (Luke 1), 446, 1213, 1407, and 1676 (Luke 1).

Profile:

Luke  1: 5, 6, 8, 21, 22, 34, 53.

Luke 10: 3, 11, 15, 18, 19, 23, 44, 57, 62, 63.

Luke 20: 4, 9, 13, 19, 35, 54, 55, 57, 62.

K^x Cl 1345 consists of MSS 808, 1345, and 2494.

Profile:

Luke  1: 6, 9, 28, 30, 34.

Luke 10: (15), (18), 44, 48, 50, 57, 60.

Luke 20: 4, 13, 19, 23, 50, 55, 62.

K^x Cl 1547 consists of MSS 1305, 1547, and 1586.

Profile:

Luke  1: 6, 9, 28, 34, 37.

Luke 10: 44, 57, 60.

Luke 20: 4, 13, 19, 35, 43, 50, 54, 62.

K^x Cl 2283 consists of MSS 1215, 2283, and 2605.

Profile:

Luke  1: 4, 18, 28, 33, 34, 36.

Luke 10:  4, 9, 15, 18, 23, 44, 57, 63.
Luke 20:  4, 35, 43, 54, 62.

K<sup>x</sup> Cl 2592 consists of MSS 967, 1110 (Luke 1 and 10), 1351, 1564 (Luke 1 and 10), 2277 (Luke 1 and 10), 2368, 2500, and 2592.

Profile:

Luke  1:  6, 34, (52).
Luke 10:  15, 18, 23, 44, 52 (ειπεν αυτω] ειπων), 55, 57.
Luke 20:  4, 13, 19, 35, 54, 55, 57, 62.

There are seventeen pairs among the K<sup>x</sup> members in addition to those which belong to the K<sup>x</sup> clusters.

MSS 53 and 902 add readings 4, 36, and 51 in Luke 1, and lack 19 in Luke 20.

MSS 219 and 2217 add reading 52 in Luke 1, and lack 50 and add 76 in Luke 20.

MSS 272 and 419 add readings 8 and 9 in Luke 1, lack 23 and add 36, 62, and 64 in Luke 10, and add 76 in Luke 20.

MSS 301 and 373 add readings 36 and 37 in Luke 1, and add 49 and lack 62 in Luke 20 (54 in Luke 20 reads ομοιως).

MSS 358 and 360 add reading 52 in Luke 1, add 52 and 55 in Luke 10, and lack 50 in Luke 20.

MSS 412 and 1394 were both written in 1301 by Theodoros Hagiopetrites. They share the following profile:

Luke  1:  6, 9, 34, (42).
Luke 10:  9, 15, 18, (23), 57, 62, 63 (ο Ιησους] omit).
Luke 20:  4, 19, 35, 50, 65, 74, (76).

MSS 439 and 877 lack readings 19, 54, and 62, and add 33 in Luke 20.

MSS 529 and 2694 add readings 9, 28, and 36 in Luke 1, add 62 and 63 in Luke 10, and lack 50 and 62 and add 5, 18, 42, and 68 in Luke 20.

MSS 568 and 1452 add readings 22 and 36 in Luke 1, and add 42 in Luke 20.

MSS 778 and 1203 add readings 36 and 37 in Luke 1, and lack 4 and 50 in Luke 20. The pair stands close to pair 875 and 971.

MSS 864 and 1609 add reading 43 in Luke 1, and lack 50 and 54 and add 30 and 43 in Luke 20. There is a clear influence of K<sup>r</sup>.

MSS 875 and 971 add readings 36 and 37 in Luke 1, and lack 50 in Luke 20. The pair stands close to pair 778 and 1203.

MSS 939 and 1693 add readings 4, 23, 28, and 36 in Luke 1, add 11 and 21 in Luke 10, and add 8 and lack 35, 50, 54, and 55 in Luke 20.

MSS 1076 and 1417 add readings 8, 14, 28, 36, and 52 in Luke 1.

MSS 1474 and 2649 add readings 28 and 36 in Luke 1, lack 15 and the secondary readings in Luke 10, and lack 50, 54, and 57 and add 60 in Luke 20.

MSS 1569 and 2455 add readings 9, 23, 28, and 37 in Luke 1, lack 15, 18, and 23 and add 16 and 62 in Luke 10, and lack 35, 55, and 57 and add 43 and 70 in Luke 20.

MSS 1671 and 2112 add readings 9, 36, and 53 in Luke 1, and lack 35 and add 42 in Luke 20.

# 4. THE M GROUPS

Among the Iota groups von Soden distinguished $I^{\varphi r}$ as a distinct entity.[9] His discovery has been confirmed by the Profile Method, although there is much more diversity than he indicated. The three subgroups von Soden identified are clearly visible in Luke[10] and they correspond to Cl M10 and M1386 and Gr M27 presented below. A significant number of members unknown to von Soden or classified differently by him could be added to these subgroups. The uncial M (021) for which the groups and clusters have been named is a divergent member of M27, and certainly not the archetype of the M groups. In addition to von Soden's three subgroups a total of nine other groups or clusters could be distinguished. Only Grs M27 and M106 have been entered among the group profiles in Appendix II, since they are the two largest subgroups and their profiles suffice for a preliminary identification of group members. The M groups and clusters are named after the leading member. The reason for the diversity among the M groups is most likely the "gravitational pull" of the $K^x$ text which was dominant during the early Middle Ages. Such a cluster as M1402 stands very close to $K^x$ and could also have been treated as a $K^x$ subgroup. The M groups formed with the $\Pi$ groups the main challenge to the $K^x$ text from the ninth to the twelfth century. Their origin and textual history before the ninth century is unclear but deserves further study. There is an obvious relationship between the M and $\Pi$ groups.

The group profiles of M27 are:

Luke  1:  6, 9, 22, 23, 34, 36, 37, 53.

Luke 10:  9, 10, 12, 15, 25, 35, 37, 41, 43, 57, 60.

Luke 20:  (2), 9, 18, 19, 22, (28), 33, 40, 42, 43, 50, 53, 60, 61, 62, 65, 68, 70, 73, 74.

The pair 569-1170 stands close to M27; it has the following profile:

Luke  1:  5, 6, 8, 9, 16, (22), 23, 33, 34, 36, 37.

Luke 10:  9, 10, 12, 15, 22, 25, 35, 41, 43, 57, 60, 62.

Luke 20:  = M27.

A little more distant stands the pair 750-1222; it has the following profile:

Luke  1:  4, 5, 6, 9, (22), 23, (28), 34, 36, 37.

Luke 10:  3, 15, (18), 35, 41, 43, 57.

Luke 20:  1, 9, 18, 22, 40, 42, 43, 50, 53, 62, 65, 68, 70, 73, 74.

Also related to M27 is the pair 1626-2705, though this is not visible in Luke 1; it has the following profile:

Luke  1:  6, 8, 16, 20, 28, 33, 34.

Luke 10:  9, 10, 12, 15, 19 (εισελθητε), 41, 57, 63.

Luke 20:  18, 19, 21, 22, 28, 31 (τους γεωργους τουτους] αυτους), 42, 43, 53, 60, 61, 62, 65, 68, 70, 73, 74.

The following MSS, including the three pairs, are members of M27 in at least part of Luke: M (021), 27, 71, 248 (Luke 20), 447 (Luke 10 and 20), 518 (Luke 10 and 20), 569, 692, 750, 830 (Luke 10), 1014 (Luke 10 and 20), 1032 (Luke 1), 1170, 1222, 1228 (Luke 20), 1413, 1415, 1458, 1626, 1663 (Luke 10 and 20), and 2705.

---

[9] *Die Schriften* I/2, 1142-47.
[10] Ibid., I/2, 1142.

Cl M10, consisting of MSS 10, 895, 1091, 1194, and 2676, is related to M27. It is equivalent to von Soden's first subgroup of I$^{φr}$ and it has the following profile:

Luke  1: 6, 9, 21, 23, 24 (ιδουσα] ακουσασα), 28, 34, 36, 37, 53.

Luke 10: 4, 9, 10, 12, 15, 19 (εισελθητε), 41, 57, 60, 62.

Luke 20: 2, 18, 19, 21, 22, 28, 31 (τους γεωργους τουτους] αυτους), 40, 42, 43, 54, 57 (δε] ουν), 60, 61, 62, 65, 68, 70, 73, 74.

Cl M350, consisting of MSS 350, 1484, and 2121, is related to M27 in Luke 20; it has the following profile:

Luke  1: 6, 8, 22, 34, 36.

Luke 10: 11, 15, (21), 22, 23, 57, 58, 64.

Luke 20: = M27.

Cl M609, consisting of MSS 609, 1047, 1220, 2098 (Luke 1), and 2661, is related to M27; it has the following profile:

Luke  1: 4, 6, 17, 34, 36, 37, (53).

Luke 10: 1, 3, 8, 9, 10, 15, (19), (22), (25), (35), (37), (47), 57, (62), 63.

Luke 20: 9, 18, 19, 28, 33, 42, 50, 60, 61, 62, 64, (65), 70, 73, 74, 76.

Cl M1386, which is equivalent to von Soden's second subgroup of I$^{φr}$, stand very close to M10 in Luke 1 and 10. It has the following profile:

Luke  1: 6, 9, (21), 23, 28, 34, 36, 37.

Luke 10: 4, 9, 10, 12, 15, 41, 57, 60, 62.

Luke 20: 2, 6 (λεγοντες] omit), (8), (12), 13, 19, 26, 30, (42), 43, 60, 62, 68, 70, 73.

This cluster consists of MSS 498, 947, 1024, 1202, 1237, 1386, 1504 (Luke 20), and 2467.

Gr M106 and the six clusters related to it were not recognized by von Soden as belonging to I$^{φr}$. He classified most of the MSS involved as K$^x$. M106 and its allies possess, however, some clear characteristics of the M groups in Luke 10 and 20, though they stand closer to K$^x$ and M27 and the clusters and the pairs associated with it. Gr M106 consists of MSS 106, 188, 552 (Luke 10), 776, 1315, 1356, 1455, 1491 (Luke 1 and 10), 1563 (Luke 10 and 20), 2394, 2567, 2590, and 2613. Among these MSS 1315 and 2590 form a pair. The group profiles of M106 are:

Luke  1: 9, 23, 27, 28, 34, 36.

Luke 10: 3, 9, 15, 18, 25, 37, 57, 62.

Luke 20: 33, 42, 43, 54, 61, 62, 73, 74.

Cl M159, consisting of MSS 159, 443, and 1557 (Luke 1 and 10), is related to Gr M106. It has the following profile:

Luke  1: 6, 9, 23, 27, 28, 33, 34.

Luke 10: 1, 15, 18, 22, 23, 25, 50, 57, 60.

Luke 20: 4, 33, 42, 43, 58, 61, 62, 73, 74.

Cl M349, consisting of MSS 191 (Luke 10 and 20), 349, 410, 414, 1208, 1466, 1630, 2141 (Luke 10 and 20), 2290, and 2388, is related to Gr M106. MSS 349 and 2388 form a pair. The cluster has the following profile:

Luke  1: 6, 9, 23, 28, 34.

Luke 10: (3), 9, 15, (19), 22, 23, 31, 57, 62.

Luke 20: 4, 42, 43, 54, 57, 61, 62, 65, 73, 74, 75.

Cl M651, consisting of MSS 651, 1549, and 2146, is related to Gr M106. It has the following profile:

Luke  1: 9, 23, 27, 28, 34, 36, 37.
Luke 10: 9, 15, 22, 23, 31, 57, 62.
Luke 20: 43, 62, 65.

Cl M1195, consisting of MSS 293, 1195, 1589, 2145 (Luke 1 and 10), 2200 (Luke 1), and 2549 (Luke 1 and 20), is related to Gr M106. It has the following profile:
Luke  1: (9), 23, 27, 28, (29), 31, 34, (52).
Luke 10: 3, 15, 18, 22, 23, 25, 57, 62.
Luke 20: 4, 33, 42, 43, 54, 57, 61, 62, 73, 74, 75.

Cl M1326, consisting of MSS 191 (Luke 1), 444, 1326, 1396, and 2521, is related to Gr M106. It has the following profile (the profile in Luke 10 is uncertain):
Luke  1: 9, 23, 27, 28, 33, 34, 36, 37, (43).
Luke 10: 3, 15, 18, 19, 22, 23, 24, 47, 62, 63.
Luke 20: 4, 33, 42, 43, 54, 61, 62, 65, 73, (74), 75.

Cl M1402, consisting of MSS 1058, 1204, 1402, and 2315, is related to Gr M106. The cluster stands close to $K^x$ in Luke 10 and 20; it has the following profile:
Luke  1: 9, 23, 27, 28, 34, 36, 37.
Luke 10: 15, 18, 22, 23, 57, 60.
Luke 20: 4, 13, 54, 55, 62, 65.


## 5. GROUP Λ

The group was first identified and described by von Soden; he called it $I^r$.[11] He considered it the most diluted form of the Iota text-type, being made up of about nine parts Kappa to one part Iota.[12] He distinguished between a main branch and two side branches which have been weakened toward $K^x$. These subgroups are not confirmed by the Profile Method. The group profile in Luke 1 is very unstable and for some MSS hard to distinguish from $K^x$ Cl Ω. The secondary readings listed have the support of only three or four MSS and would normally not qualify; they are listed to indicate the tolerance in Luke 1. There is a unique reading in Luke 1:28 (αυτην] + ευηγγελισατο αυτην και), but it is read by only half of the members (MSS Λ, 164, 199, 262, 899, 1187, 1555, and 2586) and was not used as a test reading. Classification should be on the basis of Luke 10 and 20. The group can be described best as falling between Gr 1216 and $K^x$. As von Soden concluded, it is not an important group and appears to be of little significance for the reconstruction of the original text of the NT. Its interest is mainly in the light it sheds on the early history of $K^x$. The early date of some of its members, especially MS Λ, places the origin of the group in or before the ninth century and thus contemporaneous with $K^x$ Cl Ω. The group could be represented adequately in a critical apparatus by the uncial Λ and MS 199, which stays close to the group profile.
The group profiles of Λ are:
Luke  1: 6, 8, (9), 22, (28), (29), 34, (36), (41).
Luke 10: 3, 15, 18, 23, 33, 35, 44, 57.
Luke 20: 4, 13, 17, 19, 32, 35, 39, 54, 55, 57, 62.

---

[11]*Die Schriften* I/2, 1170-80, 1238-42.
[12]He speaks of 9% and 1% (1171), but he must mean parts.

The following 23 MSS are members of Gr $\Lambda$ in at least a part of Luke: 039 ($\Lambda$), 161, 164, 166, 173 (Luke 20), 174, 199, 211, 230, 262, 709, 710 (Luke 20), 899, 1187, 1205, 1301 (Luke 20), 1502 (Luke 20), 1555, 1573 (Luke 10 and 20), 2465, 2585 (Luke 1 and 20), 2586, and 2725 (Luke 20).

## 6. THE $\Pi$ GROUPS

The $\Pi$ groups are the third largest family of MSS among the minuscules. They are traditionally named for the uncial $\Pi$, one of the leading members of the group. Von Soden made a detailed study of this group, and he called it $K^a$ in his introductory volumes and $I^\kappa$ in the apparatus to his text.[13] Kirsopp and Silva Lake changed to the name Family $\Pi$, which was also adopted by Jacob Geerlings.[14] In addition to 041 ($\Pi$), also the uncials 02 (A), 017 (K), and 034 (Y) belong to the $\Pi$ groups. Silva Lake argued that the fifth-century uncial 02 (A) is not a member of the group but a descendant of a lost ancestor. According to its profile it is clearly related to Gr $\Pi^a$, though it is an unusual member. It does not look like a direct ancestor of 017 and 041. Von Soden distinguished three subgroups, $I^{\kappa a}$, $I^{\kappa b}$, $I^{\kappa c}$, which show some correspondence to some of the main $\Pi$ groups and clusters established by the Profile Method. As with the M groups, $K^x$ has had a major influence on the members of the $\Pi$ groups. Block mixture with $K^x$ is frequent and many members have been weakened toward $K^x$. Since the characteristics of the group are very distinct, even weak members could be identified.

The main $\Pi$ group, called $\Pi^a$, involves 65 MSS and has the following profile:
Luke  1: 1, 4, (8), 12, 14, 30, (33) 34, 41, 44, (52).
Luke 10: 1, 8, 15, 22, 23, 30, 32, 37, 38, 47, 48, 53, 57, 63.
Luke 20: 2, 4, 8, 9, 19, 23, 24, 26, 28, 33, 34, 50, 61, 62, 64, 65, 70, 74, 75.

The following MSS belong to Gr $\Pi^a$ in at least a part of Luke: 02 (A), 017 (K), 041 ($\Pi$), 49 (Luke 20), 72 (Luke 1), 114, 145 (Luke 1 and 10), 158 (Luke 20), 175, 178 (Luke 1 and 10), 182 (Luke 10 and 20), 229 (Luke 1), 264 (Luke 10), 265, 270 (Luke 10 and 20), 280, 389, 391 (Luke 10 and 20), 415 (Luke 20), 481 (Luke 1), 482 (Luke 10 and 20), 489, 518 (Luke 1), 537 (Luke 1 and beginning of 10), 544 (Luke 1), 581, 652 (Luke 1), 657 (Luke 10), 718 (Luke 20), 904 (Luke 1 and 10), 989 (Luke 1 and 10), 992, 1032 (Luke 20), 1048 (last part of Luke 10), 1079, 1138, 1159, 1219, 1272, 1313, 1346, 1354 (Luke 1 and 20), 1355, 1392 (Luke 20), 1398, 1399 (Luke 20), 1546, 1553, 1561, 1663 (Luke 1), 1690, 1699 (Luke 20), 1816, 2238 (Luke 10), 2324, 2398 (Luke 1), 2400, 2404, 2405 (Luke 10 and 20), 2411, 2463, 2517, 2525 (Luke 10), 2615, and 2686 (Luke 20).

Among these $\Pi^a$ members two clusters and three pairs can be distinguished.

---

[13]*Die Schriften* I/2, 850-93, 1160-70; II, xv. The group was discovered by Wilhelm Bousset, "Die Gruppe KΠ(M) in den Evangelien," *Textkritische Studien zum Neuen Testament* (TU 11/4; Leipzig: Hinrichs, 1894).

[14]Kirsopp Lake, "The Ecclesiastical Text," *HTR* 21 (1928) 342; Silva Lake, *Family Π and the Codex Alexandrinus: The Text According to Mark* (SD 5; London: Christophers, 1937); and Jacob Geerlings, *Family Π in Luke* (SD 22; Salt Lake City: University of Utah, 1962).

Π$^a$ Cl 178, consisting of MSS 178, 391, 989, and 2525 (Luke 10 and 20), adds reading 25 in Luke 10 and has a K$^x$ profile in Luke 20.

Π$^a$ Cl 1272, consisting of MSS 1159, 1272, 1699 (Luke 20), and 2463, has the following profile:

Luke  1: 4, 9, 28, 33, 34, 36, 41, 44.

Luke 20: 2, 4, 8, 9, 19, 23, (24), 26, 28, 35, 39, (48), 50, 61, 62, 64, 65, 70, 74.

MSS 489 and 1219 add reading 47 in Luke 1.

MSS 581 and 2404 add reading 33 and lack 14 and 52 in Luke 1.

MSS 1138 and 1553 have the following profile:

Luke  1: 3, 4, 9, 30, 34, 36, 37, 44.

Luke 20: 2, 4, 8, 9, 12, 19, 23, 24, 26, 35, 50, 61, 62, 64, 65, 70, 74.

Gr Π$^b$ stands much closer to K$^x$ than Π$^a$. It could be represented in a critical apparatus by MS 2478. The group has the following profile:

Luke  1: 3, 4, 30, 34, 36, 41.

Luke 10: 15, 22, 23, 47, 48, 57, 62, 63.

Luke 20: 4, 9, 19, 24, 26, 43, 49 (επηρωτησαν] omit), 50, 61, 62, 64, 65, 70, 75.

The following 35 MSS belong to Gr Π$^b$ in at least a part of Luke: 11 (Luke 1), 29 (corr), 68, 220, 270 (Luke 1), 365, 415 (Luke 1), 557, 582 (Luke 20), 679, 706, 726, 760 (Luke 20), 931, 969 (Luke 10 and 20), 1056, 1113, 1200, 1273 (Luke 10), 1292 (Luke 1), 1318 (Luke 1), 1319, 1375, 1420 (?), 1434 (Luke 1), 1463, 1578 (Luke 20), 1683, 2238 (Luke 1 and 20), 2278, 2478, 2492, 2624, 2725 (Luke 1), and 2756.

Eight clusters are related to Gr Π$^b$. They are:

Cl Π6, consisting of MSS 6, 515 (Luke 20), and 1310, stands close to Cl Π473. It has the following profile:

Luke  1: 4, 34, 36, (37).

Luke 10: 1, 8, 15, 22, 23, 25, 30, 47, 48, 53, (55), 57, 60, (62), 63, 64.

Luke 20: 4, 8, 9, 13, 19, 24, 26, 28, 34, 61, 62.

Cl Π171 consists of MSS 034 (Y), 171, 192, 228 (Luke 1 and 10), 236, 388, 1196, 1233, 1447 (Luke 10 and 20), 1468 (Luke 10 and 20), 1469, 1515 (Luke 10 and 20), 1581 (Luke 10 and 20), 1605, 2430 (Luke 10), 2584, 2614 (Luke 10 and 20), and 2730. Cl Π171 has the following profile:

Luke  1: 4, 6, 12, (21), 34.

Luke 10: 1, 8, 15, 23, 48, 53, (55), 57, 60, 62.

Luke 20: (4), 13, 35, 43 (after επιγραφην), 50, 54, 62, 65, 70 or: 4, 13, 19, 35, 50, 54, 55, 62, 65, 70.

Among the members of Cl Π171, MSS 388 and 2584 form a pair; they share the following profile:

Luke  1: 4, 6, 30, 34, 36.

Luke 20: 4, 13, 35, 50, 54, 55, 62, 65, 70.

Cl Π200, consisting of MSS 200, 536 (Luke 10), 582 (Luke 1), 1324, and 2098 (Luke 10 and 20), has the following profile:

Luke  1: 4, 6, 23, 28, 33, 34.

Luke 10: 1, 8, 15, 22, 23, 48, 57, 60, 62, 63.

Luke 20: 4, 9, 19, 31, 43, 61, 62, 65, 70.

Cl Π266, consisting of MSS 266, 593, and 1144, has the following profile (the profile in Luke 10 is uncertain):

Luke  1: 4, 6, 12, 28, 30, 34.
Luke 10: 1, 4, 22, 23, 37, 48, 57.
Luke 20: 4, 13, 19, 50, 54, 65, 70, 76.

      Cl Π268, consisting of MSS 268, 527 (corr), 787, 1223 (Luke 20), 1478, 2280, and 2685, has the following profile:
Luke  1: 4, 22, 30, 34, 36, 41, 48.
Luke 10: 1, 9, 15, 22, (23), (25), 47, 48, 53, 57, 63.
Luke 20: 4, 8, 9, 19, 24, 26, 28, 30, 33, 43, 61, 62, 64, 65, 70, (75).
Among the members of Cl Π268, MSS 268 and 787 form a pair which adds reading 44 in Luke 1.

      Cl Π278, consisting of MSS 278, 1209, and 1510 (Luke 10 and 20), has the following profile:
Luke  1: 4, 6, 22, (33), 34.
Luke 10: 15, 18, 23, 25, 53, 57.
Luke 20: 4, 9, 13, 19, 35, 43, 50, 53, 57, 60, 62, 65, 70.

      Cl Π473, consisting of MSS 113 (Luke 10 and 20), 133, 292 (Luke 10 and 20), 473, 515 (Luke 1 and 10), 580 (Luke 20), 944, 965, 1007, 1094, 1207, 2127, and 2371, has the following profile:
Luke  1: 4, (6), 22, 33, 34, 36.
Luke 10: 1, 8, 22, 23, 25, 48, (53), 57, 60, 63.
Luke 20: 4, 19, 24, 35, 43, 61, 62, 64, 65, 70.
Among the members of Cl Π473, MSS 965 and 1007 form a pair which lacks reading 6 and adds 48 in Luke 1, and lacks 35 in Luke 20. A second pair is formed by MSS 944 and 1207 which lacks reading 22 and 36 in Luke 1, adds 15 and 30 in Luke 10, and adds 8 and 9 and lacks 35 in Luke 20.

      Cl Π1441 consists of MSS 23 (Luke 1 and 20), 295, 1085 (Luke 10 and 20), 1223 (Luke 1 and 10), and 1441, which were all classified as I$^{φc}$ by von Soden. It has the following profile:
Luke  1: 4, (9), (23), 34, 36, (37 εις τον αιωνα] omit), 41, 43.
Luke 10: 1, 9, 15, 22, 23, 25, 53, 57, 62, 63.
Luke 20: 4, 8, 9, 19, 24, 26, 33, 35-37 omit, 43, 61, 62, 64, 65, 70.

## 7. GROUP 1

The basic outline of this group was established by Kirsopp Lake in 1902. He identified MSS 1, 118, 131, 205, and 209 as members.[15] According to Lake, Gr 1 together with Gr 13 and several other MSS attest to the existence of a "Caesarean" text-type. Because of its significant divergence from the Byzantine text, Gr 1 is normally represented, under siglum, in the critical apparatus of modern editions of the Greek NT.

      Von Soden called Lake's Gr 1 "H$^r$" in the first volumes of *Die Schriften des Neuen Testaments*.[16] He added MSS 205$^{abs}$, 1582, and 2193 to the members

[15]*Codex 1 of the Gospels and Its Allies* (TextsS 7/3; Cambridge: University Press, 1902).

[16]I/2, 1042-66. He changed to the designation I$^η$ in Volume II, xiv and divided the group into I$^{ηa}$ (MSS 1, 1582, and 2193) and I$^{ηb}$ (MSS 118, 205, and 209). The results of the Profile Method in Luke do not support his grouping of MSS 22, 872, 1192, 1210, and 1365 with 118, 205, and 209 in I$^{ηb}$ (see Gr 22a and b).

discovered by Lake. Since 205[abs] is evidently a copy of 205 it can be ignored. MS 205 is closely related to 209, though not a copy of it as Lake thought. MS 2193 has been lost since von Soden consulted it and could not be profiled.

In the process of profiling Paul McReynolds discovered that MS 884 is a member of Gr 1 in Luke 20 and I identified MS 2542 as a member in Luke 10 and 20. Thus the group has now ten members if 205[abs] and the lost 2193 are included.

The division von Soden made in Gr 1 is only supported by the profiles in Luke 1. The group profile of MSS 1, 131, and 1582 in Luke 1 are:[17]
9, 11, 17, 20, (22), 23, 24, 25, 26, 28, 29, 32, (34), 36, 37, 40, 43, (47), 48, 50, 51, 53.
The group profile of MSS 118, 205, and 209 in Luke 1 are:
9, 28, 34, 36, 40, 43, 53.
The group profiles in Luke 10 and 20 for all group members are:
Luke 10: 2, 5, 6, 7, 11, 13, 15, 20, 22, (23), 27, (29), 34, 37, 40, 44, 45, 46, 49, 50, 51, 52, 54, 55, 56, 58, 59, 62.
Luke 20: 1, 5, 6, (7), 10, 11, 14, 19, 20, 25, 27, 28, 29, 31, 33, 41, 43, 44, 45, 48, 51, 56, 58, 59, 60, 61, 62, 63, 64, 66, 67, 68, 69, 72, 75, 76.

The following ten MSS are members of Gr 1 in at least part of Luke: 1, 118, 131, 205, 205[abs] (not profiled), 209, 884 (Luke 20), 1582, 2193 (on the basis of von Soden), and 2542 (Luke 10 and 20). The range of Gr 1 could be represented adequately by MSS 1 and 209.

## 8. GROUP 13

Four members of this group (MSS 13, 69, 124, and 346) were discovered as early as 1868 by William Hugh Ferrar, though the results of his studies were not published until nine years later, after his death.[18] They have been called the Ferrar group or Family 13 after one of its leading members. They are normally represented under a siglum in critical apparatus to the Greek NT. Von Soden added nine MSS to the four discovered by Ferrar and divided them into three branches which he called I[ta] (MSS 983 and 1689), I[tb] (MSS 69, 124, 174, and 788), and I[tc] (MSS 13, 230, 346, 543, 826, 828, 837). Of these thirteen MSS 837 does not contain Luke, 1689 is lost, and 174 and 230 proved not to belong to Gr 13 in Luke but to Gr Λ. The profiles do not support von Soden's subdivisions. On the basis of the apparatus to von Soden's text of Luke 1, MS 1689 is at best only a very weak member of the group. Kirsopp and Silva Lake studied the text of Gr 13 in Mark[19] and Jacob Geerlings in the other three Gospels.[20] MS 983 is a weak member in Luke 1, and 124 is weak in Luke 1 and very weak in Luke 10 and 20. Either MS 543 or 826 could represent the whole group in a

---

[17]According to the apparatus to von Soden's text MS 2193 reads with these three MSS in Luke 1.

[18]*Four Important Manuscripts of the Gospels* by the late William Hugh Ferrar, ed. T. K. Abbott (Dublin: Hodges, Foster and Figgis, 1877).

[19]*Family 13 (The Ferrar Group): The Text According to Mark* (SD 11; Philadelphia: University of Pennsylvania Press, 1941).

[20]*Family 13 in Matthew, Luke, and John* (SD 19, 20, 21; Salt Lake City: University of Utah Press, 1961-62). A basic weakness in Geerlings's method can be seen in that he mistakenly assumed that MSS 174 and 230 were members of Gr 13 in Luke. He had no way to control the unity of his group.

critical apparatus or a single siglum could be used. There are some indications to locate the archetype of Gr 13 in southern Italy or Sicily.[21]

The group profiles of 13 are:

Luke 1: 3, 4, 7, 10, 15, (16), 18, 19, 20, 21, 22, 27, 28, 32, 33, 35, 36, 37, 38, 39, 42, 46, 47, 48, 49, 50, 51.

Reading 34 can be expected to be found in surplus.

Luke 10: 1, 3, 4, 7, 12, 13, 14, 15, 16, 17, 18, 20, 21, 22, 23, 24, 25, 26, 28, 31, 36, (37), 42, 57, 58, 63.

Luke 20: 3, 13, 15, 16, 33, 37, 38, 42, 43, 45, 46, 47, 49, 50, 57, 61, 62, 71, 73, 76, 78.

The following ten MSS are members of Gr 13 in Luke: 13, 69, 124, 346, 543, 788, 826, 828, 983, and 1689 (on the basis of von Soden).

## 9. GROUP 16

This group consists mainly of MSS classified by von Soden as the weak branch of $I^\beta$. However, the group is not simply a weakened form of Gr 1216, though it stands closer to $K^x$. If there is a relationship between Grs 16 and 1216 in Luke, it is a rather distant one. The group can be represented adequately by MS 16. Gr 16 has the following profile:

Luke 1: 8, (9), 13, 23, 28, 34, 37, 43.

Luke 10: 3, 7, 15, 19, 23, (25), 58, 63.

Luke 20: 4, 13, 19, 50, 51, 54, 55, 62, 65.

The following nine MSS belong to Gr 16 in at least a part of Luke: 16, 119, 217, 330, 491, 578 (Luke 1 and 10), 693, 1528, and 1588. Among these MSS 16 and 1528 form a pair which adds reading 3 and lacks 9 in Luke 1, and lacks 19 and adds 64 in Luke 10. A second pair is formed by MSS 217 and 578 in Luke 1 and 10. They lack readings 13 and 23 and add 48 in Luke 1, and lack 25 in Luke 20.

## 10. GROUP 22a AND 22b

The relationship between most of the members of the present Gr 22 was discovered by von Soden, though he obscured the identity of the group by associating it too closely with some of the members of Gr 1.[22] At least in Luke Gr 22 is quite distinct from Gr 1. Beginning with Lake, MS 22 has been considered an important witness to the "Caesarean" text, together with Grs 1 and 13, and MSS 038 (Θ), 28, 565, and 700.[23]

Two branches can be distinguished in Gr 22. The largest, 22a, consists of nine MSS, and 22b has six members. The Cl 585 and the pairs 165-176, 401-1013,

[21]Cf. Robert Devreesse, *Les Manuscrits grecs de l'Italie meridionale (histoire, classement, paléographie* (Studi e Testi 183; Vatican City, 1955).

[22]*Die Schriften* I/2, 1043-47 and 1242-45.

[23]See Kirsopp Lake, Robert P. Blake, and Silva New, "The Caesarean Text of the Gospel of Mark," *HTR* 21 (1928) 208. These conclusions were already foreshadowed in Lake's *Codex 1 of the Gospels and Its Allies* published in 1902. These relationships as well as the hypothetical Caesarean text seem less compelling today, and the matter should be reevaluated in the light of the results of the Profile Method.

and 1604-2546 seem to be related to Gr 22.[24] The two branches could be represented in a critical apparatus by MSS 22 and 697.

The group profiles of 22a are:

Luke 1: 9, 11, 23, 26, 27, 28, 29, 34, (43).

Luke 10: 3, 15, 18, 22, 25, 29, 45, 57, 62.

Luke 20: 4, (7), 13, 36, 43, 48, 54 (+ απεθανον), 56, 60, 62, 65, 73, 74.

The following MSS are members of Gr 22a in at least part of Luke: 660, 697, 791, 924, 1005, 1278, 1365, 2372, and 2670 (Luke 10 and 20).

The group profiles of 22b are:

Luke 1: 6, 11, 23, (24), 26, 28, 29, 34, 40, 43, (48), (51), (52), 53.

Luke 10: 3, 15, 18, 22, 25, 29, (31), (37), 44, (45), 57.

Luke 20: 4, 7, 13, 19, 36, 43, 48, 54, 55, 60, 62, 64, 65.

The following MSS are members of Gr 22b in at least part of Luke: 22, 134, 149, 351 (Luke 20), 1192, and 1210.

## 11. GROUP 291

This new group shows some relationship to the Π groups. Of the members only MS 449 was classified I[k] by von Soden.

The group profiles of 291 are:

Luke 1: 4, 6, (8), 14, (22), 34, (36).

Luke 10: 15, 18, 23, 25, 53, 57, (62), 63.

Luke 20: 13, 19, 26, 50, 60, 62, 66, 70.

The following ten MSS are members of Gr 291 in Luke: 139, 291, 371, 449, 597, 1235, 1340, 2346, 2603, and 2728. Among the members MSS 449 and 2603 form a pair which lacks readings 8 and 22 and adds 23 and 28 in Luke 1, and adds 23, 29 (και ημων γενηται), and 73 in Luke 20.

## 12. GROUP 1167

This new group stands out from K[x] mainly in Luke 20. Six of its members were classified A[k] by von Soden. The group profiles of 1176 are:

Luke 1: 6, 23, 34, (52).

Luke 10: 15, 18, (36 ο Ιησους] omit), 57, 62.

Luke 20: 4, 13, 19, 21, (41), 43, 50, 53, 54, 55, (60), 61, 62, 65, (74).

The following 22 MSS belong to Gr 1167 in at least a part of Luke: 75, 116 (Luke 20), 225 (Luke 10 and 20), 245 (Luke 10 and 20), 431, 496, 546, 578 (Luke 20), 843, 896, 951, 1015, 1167, 1242 (Luke 20), 1438, 1473, 1479 (Luke 20), 1511 (Luke 20), 1570, 2095 (Luke 20), 2229, and 2604. Among these MSS 546, 1015, and 1438 form a small cluster which lacks readings 13 and 65 and adds 9 in Luke 1. MSS 75 and 2229 (corr) form a pair which adds reading 28 in Luke 1, and lacks 13, 19, 54, and the secondary readings in Luke 20.

---

[24]See below, § 15 "Clusters and Pairs."

## 13. GROUP 1216

The group was identified and described by von Soden; he called it $I^\beta$.[25] The present Gr 1216 involves only a part of the MSS which von Soden classified as $I^\beta$. Some others form Gr 16, which is only distantly related to Gr 1216. A third group of $I^\beta$ members proved to be a subgroup of $K^x$.[26] They show no relationship to Grs 1216 and 16 in Luke. E. C. Colwell confirmed von Soden's $I^\beta$ in an independent study.[27] Gr 1216 is very distinct and stands at considerable distance from $K^x$. It can be represented adequately by MS 1216. The group profiles of Gr 1216 are:

Luke 1: (8), 9, 13, 16, 17, 22, 24, 25, 26, (33), 34, 36, 37, 42, 43, (52).

Luke 10: 3, 15, 18, 25, 33, 35, 37, 39, 58, 61, (62), 63, 64.

Luke 20: 4, 12, 13, 19, 32, 35, 39, 50, 51, 54, 55, (62), 65, 77.

The following 15 MSS belong to Gr 1216 in at least a part of Luke: 152, 184, 348, 477, 513 (Luke 10 and 20), 555, 752, 829, 977, 1216, 1243, 1279, 1579, 2174, and 2726. Among these MSS 152 and 555 form a pair which lacks readings 8 and 42 in Luke 1, and lacks 39, 50, and 54 and adds 33 and 73 in Luke 20. A second pair is formed by MSS 477 and 2174 which is very weak (close to $K^x$) in Luke 1, lacks readings 18, 37, 39, 61, and 64 and adds 48 and 60 in Luke 10, and lacks 39 and adds 60 in Luke 20. A third pair is formed by MSS 1243 and 1579, which lacks readings 33 and 42 and adds 52 in Luke 1.

Chapter IV, Table 2, presents the profiles of the members of Gr 1216 in Luke 1.


## 14. GROUP 1519

This new group stands close to $K^x$ in Luke 1 and 10. Many of its members belong to other groups in these two chapters. Eight Gr 1519 members were classified as $A^k$ by von Soden. The group has the following profile:

Luke 1: 4, 6, 22, 34, 53.

Luke 10: 3, 15, 18, 55, 57, 58 (ουν] omit).

Luke 20: 1, 4, 13, 30, 35, 42, 43, 50, 55, 58, 65.

The following 19 MSS belong to Gr 1519 in at least a part of Luke: 5 (Luke 20), 32, 269, 558 (Luke 20), 844 (Luke 20), 871, 1036, 1110 (Luke 20), 1211 (Luke 20), 1309 (Luke 20), 1321, 1416 (Luke 20), 1481 (Luke 20), 1519, 1566, 2126, 2132 (Luke 20), 2277 (Luke 20), and 2437. Among these MSS 32 and 269 form a pair which skips reading 22, lacks 53 and adds 40 in Luke 1, adds 16 and 35 in Luke 10, and lacks 13 in Luke 20; they stand close to $K^x$ Cl 43 in Luke 1 and 10. Another pair is formed by MSS 1309 and 2132, which adds readings 9 and 33 and lacks 53 in Luke 1, lacks 18, 55, and 58 and adds 60 in Luke 10, and lacks 58 and adds 2 and 54 in Luke 20. Both MSS 1110 and 2277 belong to $K^x$ Cl 2592 in Luke 1 and 10.

---

[25]*Die Schriften* I/2, 1147-60.
[26]See $K^x$ Cl 17.
[27]*The Four Gospels of Karahissar, I* (Chicago: University of Chicago, 1936) 170-77.

# 15. CLUSTERS AND PAIRS

Twenty-two non-K$^x$ clusters and fourteen non-K$^x$ pairs have been identified. They will be presented with their profiles.

Cl 7, consisting of MSS 7, 267, 1651, and 1654, stands close to K$^x$ in Luke 1 and 10, but it is quite distinct in Luke 20. It has the following profile:

Luke 1: 6, 9, 28, 34.

Luke 10: 3, 15, 18, 23, 57.

Luke 20: 4, 13, 21, 24, 35, 42, 48, 54, 55, 57, 61, 62, 65, 68.

Cl 121, consisting of MSS 64, 121, 533, 662, 663, 1060, 1297, 1642 (Luke 10 and 20), and 1665, has the following profile:

Luke 1: 6, 8, 33, 34, 36, 37, 40, 42.

Luke 10: 1, 15, 18, 22, 23, 55, 57, 62.

Luke 20: 4, 8, 13, 19, 35, 62, 73.

Cl 127, consisting of MSS 78, 127, 132, 1052, 1448, 1513, and 2530, stands close to K$^x$ in Luke 1 and 20, but it is quite distinct in Luke 10. There appears to be some relationship to the M groups. The cluster has the following profile:

Luke 1: 6, 9, 22, 34, 36, 37.

Luke 10: 3, 7, 9 (ως αρνας] omit), 10, 12, 15, 18, 23, 25, 57, 60, 62, 63.

Luke 20: 4, 13, (19), 24, 35, 54, 55.

Cl 163, consisting of MSS 163, 345, 1646, and 1695, has the following profile:

Luke 1: (2), (8), 28, 29, 34, 52, (53).

Luke 10: 15, 18, 22, 23, 25, 57, 58, (60), (62), 64.

Luke 20: 11, 19, 33, 50, 54, 57, 61, 62, 68, 74.

Cl 190, consisting of MSS 190, 2472, 2695, and 2724 (Luke 1 and 10), is closely related to Gr 1519 in Luke 20. It has the following profile:

Luke 1: 4, 6, (21), (22 omit), (23), 33, 34, 36, (37), 40.

Luke 10: (11), 15, 16, 18, 57.

Luke 20: 1, 2, 4, 30, 35, 42, 43, 50, 55, 58, 63, 65.

Cl 276, consisting of MSS 276, 506, 1011, 1057, 1666, 2328, 2622, 2687, 2688, and 2751, has the following profile:

Luke 1: 4, 6, 22, 34, (37), 53.

Luke 10: 1, 3, 15, 18, 19, 25, 57, (62), 63.

Luke 20: 1, (9), 13, 19, 26, 30, 35, (43), (50), 58, 60, 65, 70.

The cluster is closely related to Gr 1519. Among the members MSS 1011, 1057, and 2328 bear some special relationship; they lack readings 1 and 19 in Luke 1, and are the only members to read 9 and 50 in Luke 20. Also MSS 1666, 2688, and 2751 form a special cluster in that they are the only ones to read 43 and lack 19 and 65 in Luke 20.

Cl 343, consisting of MSS 343, 494, and 716, is not coherent in Luke 20. It has the following profile:

Luke 1: 6, 22, 34, 36, 42.

Luke 10: 2, 3, 11, 15, 18, 22, 23, 25, 35, 37, 48, 58, 63.

Cl 475, consisting of MSS 475, 2609, and 2373, is not coherent in Luke 1, though in the range of Gr K$^x$. There appears to be some relationship to the M groups. It has the following profile:

Luke 10: 2, 15, 18, 23, 35, 44, 48, 57, 60.

110

Luke 20: 13, 19, 21, 27, 28, 33, 37, 42, 43, 44, 45, 50, 51, 55, 57, 62, 65, 76, 78.

Cl 490, consisting of MSS 395, 470, 490, 839, 926, 980, 1486, and 2321, stand close to Gr K$^x$ in Luke 1 and 20. It has the following profile:

Luke   1: (4), 6, (23), 34, (47).

Luke 10: 1, 15, 18, 22, 23, 57, 60, 62.

Luke 20: 4, 19, 28, 35, 42, 43, 50, 55, 58, 61, 62, 65, 70.

Among the members MSS 839 and 1456 form a pair which lacks reading 23 in Luke 1 and 62 in Luke 10.

Cl 585, consisting of MSS 331, 545, 574 (Luke 20), 585, and 2375, appears to be related to Gr 22. It has the following profile:

Luke   1: 6, 9, 28, 34, 36, 43, 45.

Luke 10: 3, 15, 22, 23, (25), 57, 63.

Luke 20: 4, 19, 36, 43, 48, 61, 62.

Cl 686, consisting of MSS 686, 716 (Luke 20), 748, 1198 (Luke 1 and 10), and 2693 (Luke 1), has the following profile:

Luke   1: 8 (γεννεσει), 23, 28, 34, 36, 41, (43).

Luke 10: 15, 18, 35, 57.

Luke 20: 13, 19, 33, 39, 43, 50, 60, 62, 65, 73.

The cluster bears some relationship to Gr Λ; three of the members were classified as I$^r$ (= Gr Λ) by von Soden.

Cl 827, consisting of MSS 827, 1050, 1446, 1457, 1593, and 2766 (Luke 10 and 20), appears to be related to the M groups. It has the following profile:

Luke   1: (4), 5, (6), 9, 28, 33, 34, (36), 37, 53.

Luke 10: 15, 19, 48, 51, 55, 57, 58, 62.

Luke 20: 1, (9), 21, 33, 42, 43, 48, 55, 65, 74.

Cl 1001, consisting of MSS 782, 1001, and 2397, has the following profile:

Luke   1: 6, 8, 11, 34, 43, 52, 53.

Luke 10: 3, (11), 15, 18, 22, 23, 25, (54), 57, 63.

Luke 20: 4, 13, 19, 35, 54, 55, 74.

Cl 1012, consisting of MSS 968, 1012, 1451, 2096, and 2528, stands far removed from Gr K$^x$. It has the following profile:

Luke   1: 4, 27, 33, 34, 36, 39, 42, 48, (52), (53).

Luke 10: 9, 12, 15, 18, 22, 23, 31, (45), 46, 48, 51, (54), 57, 58, 60, 62.

Luke 20: 1, 4, 8, 10, (12), 13, 19, 23, 33, 43, 46, 57, 61, 62, 72, 75, 76.

Cl 1173, consisting of MSS 1173, 1385, and 1169 (Luke 1), was discovered by Kirsopp Lake (Lake, Blake, and New, 346). Silva New made a special study of the cluster ("A Patmos Family of Gospel Manuscripts," *HTR* 25 [1932] 85-92). MS 1169 belongs to another Patmos cluster, K$^x$ Cl 1176, in Luke 10 and 20. Cl 1173 has the following profile:

Luke   1: 6, 9, 33, 34, 35 (omit), 36, 37, 42.

Luke 10: 15, 23, 24 (omit), 50, 57, 60, 62, 63.

Luke 20: 4, 13, 19, 54, 55, 62, 65, 74.

Cl 1229, consisting of MSS 251, 1229, and 2487, has the following profile:

Luke   1: 6, 34, 36, 42, 53.

Luke 10: 3, 11, 15, 18, 22, 25, 35, 48, 58.

Luke 20: 4, 19, 33, 42, 51 (αποθανη] omit), 61, 74.

Cl 1252, consisting of MSS 1252, 1327 (Luke 20), 1533, and 2459, has the following profile:

Luke 1: 6, 10, 33, 34, 36, 37.
Luke 10: 11, 15, 18, 28, 46, 57, 60, 62.
Luke 20: 4, 8, 13, (35), 45-46 omit, 49, 55, 57, 62, 64.

Cl 1442, consisting of MSS 511 (Luke 10 and 20), 987, 999, 1442, and 1450, has the following profile:
Luke 1: 4, 6, 9, 16, 28, 34, 36.
Luke 10: 15, 18, 19, (50), 57.
Luke 20: 13, 19, 35, 50, 55, 60, 61, 64, 65, 76.

Cl 1531, consisting of MSS 185, 1531, 2291, 2387, and 2771, has the following profile:
Luke 1: 4, 5, 6, 9, (16), 34, 37.
Luke 10: 3, 18, 22, 23, 35, 57.
Luke 20: 1, 4, 19, 21, 28, 50, 54 (ομοιως), 55, 57, 59, 60, 62, 65.

Cl 1675, consisting of MSS 517, 954, 1349 (Luke 1), 1424, and 1675, corresponds to von Soden's Iφa (*Die Schriften* I/2, 1109). B. H. Streeter called it Family 1424 (*The Four Gospels: A Study of Origins* [London: Macmillan, 1924] 84) which is related to Family Θ, his name for the "Caesarean" text. Though 1424 is the oldest and best known member of the cluster, it is rather divergent. The cluster has the following profile:
Luke 1: 2, 3, 5, 6, 10, 14, 23, 25, 26, 28, 29, 31, 32, 33, 34, 37, 45, 53, 54.
Luke 10: 3, 15, 16, 18, 22, 26, 28, 37, 42, 48, 51, 54, 57, 58, 62, 64.
Luke 20: 4, 8, 13, 19, 35, 50, 54, 55, 60, 62, 65, 66.

Cl 1685, consisting of MSS 60, 1454, and 1685, is closely related to Cl 7 and Kˣ Cl 1084. It has the following profile:
Luke 1: 6, 9, 16, 28, 33, 34.
Luke 10: 15, 18, 23, 50, 57, 62.
Luke 20: 13, 21, 24, 35, 42, 48, 54, 55, 57, 65, 68, 74.

Cl 2148, consisting of MSS 854 (Luke 1 and 10), 856, 2148, and 2713 (Luke 10 and 20), has the following profile:
Luke 1: 6, 9, 28, 33, 34, 36, 37.
Luke 10: 15, 18, 24, 28 (κρισει] ημερα εκεινη), 36, 47, 57, 60, 62.
Luke 20: 13, 23, 31, 35, 49, 57, 64, 74.

MSS 145 and 2680 are coherent only in Luke 20.
Luke 20: (4), (30), 36, 42, 43, 48, 50, 54, (55), (57), 60, 61, 62, (64), 65, 66, 73, 75.

MSS 165 and 176 are related to Gr 22.
Luke 1: 3, 21, 25, 26, 28, 29, 34, 43, 48, 53 omit.
Luke 10: 15, 18, (23), (44), 57.
Luke 20: 4, 13, 35, 42, 43, 48, 50, 55, 57, (60), 61, 62, 65, (66), (68), (75).

MSS 282 and 1714 are coherent only in Luke 1.
Luke 1: 4, 6, 9, 22, 28, 33, 34, 36, 37.

MSS 401 and 1013 are not coherent in Luke 1.
Luke 10: 1, 15, 18, 22, (25), 57, (62).
Luke 20: 4, 19, 33, 36, 43, 48, 50, 55, 60, 62, 65.

MSS 472 and 1009 have the following profile:
Luke 1: 4, 9, 18, 19, (22), 34, 36, 37, 53.
Luke 10: 3, 9, 15, (19), 22, (34), (44), (47), 62, 63.
Luke 20: 4, 8, 11, 19, 28, 30, 33, 38, 39, 40, 42, 60, 61, 62, 74, 76, 78.

MSS 792 and 2643 have the following profile:

Luke  1:  2, 4, 5, 9, 14-15 omit, 23, 28, 34, 36, 37, (42), 53.

Luke 10:  3, 4, (7), 15, (18), 19, 21, (51), (55), 57, 58 omit, 62.

Luke 20:  8, 13, 19, 25, 31, 32, 39, 42, 45 omit, (57), (60), 61, 62, (65), 73, (76), 77, (78).

MSS 848 and 1255 have the following profile:

Luke  1:  (3), (6), 9, 16, 33, 34, 36, 37, 45, 51.

Luke 10:  15, 18, (23), 24 omit, 25, 57, 60, (62).

Luke 20:  4, 8, 13, 35, (50), 55, 57, (62).

MSS 860 and 2108 have the following profile:

Luke  1:  4, 9, 16, 27, (31), 34, 36, 37.

Luke 10:  3, (9), 18, 19, 57, 60, 62.

Luke 20:  13, 19, 35, 50, 59-60 omit, 62, 64.

MSS 974 and 1006 have the following profile:

Luke  1:  6, 8, 9, 11, 22, 34, 53.

Luke 10:  3, 7, 15, 18, 22, 23, 25, 57, 60, 62, 63.

Luke 20:  4, 13, 19, 35, 43, 55.

MSS 996 and 1661 have the following profile:

Luke  1:  4 omit, 6, 9, 21, 28, 34, 36, (43).

Luke 10:  3, 4, 9, 15, 18, 41, (55), 57, 62, 63.

Luke 20:  13, 19, 36, 39, (50), 55, 57, 60, 61, 62, 74, 77.

MSS 1061 and 2747 have the following profile:

Luke  1:  3, 4, 6, 9, (11), (28), 33, 34, 36, 37, 42, (45), (48).

Luke 10:  18, 23, 37, 57, (58), 60, (63).

Luke 20:  4, 9, 13, 19, (31 omit), 35, (48), (54), 55, 57, 60, 62, (74).

MSS 1282 and 1443 are related to MS 164 especially in Luke 10; they have the following profile:

Luke  1:  4, 6, 9, 22, 28, 29, (33), 34, 37.

Luke 10:  15, 18, (25), 33, (35), 49, 57.

Luke 20:  4, 13, 19, 35, (39), 43, 45, 54, 55, 57.

MSS 1604 and 2546 are not coherent in Luke 1.

Luke 10:  3, (9), 23, 31, 42, (55), 57, (62), 63.

Luke 20:  36, 43, 48, 55, 61, 62, (63), 77.

The pair is related to Gr 22.

MSS 2522 and 2561 have the following profile:

Luke  1:  1-6 missing, 9, 27, 28, 33, 34, 41.

Luke 10:  3, 18, (22), 23, 34, (35), 49, 57, 60, 62.

Luke 20:  1, 4, 19, 21, 24, 28, 42, 48, 50, 54 (ομοιως), 55, 57, 59, 60, 62, 64, 65, 73, 74, 77.

## 16. MANUSCRIPTS WITH A MIXED TEXT

In addition to the non-K$^x$ pairs listed in the previous section there are some 89 MSS with a mixed text in at least a part of Luke. Only of 31 significant ones, i.e. those which are classified "Mix" in more than one chapter in Luke or which stand at a great distance from K$^x$, will the profiles be presented. The standard for a "Mix" classification is seven test readings divergence from K$^x$. Since K$^x$ members tend to have a relatively large number of non-K$^x$ readings in surplus in Luke 1, more than seven readings divergence is necessary in that chapter for a MS to be significantly mixed.

MS 04 (C) has the following profile:

Luke 1: 4, 5, 6 (corr), 8, 9, 22, 23, 28 (corr), 29, 32, 33, 34 (corr), 36, 37, 39, 41, 43, 47, 48, 52, 53.

Luke 10: 3, 7, 13, 15, 18, 20, 22, 23, 57, 58, 63 (corr).

Luke 20: 12, 21, 25, 29, 33, 43, 47, 48.

MS 032 (W) has the following profile in Luke 20:

Luke 20: 4, 10, 13, 28, 33, 36, 42, 44, 50, 61, 62, 63, 65, 73.

MS 033 (X) has the following profile:

Luke 1: 2, 4, 6, 19, 24, 25, 26, 28.

Luke 10: 3, 13, 15, 17, 22, 23, 36, 43, 46, 51, 57, 58, 59-65 Def.

MS 038 (Θ) has the following profile:

Luke 1: 4, 6, 8, 10, 19, 27, 28, 29, 32, 33, 34, 41, 53.

Luke 10: 1, 3, 5, 7, 15, 18, 19, 21, 22, 26, 31, 36, 45, 57, 63.

Luke 20: 13, 21, 33, 42, 44, 48, 50, 54, 60, 61, 62, 65, 72, 75, 78.

MS 044 (Ψ) has the following profile in Luke 10 and 20:

Luke 10: 3, 15, 18, 22, 23, 28, 52, 56, 57, 64.

Luke 20: 1, 13, 19, 25, 28, 36, 51, 55, 60, 76, 77.

MS 79 has the following profile in Luke 10 and 20:

Luke 10: 8 omit, 10 (μηδε), 15, 18, 22, 23, 28, 37, 43, 47, 48, 60, 62.

Luke 20: 14, 23, 26, 37, 48 (απαρνεομαι), 50, 60, 62, 65.

MS 157 has the following profile in Luke 10:

Luke 10: 3, 7, 15, 19, 20, 22, 23, 26, 48, 51, 52, 57, 58, 59, 60, 62, 64.

MS 168 has the following profile in Luke 1 and 10:

Luke 1: 1, 3, 4, 5, 6, 10, 16, 28, 29, 33, 34, 36, 37, 42, 53.

Luke 10: 10-12 omit, 15, 18, 21, 22, 23, 33, 35, 57, 58, 64-68 illeg.

MS 173 has the following profile in Luke 1 and 10:

Luke 1: 3, 4, 6, 16, 22, 34, 36, 37, 42.

Luke 10: 3, 7, 9, 10-29 illeg, 35, 39, 48, 51, 55, 57 (πλησιον] omit), 58, 61, 63.

MS 213 has the following profile:

Luke 1: 18, 19, 27, 28, 33, 34, 36, 37, 39, 43.

Luke 10: 3, 13, 15, 22, 43, 46, 50, 51, 57, 58, 62, 63.

Luke 20: 1, 13, 14, 17, 19, 36, 38, 43, 45, 48, 50, 51, 55, 60, 64, 65, 74, 76, 77, 78.

MS 372 has the following profile:

Luke 1: 11, 20, 29, 41.

Luke 10: 37, 44, 45, 46, 51, 52, 56, 62.

Luke 20: 38, 44, 48, 51, 55.

MS 377 has the following profile:

Luke 1: 4, 5, 6, 9, 19 omit, 28, 29, 35, 36, 40, 53.

Luke 10: 1, 3, 15, 18, 22, 23, 57, 60, 62, 63.

Luke 20: 8, 13, 33, 38, 42, 51, 57, 61, 62, 64, 74.

MS 382 has the following profile:

Luke 1: 1, 2, 9, 22, 33, 34 omit, 36, 37, 48, 53.

Luke 10: 11, 13, 15, 18, 19, 21, 22, 23, 25, 33, 36, 57, 58, 64.

Luke 20: 11, 13, 19, 23, 28, 33, 54, 61, 62, 63, 74.

MS 700 has the following profile in Luke 1:
Luke  1: 4, 6, 10, 20, 23, 28, 36, 37, 48.
     MS 713 has the following profile:
Luke  1: 4, 6, 8, 9, 28, 33, 34, 36, 41, 49, 52.
Luke 10: 1, 3, 5, 15, 18, 22, 48, 57, 59, 60.
Luke 20: 1, 11, 28, 33, 36, 42, 50, 51, 61, 62, 65, 72, 74.
     MS 851 has the following profile:
Luke  1: 4, 5, 6, 17, 34, 36, 37, 48, 53.
Luke 10: 3, 9, 18, 21, 22, 23, 35, 57, 62.
Luke 20: 4, 13, 19, 21, 28, 42, 48, 50, 54 (ομοιως), 55, 57, 59, 60, 62, 65.
     MS 903 has the following profile:
Luke  1: 4, 9, 27, 28, 30-31 omit, 34, 36, 37, 48.
Luke 10: 1 (corr), 3, 15, 19, 21, 24, 50, 51, 59, 62, 63.
Luke 20: 1, 4, 33, 43, 61, 62, 74.
     MS 1048 has the following profile in Luke 1 and 20:
Luke  1: 1, 4, 9, 12, 17, 23, 34, 37, 42.
Luke 20: 1, 9, 11, 13, 26, 30, 35, 50, 58, 60, 65, 70.
     MS 1071 has the following profile:
Luke  1: 2, 4, 5, 6, 10, 28, 32, 33, 34, 36, 37, 43, 47, 48, 53.
Luke 10: 3, 5, 7, 11, 13, 15, 18, 19, 22, 23, 26, 29, 36, 43, 48, 51, 57, 64.
Luke 20: 8, 13 (corr), 23, 27, 42, 43, 45, 48, 49, 50, 51, 60, 61, 62, 65, 72, 76, 78.
     MS 1087 has the following profile in Luke 10 and 20:
Luke 10: 3, 15, 18, 19, 23, 24, 35, 44, 57, 62.
Luke 20: 1, 6, 12, 13, 19, 24, 25, 26, 27, 32, 38, 45, 49, 50, 51, 55, 56, 59, 60, 62, 65.
     MS 1093 has the following profile:
Luke  1: 2, 16, 21, 33, 34, 36, 37, 42.
Luke 10: 11, 15, 18, 22, 23, 25, 28, 34, 48, 55, 57, 58.
Luke 20: 6 omit, 11, 13, 54 (ομοιως), 57-58 omit, 61, 62, 64, 71.
     MS 1230 has the following profile:
Luke  1: 2, 5, 9, 28, 29, 34, 36, 52, 53.
Luke 10: 15, 18, 22, 23, 28, 31, 58, 64.
Luke 20: 11, 19, 43, 48, 50, 54, 57, 60, 61, 62, 65, 72, 74, 78.
     MS 1253 has the following profile:
Luke  1: 2, 3, 4, 5, 9, 21, 28, 29, 34, 36, 37, 41, 42, 43, 52.
Luke 10: 15, 18, 19-20 omit, 28, 50, 58, 59, 62.
Luke 20: 11, 12, 13, 19, 43, 48, 50, 57, 60, 61, 62, 65, 68, 72.
     MS 1325 has the following profile:
Luke  1: 9, 11, 31, 36, 37.
Luke 10: 37, 50.
Luke 20: 13, 19, 30, 55, 62.
     MS 1337 has the following profile:
Luke  1: 3, 4, 6, 9, 28, 33, 34, 36, 40, 41, 43.
Luke 10: 15, 18, 19, 22, 46-48 omit, 55, 57, 62.
Luke 20: 2, 4, 13, 32, 35, 39, 49, 50, 55, 57, 60, 61, 62, 63, 64.
     MS 1342 has the following profile in Luke 1:

115

Luke 1: 4, 9, 14, 23, 28, 33, 34, 36, 37, 53.
    MS 1574 has the following profile:
Luke 1: 1, 6, 9, 27, 28, 31, 34, 36, 37, 40, 43, 52 omit.
Luke 10: 3, 15, 18, 21, 24, 25, 36, 48, 55, 57, 58, 62, 63.
Luke 20: 4, 9, 12, 13, 19, 21, 35, 54, 55, 60, 64, 65, 68.
    MS 1647 has the following profile:
Luke 1: 4, 6, 9, 23, 27, 28, 34, 36, 37, 51, 53.
Luke 10: 15, 18, 22, 24, 28, 42, 48, 57, 60, 62.
Luke 20: 4, 8, 13, 35, 55.
    MS 1692 has the following profile:
Luke 1: 3, 4, 6, 21, 33, 34, 36, 37, 39, 42, 53.
Luke 10: 15, 24, 25, 38-39 missing, 48, 51, 57, 62.
Luke 20: 4, 13, 31, 36, 50, 60, 62, 65, 76.
    MS 2533 has the following profile in Luke 1 and 10:
Luke 1: 3, 9, 11, 16, 23, 28, 33, 34, 36, 37, 53.
Luke 10: 15, 23, 25, 34, 37, 44, 47, 57, 62.
    Luke 2542 has the following profile in Luke 1:
Luke 1: 1, 5, 6, 9, 16, 19, 20-21 omit, 28, 34, 36, 37, 51.

# CHAPTER VII

# THE APPLICATION OF THE PROFILE METHOD TO OTHER TEXTS

In this volume the Profile Method has been applied to MSS of the Gospel of Luke. Nothing in the method, however, limits its application to this Gospel or, for that matter, to biblical texts. It can be applied with profit to any ancient text with a large MS attestation. My experiences with the Gospel of Luke are here incorporated in a set of general guidelines. Reference will be made to the work of W. L. Richards who, in a recent study, applied the Profile Method to the Johannine Epistles.[1]

## 1. WHEN SHOULD THE PROFILE METHOD BE USED?

The Profile Method is basically a classification tool. Classification of MSS in terms of groups is necessary to reconstruct the history of the transmission of a text and to select representatives when the total number of witnesses is too large to be included in a critical apparatus. If fewer than one hundred MSS of a text are extant or available it may be feasible to collate all in full and to consult and cite them. In such a case there is little need for the Profile Method. When there exist several hundred witnesses to a text, however, the work involved to assemble the data becomes so enormous and the results so hard to interpret, that a classification tool is needed.

## 2. THE TEST PASSAGES

In the Profile Method a text is normally not analyzed in full but in test passages. A bona fide group will show its identity already in a relatively short selection of text. This allows for a major reduction of effort and time, and it gives results which are much more easily analyzed. To select the test chapters or passages the following practical considerations should be kept in mind.

a. The number of test passages chosen depends on the length of the document. A short text such as the Letter of Paul to Philemon would be analyzed in its entirety. For a medium-sized text such as I Corinthians two test passages suffice, one taken near the beginning and one near the end. The first and last chapters are best avoided since they have the greatest chance of being defective. In the case of a relatively long text, such as the Gospel of Luke, it is best to select three passages, for the following reasons.[2] First, a text can be classified even if a major section is

---

[1]*The Classification of the Greek Manuscripts of the Johannine Epistles* (SBLDS 35; Missoula: Scholars, 1977).

[2]Some texts, such as the Catholic Epistles, have been transmitted as a unit and can be treated as one text.

lost. Second, a change of group affiliation within a text, called block mixture, can be spotted. Third, it is useful to have the classification on the basis of one test passage confirmed by another.

b. It is advisable to choose test passages of which the beginning can be located easily in the MS. Some ancient texts include marginal equipment which can help the reader to find certain passages. Other texts are divided into books or chapters. Since these do not always coincide with modern divisions it is best to consult several MSS to find convenient places to begin the test passages. The time spent searching for the test passages in a MS is wasted and a source of frustration.

c. It is difficult to specify the length of a test passage. The point is that the passage should include enough test readings to show clear profiles. The number of test readings in a passage cannot be predicted. In Luke 20 there are two-and-a-half times as many test readings per line of printed text as in Luke 1. If a passage proves to have fewer than fifty meaningful test readings it is probably too short, and more than seventy makes it unnecessarily long.

## 3. THE TEST READINGS

The crucial and most difficult step is the selection of test readings. First of all a significant number of MSS should be collated in the test passages. Richards used 81 MSS of the 600 known to contain the Johannine Epistles. It is not advisable to use fewer than 100 MSS for the selection of test readings. The more MSS one uses the easier it is to select meaningful test readings.[3] The collating can be done against any readily available text. The advantages of using the TR for the NT have been stated above,[4] but there are no strong arguments against using a modern critical edition. There is a significant reduction of work if variants depending on orthographic or stylistic preference such as abbreviations, all types of itacisms, *nu*-movables, and ουτω-ουτως are ignored already in the initial collation of the test passages.[5]

After all the variants with their MS support have been collected, those which are likely nongenetic need to be eliminated. A reading which has been incorrectly eliminated will hardly be missed if the test passage is long enough, but if variants due to scribal habit or accident are selected as test readings they will clutter the profile and make classification more difficult. Obviously the single readings and those supported by only a few MSS can be removed. Most of these are nonsense readings and other scribal errors, but even if a few of them do show relationship among MSS they are only relevant to pairs, small clusters, or subgroups and not needed for classification.[6] This will result in a major reduction of variants.

Any further reduction becomes more difficult. In the case of the Gospel of Luke use was made of previous group studies. A number of MS groups had been known for some time and had been studied by a number of scholars. When the

---

[3]One should try to include all those which have been identified in previous studies as significant witnesses. In addition there should be a considerable number chosen at random.

[4]Chapter IV, 37-38.

[5]Richards took the trouble of testing the value of these variants. He proved the obvious by showing that they have no value for group classification (*Classification,* 33-41). Cf. E. J. Epp, ''Toward the Clarification of the Term 'Textual Variant,''' *Studies in New Testament Language and Text* (George D. Kilpatrick Festschrift) [ed. W. J. Elliott; Leiden: Brill, 1976] 153-73.

[6]Pairs and subgroups are generally so close-knit that they are easy to identify.

majority of the members of one or more groups would read a variant in a test passage against one or more other groups it could be assumed that this variant was of value for showing relationships among MSS. On the other hand, variants which had scattered minority support of members of several groups were likely nongenetic and could be eliminated. This is the surest way of selecting meaningful test readings, but it can be used only if a significant number of groups have already been identified in the MS tradition.

Richards has criticized this use of previous group studies and had tried an alternative.[7] He started with about 1600 variants in the Johannine Epistles found in 80 MSS which were fully collated.[8] The choice of MSS had not been at random for he made an effort to include at least three members of the eleven groups discovered by von Soden in the MS tradition of the Catholic Epistles. Only twenty of the MSS he used had not been classified previously. Thus Richards's study is also not completely independent from previous group studies, and it is none the worse for it. Of the 1600 variants more than one thousand were singular and thus eliminated. The remaining 587 variants were divided into 209 nonquestionable and 378 questionable ones. The latter category included *nu*-movables, itacisms, interchange of pronouns, and stylistic patterns. They were eliminated after a laborious and largely superfluous process of testing their value to show group relationships. The 209 nonquestionable units of variation could have served as test readings for establishing the profiles of MSS and groups. However, Richards had understood the purpose and principle of the Profile Method only imperfectly and instead turned first to statistical analysis.

The results of this statistical analysis, which fills most of Richards's book, are mainly negative. They are instructive in that they show how little help the computer is in showing relationships among MSS. Richards became aware of the problem, but one wonders why he burdened his readers with many pages of tables which he admits were of little or no use in establishing his groups.[9] How he finally made his tentative groupings on the basis of statistical analysis remains unclear. He could have moved with his 209 nonquestionable units of variation directly to the application of the Profile Method. Even though these nonquestionable readings may include a considerable number of nongenetic readings, they would have formed an adequate grid to project and compare the profiles of MSS and groups. With only 81 MSS to compare, it would have been relatively easy to identify the groups. The large effort which was now spent on statistical analysis could have been directed to the profiling and classification of the 520 MSS of the Johannine Epistles that remain to be studied.

In those cases in which there are no previous group studies to guide the selection of test readings, it would be advisable to analyze the variants from a textual-critical viewpoint. An experienced textual critic will be able to spot those

---

[7]His criticism is based on a misunderstanding of the function of test readings (see above, Chapter IV, 36. The kind of use of predetermined groups that he shows to be deficient ("A Critique of a New Testament Text-Critical Methodology — The Claremont Profile Method," *JBL* 96 [1977] 562-66) bears no relationship to the Profile Method as developed and applied by me. Richards adopted the standard of at least 66% agreement with the group profile for group membership that McReynolds and I entertained at one point but abandoned as unnecessary and misleading. It goes against the principle of the Profile Method to use percentages for group requirements.

[8]Richards counts one MS twice since it was corrected extensively.

[9]*Classification,* 56 and 69.

due to stylistic convention, influence of parallels and lectionaries, and others which depend more likely on the scribe than on his model. After these have been eliminated the selection of test readings is complete.

## 4. THE PROFILES

The next step is to assign numbers to the test readings and to collate as many MSS as possible in the test readings. The profiles are formed by the numbers of the test readings which the MS supports against the collation base. The profiles are best entered in duplicate on file cards, one set to be kept in the numerical order of the MSS and the other to be filed according to the groups which emerge. Each file card should list the MS number, the date, and the previous classification, if available, in addition to the profile in numbers for each test passage. The profile can also be drawn graphically for easy comparison. With about two hundred readings to collate in the three test chapters of Luke, an experienced person can profile a MS within half an hour. Not just the profiles of the MSS used for the selection of the test readings should be collected but ideally the profiles of all existing witnesses.

## 5. THE CLASSIFICATION

By comparing the profiles of the MSS in the test passages patterns of readings will emerge. MSS which have a high degree of agreement in their profile form a group. By noting the test readings in which about two-thirds of the members agree the primary group readings are determined. Those readings shared by about one-third to two-thirds of the members are secondary group readings. Thus a group profile emerges. The group profiles of all the groups should be compared to see whether they are sufficiently distinct to warrant their separation. At this point it will become clear which test readings are useless for group classification. If desired they can be eliminated to achieve less cluttered profiles.

The next step is the classification of the MSS which did not fall readily into a group during the first search. Many of these will prove to be weak group members which can be classified when studied in terms of all the group profiles. A residue of nonconformist MSS will remain that can be classified as mixed. This is a lengthy and complicated process since one must become familiar with the typical features of each group.

## 6. THE SELECTION OF REPRESENTATIVES

The classification of MSS is no end in itself but the basic step to the representation of the whole MS tradition in a comprehensible critical apparatus. A group can be represented by means of a siglum which stands for the majority reading of the group members or by a core member of the group, i.e. a MS which conforms closely to the group profile. In case of considerable divergence within a group or the existence of subgroups it may be useful to select several group members to represent the whole range. It would be a mistake to select more members than is necessary for representation in the case of groups which have traditionally been considered important. Of course, large groups do not deserve fuller representation than small ones. A textual apparatus should be balanced and neutral.

The greatest difficulty lies in the selection of the nonconformist or mixed MSS. In the case of the Gospel of Luke there are probably too many to include all of them in a critical apparatus. If a selection needs to be made it should not be on the basis of the divergence from the collation base but in terms of their divergence from the group profiles. Those which do not stand too far removed from one or more of the groups could be eliminated. Sometimes one group is so dominant, e.g. $K^x$ in the Gospels, that significant mixture can be measured in terms of the divergence from that group. The selection of each witness needs to be justified and explained in the introduction to the critical edition. This makes it possible for the reader to judge the value of the support of each MS for a variant.

# APPENDIX I

# THE TEST READINGS IN
# LUKE 1, 10, AND 20

For convenience the readings have been keyed to the UBS edition of *The Greek New Testament* rather than the TR, i.e. the word before the bracket is the reading of the UBS edition. The profile of a MS is formed by noting the numbers of those test readings where the MS agrees with the bold reading. The readings which are not bold are those of the TR.

*Luke 1:*

| READING NO. | VERSE NO. | | |
|---|---|---|---|
| 1. | 2 | παρεδοσαν ] | **παρεδωκαν** |
| 2. | 7 | **ην η ελισαβετ** ] | η ελισαβετ ην |
| 3. | 7 | η ] | omit |
| 4. | 8 | εναντι ] | **εναντιον** |
| 5. | 9 | κυριου ] | **θεου** |
| 6. | 10 | **ην του λαου** ] | του λαου ην |
| 7. | 14 | επι ] | **εν** |
| 8. | 14 | **γενεσει** ] | γεννησει |
| 9. | 15 | του ] | omit |
| 10. | 15 | κυριου ] | **θεου** |
| 11. | 16 | επι ] | **προς** |
| 12. | 17 | ετοιμασαι ] | + **τω** |
| 13. | 21 | εθαυμαζον ] | **εθαυμαζεν** |
| 14. | 22 | **εδυνατο** ] | ηδυνατο |
| 15. | 22 | αυτοις ] | omit |
| 16. | 22 | διεμενε(ν) ] | **διεμεινε** |
| 17. | 23 | επλησθησαν ] | **επληρωθησαν** |
| 18. | 24 | ταυτας τας ημερας ] | **τας ημερας ταυτας** |
| 19. | 25 | επειδεν ] | **εφειδεν** |
| 20. | 26 | **απο** ] | υπο |
| 21. | 26 | του ] | omit |
| 22. | 26 | **Ναζαρεθ** ] | Ναζαρετ |

| READING NO. | VERSE NO. | | |
|---|---|---|---|
| 23. | 27 | οικου ] | + **και πατριας** |
| 24. | 29 | **δε** ] | + **ιδουσα** |
| 25. | 29 | **επι τω λογω διεταραχθη** ] | 4.1.2.3 |
| 26. | 29 | **τω λογω** ] | + αυτου |
| 27. | 30 | ο αγγελος αυτη ] | **αυτη ο αγγελος** |
| 28. | 34 | εσται ] | + **μοι** |
| 29. | 35 | γεννωμενον ] | + **εκ σου** |
| 30. | 39 | αναστασα δε ] | **και αναστασα** |
| 31. | 39 | δε ] | omit |
| 32. | 41 | **τον ασπασμον της μαριας η ελισαβετ** ] | 5.6.1.2.3.4 |
| 33. | 42 | ανεφωνησε(ν) ] | **ανεβοησε(ν)** |
| 34. | 44 | εν αγαλλιασει το βρεφος ] | **το βρεφος εν αγαλλιασει** |
| 35. | 45 | εσται ] | + **η** |
| 36. | 50 | γενεας και γενεας ] | **γενεαν και γενεαν**   TR reads: γενεας γενεων |
| 37. | 55 | εις τον αιωνα ] | **εως αιωνος** |
| 38. | 57 | τη ] | **της** |
| 39. | 59 | **ημερα τη ογδοη** ] | ογδοη ημερα |
| 40. | 61 | οτι ] | omit |
| 41. | 61 | **εκ της συγγενειας** ] | εν τη συγγενεια |

42. 62 **αυτο** ] αυτον

43. 63 εστι(ν) ] **εσται**

44. 65 και εγενετο ] **εγενετο δε**

45. 65 παντα ] omit

46. 66 αυτου ] **αυτων**

47. 67 **επροφητευσε(ν)** ] προεφητευσε

48. 69 **εν** ] + τω

49. 70 **αγιων** ] + των

50. 74 **χειρος** ] + των

51. 74 **εχθρων** ] + ημων

52. 75 **ημεραις** ] + της ζωης

53. 77 αυτων ] **ημων**

54. 80 ισραηλ ] **λαον**

## Luke 10:

1. 1 **δυο δυο** ] δυο

2. 1 αυτου ] **εαυτου**

3. 1 **ημελλεν** ] εμελλεν

4. 1 ερχεσθαι ] **διερχεσθαι**

5. 1 ] **εισερχεσθαι**

6. 2 ελεγεν ] **ειπεν**

7. 2 δε¹ ] ουν

8. 2 οπως ] + **αν**

9. 3 αρνας ] **προβατα**

10. 4 μη² ] **μητε**

11. 4 **μη³** ] μηδε

12. 4 ] **μητε**

13. 5 **εισελθητε** ] εισερχησθε

14. 5 ειρηνη ] + **εν**

15. 6 **εαν** ] + μεν

16. 6 εφ ] **προς**

17. 7 οικιας ] **οικιαν**

18. 8 **ην** ] + δ·

19. 8 εισερχησθε ] **εισερχεσθε**

20. 10 **εισελθητε** ] εισερχησθε

21. 11 ημιν ] **υμιν**

22. 11 **εις τους ποδας** ] omit

23. 12 **λεγω** ] + δε

24. 12 εν τη ημερα εκεινη ανεκτοτερον εσται ] **5.6.1.2.3.4**

25. 13 Βηθσαιδα ] **Βηθσαιδαν**

26. 13 **εγενηθησαν** ] εγενοντο

27. 14 ανεκτοτερον εσται εν τη κρισει ] **3.4.5.1.2**

28. 14 εν τη κρισει ] **(εν) ημερα κρισεως**

29. 15 **υψωθεισ η** ] υψωθεισα

30. 16 ακουων υμων ] **υμων ακουων**

31. 16 με ] + **και ο ακουων εμου ακουει του αποστειλαντος με**

32. 17 οι εβδομηκοντα μετα χαρας ] **3.4.1.2**

33. 17 εβδομηκοντα ] + **μαθηται**

34. 17 υποτασσεται ημιν ] **ημιν υποτασσεται**

35. 21 αυτη ] + **δε**

36. 21 τω πνευματι τω αγιω ] **ο Ιησους τω πνευματι**
TR reads: τω πνευματι ο Ιησους

37. 22 **παντα** ] και στραφεις προς τους μαθητας ειπε παντα

38. 22 παρεδοθη ] **παρα δεδοται**

39. 22 τις εστιν ο υιος ει μη ο πατηρ ] omit

40. 23 ειπε(ν) ] + **αυτοις**

41. 24 γαρ ] **δε**

42. 26 δε ] + **Ιησους**

43. 28 αυτω ] + **Ιησους**

44. 30 εκδυσαντες ] εξεδυσαν

45. 30 **ημιθανη** ] + τυγχανοντα

46. 32 γενομενος ] omit

47. 32 ελθων ] omit
48. 32 ιδων ] + **αυτον**
49. 33 **ιδων** ] + αυτον
50. 34 αυτον² ] omit
51. 35 **αυριον** ] + εξελθων
52. 35 **ειπεν** ] + αυτω
53. 35 τι ] + **δ'**
54. 35 εγω ] omit
55. 35 με ] **μοι**
56. 36 **τις** ] + ουν

57. 36 **πλησιον δοκει σοι** ] δοκει σοι πλησιον
58. 37 **δε** ] ουν
59. 38 αυτους ] **αυτον**
60. 39 τον λογον ] **των λογων**
61. 39  ] **τους λογους**
62. 40 μελει ] **μελλει**
63. 41 ειπεν αυτη ο κυριος (or Ιησους) ] **3.4.1.2**
64. 42 **γαρ** ] δε

## Luke 20:

1. 1 **ημερων** ] + εκεινων
2. 1 εν τω ιερω ] omit
3. 1 αρχιερεις και οι γραμματεις ] **4.2.3.1**
4. 1 αρχιερεις ] **ιερεις**
5. 2 και ειπαν ] omit TR reads: και ειπον
6. 2 **λεγοντες προς αυτον** ] 2.3.1
7. 2 **ειπον** ] ειπε
8. 3 υμας καγω ] **καγω υμας**
9. 3 ενα λογον (=TR) ] **λογον ενα**
10. 3 ενα ] omit (=UBS edition)
11. 5 συνελογισαντο ] **διελογισαντο**
12. 5 οτι ] omit
13. 5 **δια τι** ] + ουν
14. 6 **ο λαος απας** ] πας ο λαος
15. 6 ειναι ] **γεγονεναι**
16. 7 ειδεναι ] + **το**
17. 7 ποθεν ] omit
18. 8 και ο ] **ο δε**
19. 9 τις ] omit
20. 10 και ] + **τω**
21. 10  ] + **εν τω** (TR reads: και εν)
22. 10 απο του καρπου του αμπελωνος

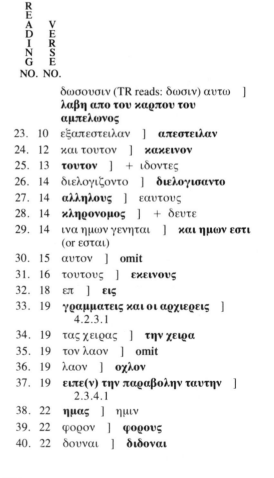

δωσουσιν (TR reads: δωσιν) αυτω ] **λαβη απο του καρπου του αμπελωνος**
23. 10 εξαπεστειλαν ] **απεστειλαν**
24. 12 και τουτον ] **κακεινον**
25. 13 **τουτον** ] + ιδοντες
26. 14 διελογιζοντο ] **διελογισαντο**
27. 14 **αλληλους** ] εαυτους
28. 14 **κληρονομος** ] + δευτε
29. 14 ινα ημων γενηται ] **και ημων εστι** (or εσται)
30. 15 αυτον ] omit
31. 16 τουτους ] **εκεινους**
32. 18 επ ] **εις**
33. 19 **γραμματεις και οι αρχιερεις** ] **4.2.3.1**
34. 19 τας χειρας ] **την χειρα**
35. 19 τον λαον ] omit
36. 19 λαον ] **οχλον**
37. 19 **ειπε(ν) την παραβολην ταυτην** ] **2.3.4.1**
38. 22 **ημας** ] ημιν
39. 22 φορον ] **φορους**
40. 22 δουναι ] **διδοναι**

| 41. | 23 | **αυτους** ] + τι με πειραζετε |
| 42. | 24 | **δειξατε** ] επιδειξατε |
| 43. | 24 | δηναριον ] + **οι δε εδειξαν και ειπε** |
| 44. | 25 | δε¹ ] omit |
| 45. | 25 | **προς αυτους** ] αυτοις |
| 46. | 25 | **τοινυν αποδοτε** ] αποδοτε τοινυν |
| 47. | 25 | Καισαρος ] + **τω** |
| 48. | 27 | αντιλεγοντες ] **λεγοντες** |
| 49. | 27 | επηρωτησαν ] **επηρωτουν** |
| 50. | 28 | **Μωυσης** ] Μωσης |
| 51. | 28 | **η** ] αποθανη |
| 52. | 28 | λαβη ο αδελφος αυτου ] **2.3.4.1** |
| 53. | 29 | ησαν ] + **παρ ημιν** |
| 54. | 31 | ωσαυτως ] + **ως αυτως** |
| 55. | 31 | **επτα** ] + και |
| 56. | 31 | και απεθανον ] omit |
| 57. | 32 | υστερον ] + **παντων** |
| 58. | 32 | ] + **δε** (TR reads: υστερον δε παντων) |
| 59. | 33 | ουν εν τη αναστασει ] **2.3.4.1** (TR reads: 2.3.1.4) |
| 60. | 33 | γινεται ] **εσται** |

| 61. | 34 | γαμισκονται ] **εκγαμιζονται** (TR reads: εκγαμισκονται) |
| 62. | 35 | γαμιζονται ] **εκγαμιζονται** (TR reads: εκγαμισκονται) |
| 63. | 36 | ετι ] omit |
| 64. | 36 | εισι(ν)² ] omit |
| 65. | 37 | **Μωυσης** ] Μωσης |
| 66. | 37 | εμηνυσεν ] **εμνημονευσεν** |
| 67. | 39 | ειπας ] **λεγεις** |
| 68. | 40 | επερωταν ] **επερωτησαι** |
| 69. | 40 | ουδεν ] **ουδε εν** |
| 70. | 41 | λεγουσι(ν) ] + **τινες** |
| 71. | 41 | τον Χριστον ειναι Δαυιδ υιον ] **οι γραμματεις οτι ο Χριστος υιος δαυιδ εστιν** (TR reads: 1.2.5.3.4) |
| 72. | 42 | **αυτος γαρ** ] και αυτος |
| 73. | 42 | βιβλω ] + **των** |
| 74. | 44 | κυριον αυτον ] **αυτον κυριον** |
| 75. | 44 | **αυτου υιος** ] υιος αυτου |
| 76. | 46 | περιπατειν εν στολαις ] **2.3.1** |
| 77. | 47 | κατεσθιουσι ] **κατεσθιοντες** |
| 78. | 47 | προσευχονται ] **προσευχομενοι** |

APPENDIX II

# THE GROUP PROFILES IN
# LUKE 1, 10, AND 20

The group profiles of the sixteen main groups[1] are here presented graphically. The test readings are represented by the numbers at the left; the groups are listed at the top in the same order as in Chapter VI. Primary group readings, which have the support of at least two-thirds of the main group members, are indicated by an "x." Secondary readings, which have the support of about one-third to two-thirds of the group members, are indicated by a dot. An asterisk stands for a special group reading.[2]

A MS can be classified by collating it in the test readings in Luke 1, 10, and 20 (see Appendix I). The resulting profile made up of the numbers of the test readings which the MS supports can be compared with the group profiles. If the profile conforms more or less with one of the group profiles, the group description in Chapter VI should be consulted for confirmation and for possible further classification in terms of a subgroup.[3] If the profile of the MS in question does not conform to one of the group profiles, the sections on the non-K$^x$ clusters and significantly mixed MSS in Chapter VI should be consulted. If this does not lead to classification, the MS should be designated "Mix(ed)" if it has at least seven non-K$^x$ readings in a chapter or "Kmix" if it has five or six non-K$^x$ readings in a chapter.

---

[1]Gr 22$^a$ and 22$^b$ are presented separately though they belong together.
[2]These are specified in Chapter VI.
[3]Ideally the profile should be compared with the profiles of the other group members.

126

# GROUP PROFILES IN LUKE 1

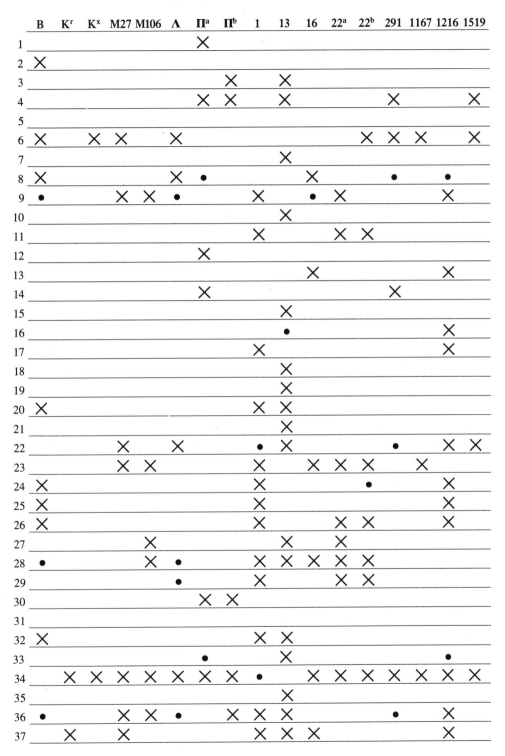

| | B | Kʳ | Kˣ | M27 | M106 | Λ | Πᵃ | Πᵇ | 1 | 13 | 16 | 22ᵃ | 22ᵇ | 291 | 1167 | 1216 | 1519 |
|---|---|---|---|---|---|---|---|---|---|---|---|---|---|---|---|---|---|
| 1 | | | | | | | X | | | | | | | | | | |
| 2 | X | | | | | | | | | | | | | | | | |
| 3 | | | | | | | | X | | X | | | | | | | |
| 4 | | | | | | | X | X | | X | | | | X | | | X |
| 5 | | | | | | | | | | | | | | | | | |
| 6 | X | | X | X | | X | | | | | | | X | X | X | | X |
| 7 | | | | | | | | | | X | | | | | | | |
| 8 | X | | | | | X | • | | | | X | | | • | | • | |
| 9 | • | | X | X | | • | | | X | • | X | | | | | X | |
| 10 | | | | | | | | | | X | | | | | | | |
| 11 | | | | | | | | | X | | | X | X | | | | |
| 12 | | | | | | | X | | | | | | | | | | |
| 13 | | | | | | | | | | | X | | | | | X | |
| 14 | | | | | | | X | | | | | | X | | | | |
| 15 | | | | | | | | | | X | | | | | | | |
| 16 | | | | | | | | | | • | | | | | | X | |
| 17 | | | | | | | | | X | | | | | | | X | |
| 18 | | | | | | | | | | X | | | | | | | |
| 19 | | | | | | | | | | X | | | | | | | |
| 20 | X | | | | | | | | X | X | | | | | | | |
| 21 | | | | | | | | | | X | | | | | | | |
| 22 | | | X | | | X | | | • | X | | | • | | | X | X |
| 23 | | | X | X | | | | | X | | X | X | X | X | | | |
| 24 | X | | | | | | | | X | | | | • | | | X | |
| 25 | X | | | | | | | | X | | | | | | | X | |
| 26 | X | | | | | | | | X | | | X | X | | | X | |
| 27 | | | | | X | | | | | X | | X | | | | | |
| 28 | • | | | | X | • | | | X | X | X | X | X | | | | |
| 29 | | | | | | • | | | X | | | X | X | | | | |
| 30 | | | | | | | X | X | | | | | | | | | |
| 31 | | | | | | | | | | | | | | | | | |
| 32 | X | | | | | | | | X | X | | | | | | | |
| 33 | | | | | | | • | | | X | | | | | | • | |
| 34 | | X | X | X | X | X | X | X | • | | X | X | X | X | X | X | X |
| 35 | | | | | | | | | | X | | | | | | | |
| 36 | • | | X | X | | • | | X | X | X | | | | • | | X | |
| 37 | | X | | X | | | | | X | X | X | | | | | X | |

127

# GROUP PROFILES IN LUKE 1

| | B | Kʳ | Kˣ | M27 | M106 | Λ | Πᵃ | Πᵇ | 1 | 13 | 16 | 22ᵃ | 22ᵇ | 291 | 1167 | 1216 | 1519 |
|---|---|---|---|---|---|---|---|---|---|---|---|---|---|---|---|---|---|
| 38 | | | | | | | | | | X | | | | | | | |
| 39 | X | | | | | | | | | X | | | | | | | |
| 40 | | | | | | | | | X | | | | X | | | | |
| 41 | X | | | | • | X | X | | | | | | | | | | |
| 42 | • | | | | | | | | | X | | | | | | X | |
| 43 | | X | | | | | | | X | | X | • | X | | | X | |
| 44 | | | | | | X | | | | | | | | | | | |
| 45 | | | | | | | | | | | | | | | | | |
| 46 | | | | | | | | | | X | | | | | | | |
| 47 | X | | | | | | | | • | X | | | | | | | |
| 48 | X | | | | | | | | X | X | | | • | | | | |
| 49 | • | | | | | | | | | X | | | | | | | |
| 50 | X | | | | | | | | X | X | | | | | | | |
| 51 | • | | | | | | | | X | X | | | • | | | | |
| 52 | X | | | | | | • | | | | | | • | | • | • | |
| 53 | | | X | | | | | | X | | | | X | | | | X |
| 54 | | | | | | | | | | | | | | | | | |

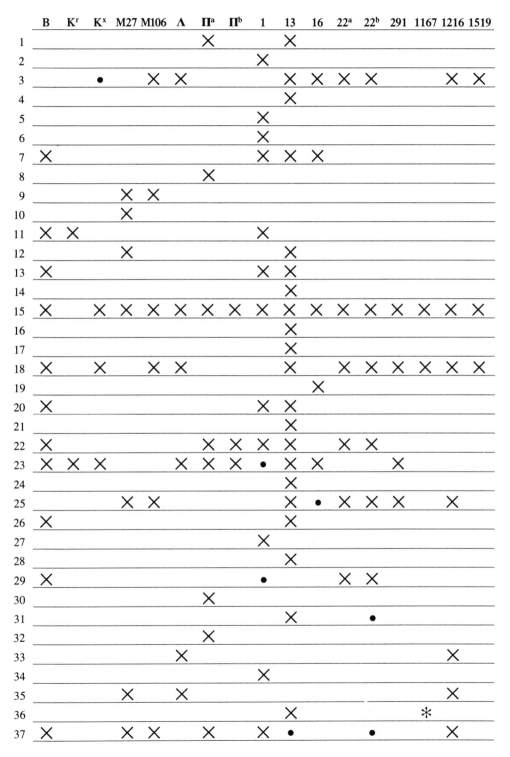

| | B | K$^r$ | K$^x$ | M27 | M106 | Λ | Π$^a$ | Π$^b$ | 1 | 13 | 16 | 22$^a$ | 22$^b$ | 291 | 1167 | 1216 | 1519 |
|---|---|---|---|---|---|---|---|---|---|---|---|---|---|---|---|---|---|
| 1 | | | | | | | X | | | X | | | | | | | |
| 2 | | | | | | | | | X | | | | | | | | |
| 3 | | | • | | X | X | | | | X | X | X | X | | | X | X |
| 4 | | | | | | | | | | X | | | | | | | |
| 5 | | | | | | | | | X | | | | | | | | |
| 6 | | | | | | | | | X | | | | | | | | |
| 7 | X | | | | | | | | X | X | X | | | | | | |
| 8 | | | | | | | X | | | | | | | | | | |
| 9 | | | X | X | | | | | | | | | | | | | |
| 10 | | | X | | | | | | | | | | | | | | |
| 11 | X | X | | | | | | | X | | | | | | | | |
| 12 | | | X | | | | | | | X | | | | | | | |
| 13 | X | | | | | | | | X | X | | | | | | | |
| 14 | | | | | | | | | | X | | | | | | | |
| 15 | X | | X | X | X | X | X | X | X | X | X | X | X | X | X | X | X |
| 16 | | | | | | | | | | X | | | | | | | |
| 17 | | | | | | | | | | X | | | | | | | |
| 18 | X | | X | | X | X | | | | X | | X | X | X | X | X | X |
| 19 | | | | | | | | | | | X | | | | | | |
| 20 | X | | | | | | | | X | X | | | | | | | |
| 21 | | | | | | | | | | X | | | | | | | |
| 22 | X | | | | | X | X | X | X | | X | X | | | | | |
| 23 | X | X | X | | | X | X | X | • | X | X | | | X | | | |
| 24 | | | | | | | | | | X | | | | | | | |
| 25 | | | X | X | | | | | | X | • | X | X | X | | X | |
| 26 | X | | | | | | | | | X | | | | | | | |
| 27 | | | | | | | | | X | | | | | | | | |
| 28 | | | | | | | | | | X | | | | | | | |
| 29 | X | | | | | | | | • | | | X | X | | | | |
| 30 | | | | | | X | | | | | | | | | | | |
| 31 | | | | | | | | | | X | | | • | | | | |
| 32 | | | | | | X | | | | | | | | | | | |
| 33 | | | | | X | | | | | | | | | | | X | |
| 34 | | | | | | | | | X | | | | | | | | |
| 35 | | | X | | X | | | | | | | | | | | X | |
| 36 | | | | | | | | | | X | | | | | ✳ | | |
| 37 | X | | | X | X | | X | | X | • | | | • | | | X | |

# GROUP PROFILES IN LUKE 10

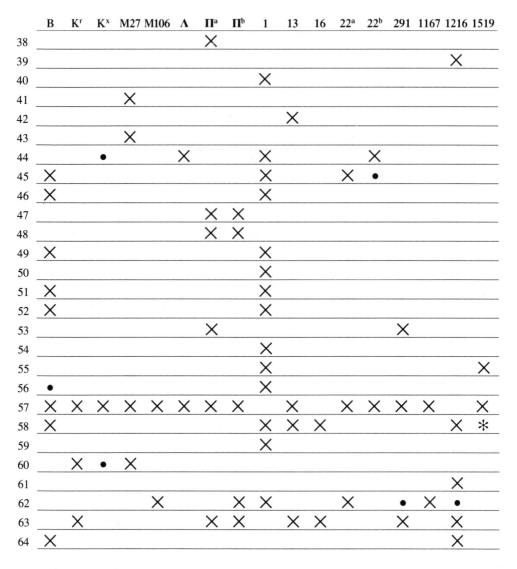

GROUP PROFILES IN LUKE 20

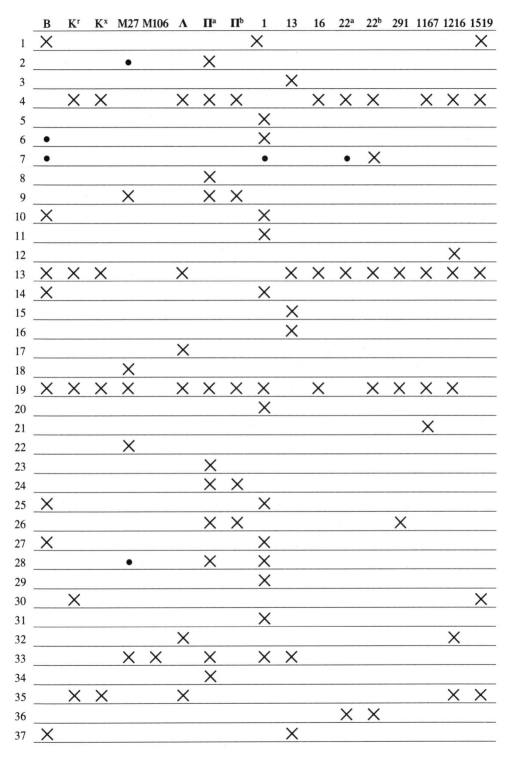

# GROUP PROFILES IN LUKE 20

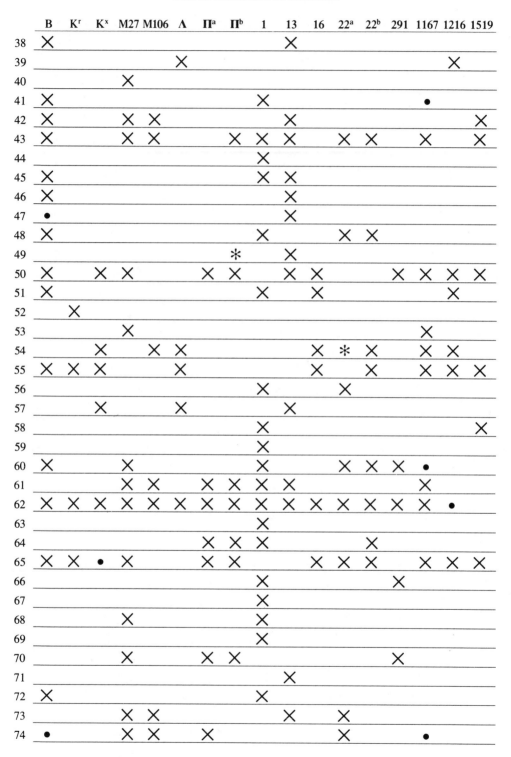

# GROUP PROFILES IN LUKE 20

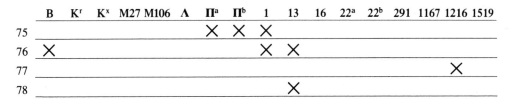

| | B | Kʳ | Kˣ | M27 | M106 | Λ | Πᵃ | Πᵇ | 1 | 13 | 16 | 22ᵃ | 22ᵇ | 291 | 1167 | 1216 | 1519 |
|---|---|---|---|---|---|---|---|---|---|---|---|---|---|---|---|---|---|
| 75 | | | | | | | X | X | X | | | | | | | | |
| 76 | X | | | | | | | | X | X | | | | | | | |
| 77 | | | | | | | | | | | | | | | | X | |
| 78 | | | | | | | | | | X | | | | | | | |

APPENDIX III

# THE WITNESSES TO THE
# CONTINUOUS GREEK TEXT
# OF LUKE IN THE
# UNITED BIBLE SOCIETIES EDITION[1]

In view of its handsome and lucid format it is not surprising that the UBS edition is widely used by students of the NT. The overall strengths and weaknesses of this edition have been pointed out repeatedly and need not concern us here.[2] Though one may regret that so few variants are presented and may question the principle of selection,[3] the fact remains that the extent of attestation presented with each variant is unprecedented. Reviewers have generally praised the edition for the large number of minuscules which it has cited or consulted. The expectation has been raised that in contrast with previous editions the reader has been given enough information about the MS support of the variants to allow for an independent and well-founded choice. It is this contention which will be tested here in terms of the witnesses to the continuous Greek text of Luke on the basis of the results of the Profile Method. The intent is not so much to find fault as to assist the reader in the evaluation of the Greek witnesses presented in the apparatus of the UBS edition, and to make suggestions for a better selection and more meaningful citation of Greek MS evidence.

The obvious questions in the mind of the user of a critical apparatus are why a certain witness is included and what value should be attached to its support of certain readings. If only internal considerations were of importance it would be sufficient to list all the surviving variants in a passage without MS attestation. That the support is usually specified means that also external factors are considered important. The support of certain MSS, versions, or Church Fathers can strengthen or weaken the claim of a variant to be the best or original reading. In the case of the versional and patristic evidence the situation is fairly clear; it provides information about the date and provenance of a reading or a text-type.[4] The problem lies with the

---

[1]*The Greek New Testament* (ed. Kurt Aland, Matthew Black, Bruce M. Metzger, and Allan Wikgren; 3rd edition; London: United Bible Societies, 1975). All comments apply equally to the first edition (UBS[1]).

[2]See e.g. the penetrating review of UBS[1] by Irving Alan Sparks in *Int* 22 (1968) 92-96.

[3]It should be remembered that the edition was designed to cater primarily to the needs of Bible translators.

[4]Some textual critics assign a more basic role to the patristic evidence. Hermann von Soden thought that Tertullian and Origen stood close enough to the autographa and had sufficient textual-critical interest and competence to lend great weight to their readings (*Griechisches Neues Testament, Text mit kurzem Apparat* [*Handausgabe*] [Göttingen: Vandenhoeck and Ruprecht, 1913] x-xii).

witnesses to the continuous Greek text. It is far from clear what valid information can be derived from them for the evaluation of variants. The reasons for calling one MS a valuable witness to the text and another untrustworthy are much less clear and adequate than is generally believed.[5]

Since there are so many witnesses to the continuous Greek text of the NT, the problem already comes to the fore in the necessary selection process. Some of the criteria which guided the editors of the UBS edition are apparent. Their main value judgment is that the more ancient MSS are better witnesses to the text. This means that the readings of the papyri would tend to receive more weight than those of the uncials,[6] and those of the early uncials more than the minuscules. In agreement with this principle the editors included all the available papyri and most of the uncials, but only a small fraction of the available minuscules.[7] The minuscules were not selected on the basis of their date but in view of the character of their text.

There is, of course, something obvious about preferring older witnesses to later ones, but this principle has severe limitations. It starts from the assumption that, since older MSS stand closer to the autographa in time, they must stand closer also in the quality of their text. This assumption is questionable. The history of the transmission of the text of the NT is not characterized by continuously increasing corruption, but by a concerted effort to eliminate it. That this effort, which involved also stylistic and orthographical standardization and harmonization of parallel passages, sometimes made matters worse is beside the point. The main corruption of the text came very early, before or at the time our earliest NT papyri were written. Later generations were preoccupied with eliminating variants rather than creating new ones. The early papyri have a large number of variants shared by no other MSS. Later copyists, in so far as they were aware of them, did not think these had a claim to being original. Theoretically the original reading may have been lost in some cases through this process of elimination.

Not all that many readings can be condemned at present because they lack early attestation. $P^{66}$ serves as a warning here for it contains some variants which had been considered late and thus secondary.[8] A reading which has only early attestation has no claim to being better than a reading which has mainly late support. It is only when late attestation is supported by intrinsic arguments that a reading can

[5]The supremacy of Codex Vaticanus (03=B) and its allies during the last hundred years depends more on uncritical scholarly consensus than on scientific proof. F. J. A. Hort's ingenious case for calling the "Neutrals" good and the Byzantine text late and secondary rests on limited evidence and dangerous generalizations (see pp. 2-6). One cannot condemn all "Byzantine" readings because some are demonstrably secondary! Each reading deserves to be judged on its own merits and not simply on the basis of the assumed quality of the MS in which it appears. In this the "eclectic school" of textual criticism is certainly correct. External evidence should not be used as a short cut to a full consideration of the evidence.

[6]Sparks noted that the editors were not consistent in this in that they favored $P^{75}$ over Codex Vaticanus, but in the Pauline Epistles they preferred Vaticanus to $P^{46}$ (*Int* 22 [1968] 95).

[7]The list of uncials used for the edition (pp. xv-xix) is incorrect. MSS 09 (F), 011 (G), 013 (H), 021 (M), 027 (R), 028 (S), 030 (U), 031 (V), 034 (Y), 039 (Λ), 045 (Ω), 047, and 0211 were not cited at all in Luke, 07 (E) and 026 (Q) only once, and 036 (Γ) only twice. These MSS were probably considered too "Byzantine" in character to be included. MSS 027, 045, and 0211 were not listed among the uncials used in UBS[1]. For the classification of the uncials that are extant in at least one of the test chapters in Luke see Chapter V.

[8]It is often forgotten that such major early uncials as 02 (A), 04 (C), and 032 (W) are at least in certain parts witnesses to the text which became dominant in the late Byzantine period.

be called secondary with confidence. The "lectio anterior potior" principle is seldom applicable in the evaluation of readings, yet it remains one of the main guides for the selection of MSS for a critical apparatus.

For the selection of minuscules — and apparently also for the late uncials — the editors used another principle which also has been taken for granted during the past century. Mainly on the basis of F. J. A. Hort's claim that Byzantine readings are generally secondary in nature, the value of a MS has been considered proportional to its distance from the Byzantine text, which in practice meant Erasmus's TR.[9] Thus for the UBS edition more than one thousand minuscules were examined to find those which "exhibit a significant degree of independence from the so-called Byzantine manuscript tradition."[10] The result was a total of 23 minuscules cited systematically in Luke.[11] Among these are nine well-known and much cited members of the "Neutral" group (MSS 33, 892, and 1241) and the so-called Caesarean text (MSS 1, 13, 28, 565, 700, and 1071). The other fourteen minuscules are, at least in Luke, mostly unremarkable MSS which stand surprisingly close to the Byzantine text. Two of them, MSS 1010 and 1344, are actually members of $K^x$, the majority text of the early Middle Ages! The classification of the 23 minuscules is presented in Table 3.

When one observes the group classifications of the minuscules systematically cited in the textual apparatus of Luke it becomes clear that several of them could have been left out without loss. The two $K^x$ members (1010 and 1344) add nothing to the majority of the Byzantine MS tradition which is cited under the siglum *Byz*.[12] The readings of the "Neutral" minuscules 33, 565 (beginning of Luke), 892, and 1241 are already overrepresented by uncial members of this group. MSS 1216 and 2174 are both members of Gr 1216; nothing would have been lost by dropping MS 2174. MSS 1079 and 1546 are members of $\Pi^a$ and already more than adequately represented by the uncials A (02), K (017), and $\Pi$ (041). If the redundant MSS are eliminated we are left with only 14 minuscules (MSS 1, 13, 28, 700, 1009, 1071, 1195, 1216, 1230, 1242, 1253, 1365, 1646, 2148) for which the presence in the apparatus has some justification.

However, redundancy is only a minor problem compared with the failure of omission. The selection tool, developed by the INTF in Münster, and applied to more than one thousand MSS, clearly failed. Most of the minuscules designated "Mixed" by the Profile Method went unnoticed even though they diverge signifi-

---

[9]See pp. 2-6.

[10]*The Greek New Testament*, xix. This selection tool is apparently Aland's "1000 cursives examined in 1000 passages with a view to evaluate their text" (see pp. 3-4 and 21-22). His definition of a Byzantine reading remains unclear.

[11]The list of minuscules which are cited consistently (pp. xix-xx) is incorrect. MSS 330, 1006, 1505, 2127, 2492, and 2495 were not cited in Luke though they are extant. MS 945 is cited only with a variant in Luke 1:17 and should have been in the list of MSS cited cursorily (pp. xx-xxvii). MSS 1 and 13 were cited under the group symbols f[1] and f[13]. However, it appears that the family readings were assumed to be identical to the readings of these two MSS.

[12]In the 187 variants in the apparatus of Luke, MSS 1010 and 1344 read only twice against the siglum *Byz*. In addition, MS 1010 reads four times against 1344 and *Byz*, and 1344 six times against 1010 and *Byz*. The Byzantine minuscules do not form a unified entity which can be represented by a siglum based on the reading of the majority. They divide into distinct groups which differ so greatly in size that the majority will almost always be identical to $K^x$.

*TABLE 3*

## TWENTY-THREE MINUSCULES CITED SYSTEMATICALLY IN THE UBS EDITION OF THE GOSPEL OF LUKE

| Gregory Number | Classification | Comments |
|---|---|---|
| 1 | 1 | apparently identical to the siglum f¹ |
| 13 | 13 | apparently identical to the siglum f¹³ |
| 28 | Mix-Kˣ | not significantly mixed in Luke |
| 33 | B | weak member at the beginning of Luke |
| 565 | B-Kˣ | Gr B at the beginning of Luke |
| 700 | Mix-B-Kˣ | Gr B in the middle of Luke |
| 892 | B | core member of Gr B |
| 1009 | Mix | pair with 472 |
| 1010 | Kˣ | member of Kˣ Cl 160 |
| 1071 | Mix | some relationship to Gr B |
| 1079 | Πᵃ | core member |
| 1195 | M1195 | one of the less important M groups |
| 1216 | 1216 | core member |
| 1230 | Mix | related to Cl 163 |
| 1241 | B | last part of Luke 1 is not Gr B |
| 1242 | Kmix-1167 | |
| 1253 | Mix | |
| 1344 | Kˣ | |
| 1365 | 22a | |
| 1546 | Πᵃ | not a core member |
| 1646 | Cl 163 | |
| 2148 | Cl 2148 | core member |
| 2174 | 1216 | weak member |

cantly from the Byzantine majority text $K^x$.[13] Also the Grs M27, M106, and $\Pi^b$, and the Cls M10, M609, $\Pi$268, 475, 686, 827, 1012, 1229, and 1675, which stand at considerable distance from $K^x$, were ignored. Furthermore, the selection tool could not make distinctions among the Byzantine minuscules and select representatives from the different groups. Thus most of the M and $\Pi$ groups, Grs $\Lambda$, 16, 291, 1519,

---

[13]Only five of the 34 significantly "Mixed" minuscules in Luke were included (MSS 700, 1009, 1071, 1230, and 1253). The 29 "Mixed" minuscules which were ignored in the UBS edition are MSS 79, 157, 168, 173, 176, 213 (listed in UBS³, xxi, but not cited in Luke), 372, 377, 382, 401, 713, 792, 851, 903, 1048, 1061, 1087, 1093, 1325, 1337, 1342, 1574, 1647, 1692, 2533, 2542, 2546, 2561, and 2680. Of these 157, 372, and 1574 appear in the list of MSS which are cited cursorily (see Table 4), but this involves at best only a few variants in Luke. MSS which are classified "Mixed" in only one of the three test chapters were generally not considered significantly mixed and were thus not included in the total of 34 MSS.

and $K^r$ — not to speak of the non-$K^x$ clusters — were all swallowed up by the siglum "Byz" which actually only represents Gr $K^x$. We are forced to conclude that as far as Luke is concerned the UBS edition has made no appreciable advance over other editions in the citation of minuscules. The variety of evidence contained in the minuscules remains to a large extent unrepresented.

The editors chose to cite in addition three uncials and thirty-one minuscules in Luke "when they are of special significance for certain variants."[14] They are listed with their classification and frequency of citation in Luke in Table 4. The principle which guided their citation is not stated, though it can be deduced readily. These 34 MSS, taken from various printed editions, are cited only when they support one or more of the ancient versions against the Greek MSS which have been cited systematically. There is indeed some merit in knowing whether the reading of a version has Greek support.[15] One wonders, however, what meaning to attach to the support of a versional reading by one or a few late medieval MSS. One suspects that in most cases there is no genetic relationship but only accidental agreement. Furthermore, there has been no exhaustive search for such support and thus one cannot assume that Greek support is actually lacking for the many variants cited with only versional support. This kind of citation is too sporadic and haphazard to be of value. The addition of these 34 MSS may sound impressive but lacks real significance.

Some lessons can be drawn from the weaknesses of the Greek MS citation in the UBS edition:

1. For a meaningful evaluation of MS evidence it is necessary to know something about the character of the text of each MS. This will prevent redundancy and allow that the largest possible part of the MS tradition be represented in the apparatus.

2. Minuscules for a critical apparatus should be selected not on the basis of their distance from the "Byzantine" majority, but on the basis of their ability to represent a distinct group which is not attested by any of the uncials. Also so-called mixed minuscules deserve to be included, i.e. MSS of which the text differs significantly from all the groups represented in the apparatus.

3. The so-called Byzantine text should not be represented by one siglum, but by MSS or sigla which can represent all the different groups among the minuscules.

4. The inclusion of uncials in a critical apparatus needs to be justified in the same way as the minuscules. The relatively early date of an uncial is not sufficient reason for inclusion if its text is already adequately represented by another early uncial.

5. Since a change of text between the main sections of the NT is very common it is necessary to select representatives separately for each Gospel, for Acts, the Pauline Epistles as a unit, the Catholic Epistles as a unit, and Revelation.

---

[14]*The Greek New Testament*, xx-xxxi. The uncials 07 (E), 026 (Q), and 036 (Γ), and the minuscule 945 should also have been in this list rather than among the MSS cited systematically (pp. xv-xvii). Though 115 minuscules containing the Gospels were added to the list of MSS cited cursorily in UBS³, none of these was actually cited in Luke.

[15]It is questionable whether the readings of a version that lack Greek support deserve citation in the apparatus of a critical edition of the Greek text. There are many such instances in the UBS edition.

## TABLE 4

### THREE UNCIALS AND THIRTY-ONE MINUSCULES CITED CURSORILY IN THE UBS[3] EDITION OF THE GOSPEL OF LUKE

| Gregory Number | Classification | Times Cited | Comments |
|---|---|---|---|
| 07 (E) | K$^x$ (Cl Ω) | 1 | |
| 026 (Q) | Mix | 1 | not significantly mixed |
| 036 (Γ) | K$^x$ | 2 | |
| 5 | Mix-1519 | 1 | |
| 38 | K$^x$ (Cl 1053) | 1 | |
| 53 | K$^x$ | 1 | pair with 902 |
| 56 | K$^r$ (Cl 56) | 1 | |
| 57 | | 2 | INTF microfilm illeg |
| 61 | | 1 | not profiled due to late date |
| 69 | 13 | 3 | |
| 71 | M27 | 2 | core member |
| 76 | K$^x$ (Cl 1193) | 1 | |
| 124 | 13 | 2 | weak member |
| 157 | K$^x$-Mix-B | 3 | related to Gr B in Luke 10 |
| 162 | K$^x$ | 1 | |
| 174 | Λ | 1 | member of Gr 13 in Mark |
| 230 | Λ | 1 | member of Gr 13 in Mark |
| 235 | K$^x$ | 1 | |
| 238 | | 1 | not profiled due to commentary |
| 248 | Kmix-M27 | 1 | weak member of M27 |
| 259 | | 1 | not profiled due to commentary |
| 274 | K$^x$ | 1 | |
| 291 | 291 | 1 | core member |
| 346 | 13 | 4 | core member |
| 348 | 1216 | 1 | core member |
| 372 | Mix | 1 | very strange text |
| 407 | K$^x$ | 1 | K$^x$ Cl 1053 in Luke 10 |
| 435 | K$^x$ (Cl 1053) | 2 | |
| 472 | Mix | 1 | pair with 1009 |
| 692 | M27 | 2 | |
| 788 | 13 | 2 | core member |
| 945 | Kmix-K$^x$ | 1 | |
| 1012 | Cl 1012 | 2 | very distinct cluster |
| 1574 | Mix | 1 | |

A number of test passages are needed to spot block mixture in each of these sections.

6. The introduction of a critical edition should include a justification for each MS which has been included in the apparatus. It should provide all the information necessary to evaluate its support of variants.

7. A critical apparatus should be objective and balanced. It should be clear from the introduction that no group is overrepresented or ignored. While it may be difficult to represent every aspect of the MS tradition, there is no excuse for the obvious bias toward Gr B which has characterized modern editions with the exception of the one produced by von Soden.